THE AMERICAN CENTURY SERIES

STATEN ISLAND

IN THE TWENTIETH CENTURY

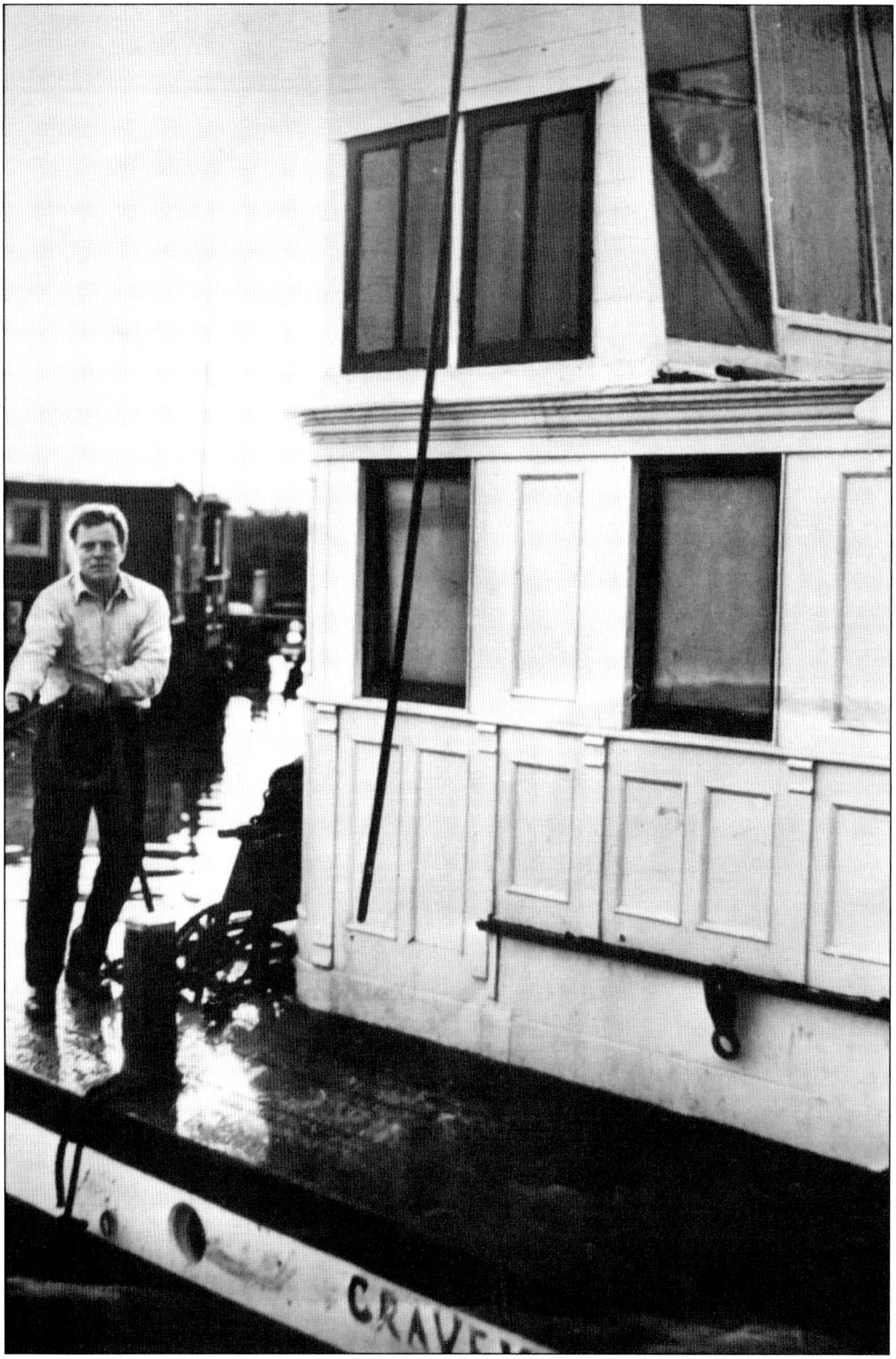

Artist John A. Noble on his houseboat/studio, 1948.

THE AMERICAN CENTURY SERIES

STATEN ISLAND

IN THE TWENTIETH CENTURY

Margaret Lundrigan and Tova Navarra

ARCADIA
PUBLISHING

ISBN 978-0-7385-9041-7

Published by Arcadia Publishing
Charleston, South Carolina

Printed in the United States of America

Library of Congress Catalog Card Number: 98-85877

For all general information contact Arcadia Publishing at:
Telephone 843-853-2070
Fax 843-853-0044
E-mail sales@arcadiapublishing.com
For customer service and orders:
Toll-Free 1-888-313-2665

Visit us on the Internet at www.arcadiapublishing.com

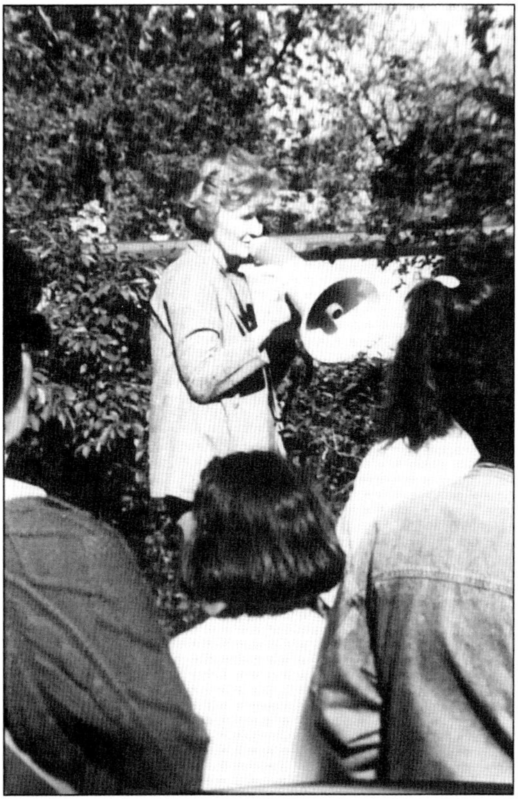

The authors fondly dedicate this book to Staten Island historian Marjorie Johnson, who has been associated with the Staten Island Historical Society for 21 years. Mrs. Johnson has been instrumental in the production of this volume, enormously giving of her time, her personal photographic collection, her incredible knowledge, and infectious love of Staten Island history. She was named a Woman of Achievement by the Staten Island Advance, served on the board of directors of the Alice Austen House, and devoted much time to helping developmentally disabled children. It is our great good fortune to know her.

ML and TN

I would like also to dedicate this book to my brother, James Lundrigan, and my sister, Noreen Harris, who are always there for me.

ML

Contents

Acknowledgments

As authors of photographic history books, we recall the famous line in Tennessee Williams' play *A Streetcar Named Desire*, spoken by the character Blanche du Bois, "I have always depended upon the kindness of strangers."

Indeed, we acknowledge the kindness of strangers (some of whom have become wonderful friends), family members, organizations, and the community at large. We have not been disappointed. In fact, one of the most enjoyable parts of the putting the book together was meeting people who gave generously of their photographs, time, knowledge, and love of local history.

We are indebted to the Staten Island Historical Society, including special thanks to its terrific "rare birds" Marjorie Johnson, William and Judy McMillen, Barnett Shepherd, Carlotta DeFillo, Marjorie Holtermann Fandrei, and photographer Tom Shidemantle. We also appreciate the contributions of David Kleiser, board president; Brian Rehr of the Snug Harbor Cultural Center; author Erin Urban of the John A. Noble Collection; indefatigable artist Jack Demyan; talented and energetic photographers Jim and Ron Star Romano; the delightful Drinnans, Bill and Claire; Edith and Al Holtermann and the Holtermann family; good friends Richard and Marion Dutka and their family; lovely Arleen Brahn; the gracious Jack Casey; historian and community leader Evelyn King; dear family members Ted, Noreen, Brian, Teddy, and Suzanne Harris; the irrepressible Dorothy Cugini Nolan and the Cugini family; Catherine Cass, owner of the "Crimson Beech" residence designed by Frank Lloyd Wright; Vermont resident A. Richard Boera, former business manager of Staten Island Community College; Rudolph Ayoub of Jerry's Confectionery; Patricia Kelly, manager of the photography collection, Baseball Hall of Fame and Museum, Inc.; Mary Ann Peters and her daughters Lauren and Erica; William P. Blaine; Troy Taylor, manager of MotoPhoto in Ocean Township, New Jersey, and his staff for high quality service; fellow Arcadia author Randall Gabrielan; our publishers and editors Kirsty Sutton, Jim Burkinshaw, Rebecca Heflin, Mark Berry, Jaime Carter, Sarah Maineri, Becky Cooper, and the entire staff of Arcadia. All these wonderful people have enriched our lives and, as Shakespeare wrote, "We shall note you in our book of memory."

Introduction

We were very tired, we were very merry,
We had gone back and forth all night on the ferry . . .

—from *Recuerdo*, by Edna St. Vincent Millay

The story of Staten Island in the 20th century unfolds largely as a story of connection. From the earliest European settlement days, the question of "How do you get there from here?" loomed large. One of the first Dutch ministers, Samuel Drisius, who was assigned the care of both Manhattan and Staten Island, felt the effects of the difficult journey involved in ministering to the two communities. Even American writer Henry David Thoreau, during his short stay as tutor to Judge Emerson's children, wrote in a letter of going to Stapleton to board the ferry to Manhattan. Prior to the turn of the century, a commission studied Staten Island's meager population and attributed its lack of growth "to poor transportation and malaria." But, ironically, the connection issue was a double-edged sword, because near inaccessibility had guarded Staten Island's revered rural character for many years and allowed the preservation of its historic sites.

In the early 1820s, however, Governor Daniel Tompkins earnestly attended to ameliorating transportation to and from Staten Island with the inauguration of the Steamship *Nautilus* and the founding of Richmond Turnpike, which was later renamed Victory Boulevard in honor of the U.S. victory in World War II. Entrepreneur and captain of industry Cornelius Vanderbilt established the basis for one of America's great fortunes by providing ferry service to Manhattan. And community leader Erastus Wiman (1834–1904) went on to become the "heart and soul" of the transportation movement. A showman and visionary, Wiman talked with William H. Pendleton, manager of the North Shore Ferry from 1872 to 1876. Pendleton (and others) suggested there be a concentration of communication with New York at St. George. In volume one of their historical reference *Staten Island and Its People*, Leng and Davis recounted that the fruits of Wiman's tireless labor included musical shows, an illuminated fountain, amusements and exhibits at the ferry terminal, the construction of a railroad along the north and east shores, and the completion in 1889 of a bridge across the Arthur Kill. Rapid transit had finally taken hold.

In 1898, Staten Islanders voted by referendum to become part of the city of New York. In 1905, the City took control of the ferries, and government began moving to the North Shore, seen most vividly in the building of borough hall, the courthouse, and the library. This growth and consolidation ushered in what borough historian of 54 years, Loring McMillen, called the "Cosmopolitan Era." Increasingly efficient modes of transportation—ferries, trains, trolleys (affectionately known as "Red Mikes"), and later buses and automobiles—eliminated former "barriers" between the island and the other New York boroughs. The 1930s brought the construction of the Bayonne, Goethals, and Outerbridge Crossing bridges, although connection to Brooklyn from Staten Island remained yet a dream. Historian Barnett Shepherd points out that the building of the Verrazano Narrows Bridge in 1964 marked a watershed for Staten Island development. The population grew from 67,000 in 1900 to approximately 379,000 by 1990.

The past one hundred years on Staten Island have been exciting. Major events include disputes such as the garbage wars, disasters—the collapse of the Jersey Street building in 1937, the 1946 burning of the St. George Ferry Terminal, the crash of a DC8 over Staten Island, the brush fires on the South Shore that became known as "Black Saturday," and the explosion of the gas tanks that killed 40 people—as well as celebrations, such as the openings of the bridges, historic visits by John F. Kennedy, Jacqueline Kennedy Onassis, President Bill Clinton, and former president George Bush, and movies made on Staten Island, particularly the 1960s classic *Splendor in the Grass* and the Academy Award-winning *The Godfather* of the 1970s. And in November 1990, almost one hundred years after voting to become one of New York City's five boroughs, Staten Islanders voted overwhelmingly to form a commission to study the feasibility of seceding. All these events and people, famous and not so famous, have helped create the Staten Island of today.

We selected photographs that highlight significant events in Staten Island history and everyday life on the island in the past one hundred years. Because poet John Donne convinced us long ago that no man is an island, we further interpret that no island is an island, and we daresay no community on earth truly exists in secret or in total isolation from the rest of the world. In keeping with the theme of community in the 20th century, then, we set forth timelines as chapter openers. Timelines offer a comprehensive profile of national and world events that had an impact on American life in each decade. They augment each decade's image and evolution, from what controversy hit the headlines to what fads captured people's fancy. The timelines also support not only the idea of connection between locations, but between people and cultures. Surely, even after having done three Staten Island history books, the first being *Images of America: Richmondtown and Lighthouse Hill*, we view this precious piece of New York as infinitely "book worthy."

Considering the practical limitations of a 128-page format and at times an inability to locate certain photographs, we realize (and regret) that many individuals and organizations are not included herein. Therefore, we always welcome comments and suggestions for picture sources for future volumes. As our colleague Randall Gabrielan quips, we've come to think our middle names are now officially "Got any pictures?" Once again, our thanks to all who participated so generously in the production of this book and added their portraits, landscapes, and insights to posterity. Readers may contact us in care of Arcadia Publishers, 24 Chestnut Street, Suite 2, Dover, NH 03820.

Margaret "Got any pictures?" Lundrigan
Tova "Got any pictures?" Navarra
February 1998

One

1900–1909

The Turn of the Century

*The Commonwealth of Australia founded, 1900.
*25th U.S. President William McKinley reelected, 1900.
*Joseph Conrad writes *Lord Jim*, and Anton Chekhov writes *Uncle Vanya*, 1900.
*Authors Oscar Wilde and Thomas Wolfe die, and Sigmund Freud writes *The Interpretation of Dreams*, 1900.
*American composer Aaron Copland born, 1900.
*World Exhibition held in Paris, 1900.
*The "Cake Walk" dance becomes popular, 1900.
*Picasso's *Blue Period*, 1901.
*American film producer Walt Disney born, 1901.
*Queen Victoria dies, 1901.
*The hormone adrenaline is first isolated, 1901.
*American suffragette leader Elizabeth Cady Stanton dies, 1902.
*Operatic tenor Enrico Caruso makes his first recording, 1902.
*Beatrix Potter writes *Peter Rabbit* children's story series, 1902.
*Aswan Dam opens, 1902.
*Jack London writes *The Call of the Wild*, 1903.
*Orville and Wilbur Wright fly in a powered airplane, 1903.
*Pope Leo XIII dies, succeeded by Pope Pius X, 1903.
**The Great Train Robbery* becomes the longest film to date (12 minutes), 1903.
*Henry Ford creates the Ford Motor Company, 1903.
*Richard Steiff designs the first "teddy bears," named for Theodore "Teddy" Roosevelt, 1903.
*Theodore Roosevelt becomes the 26th U.S. president, 1904.

*Abbey Theatre founded in Dublin, 1904.

*Deaf and blind Helen Keller graduates from Radcliffe College, 1904.

*Albert Einstein formulates the Special Theory of Relativity, 1905.

*Ruth St. Denis introduces modern dance, 1906.

*"Typhoid Mary" incarcerated for spreading disease, 1906.

*French Impressionist Paul Cezanne and P.L. Dunbar, African-American poet, die, 1906.

*Swedish film star Greta Garbo born, 1906.

*The first *Ziegfeld Follies* staged in New York, 1907.

*In Philadelphia, the second Sunday in May established as "Mother's Day," 1907.

*Ivan Pavlov establishes "Pavlov's Dogs" as model for conditioned reflexes, 1907.

*Union of South Africa established, 1908.

*King Carlos I of Portugal and the crown prince both assassinated, 1908.

*The first "Model T" created, 1908.

*William Howard Taft elected U.S. president, 1908.

*Jack Johnson becomes the first black world-heavyweight boxing champion, 1908.

*Scientist Paul Ehrlich prepares Salvarsan to cure syphilis, 1909.

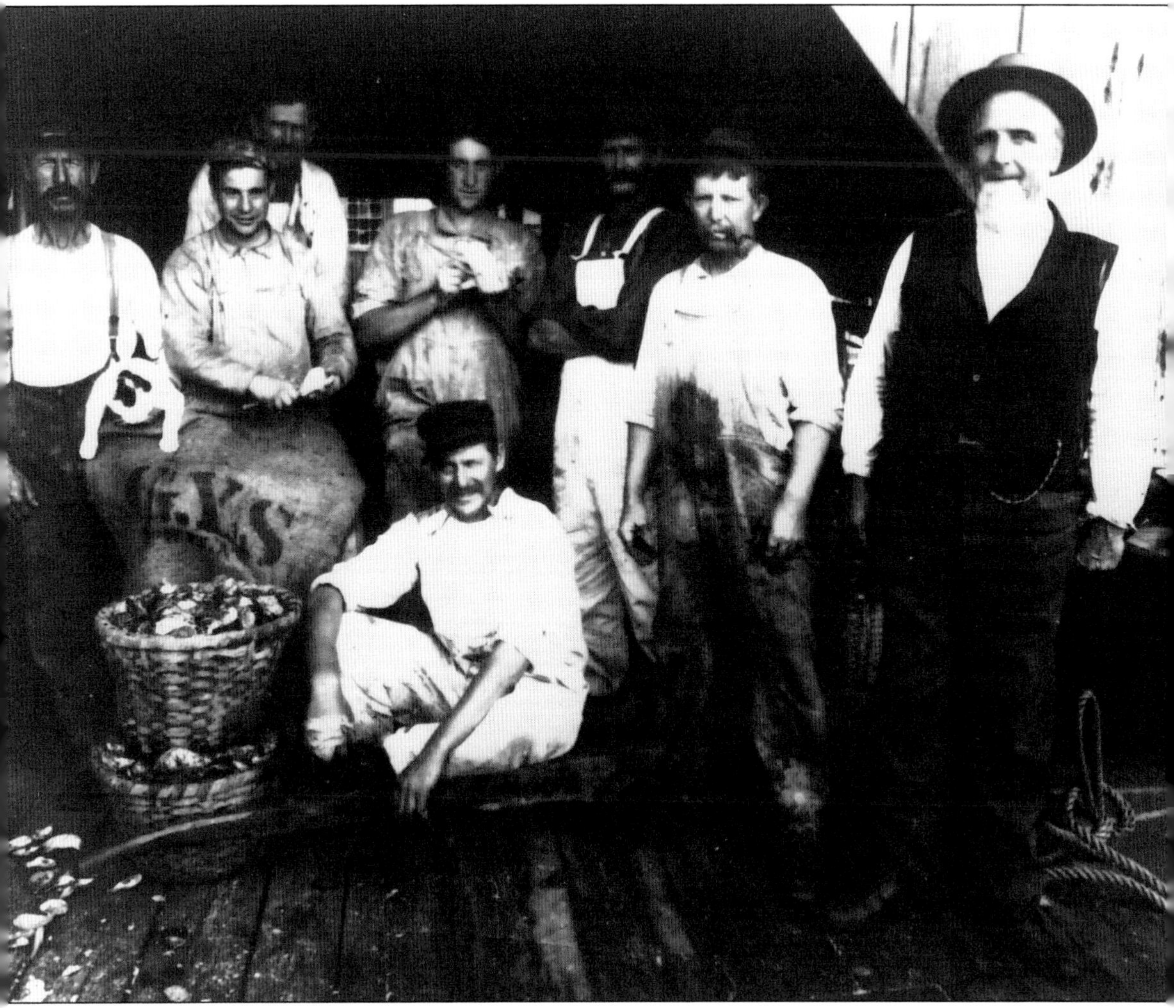

Staten Island oystermen around the turn of the century. This wonderful image was possibly from Mariner Harbor depicting an industry that had constituted a significant part of the island's economy. Cocclestown, the original name of Richmondtown, was so named because of piles of shells left by Native American tribes. This suggests that oystering pre-dates European settlement. By the early 1800s many of the oyster beds were played out from harvesting. To restore the beds, the watermen began to "seed" the beds with oysters from Virginia and neighboring waters. The process proved successful, and by the 1870s, as Charles Sachs notes in *Made On Staten Island*, Staten Island planters were providing oysters as far west as the Rocky Mountains. The Staten Island Historical Society received this print from the collection of Bob Anderson.

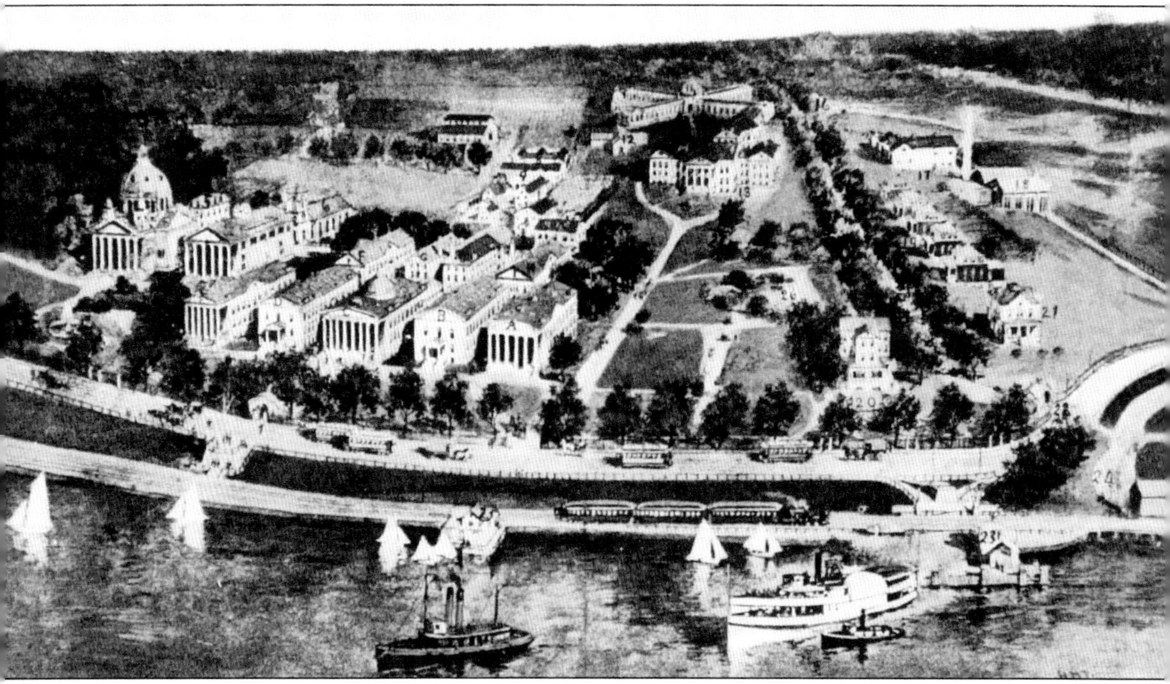

A bird's-eye view of Sailors' Snug Harbor, *c.* 1900. Founded in 1801 from a bequest from Capt. Randall to care for "aged and decrepit seaman," a description some of the residents took exception to. The first building opened in 1833 following the resolution of legal entanglements relating to the will. Since the opening of its first building on Staten Island, Snug Harbor had evolved into a highly self-contained community with a reputation as one of the island's wealthiest charities. In this photograph are the main building with wings, the dormitories, dining hall, the Randall Church (with dome), and Music Hall to the left; in the rear are the hospital and x-shaped sanitarium; and to the right is the governor's residence. (Collection of Randall Gabrielan.)

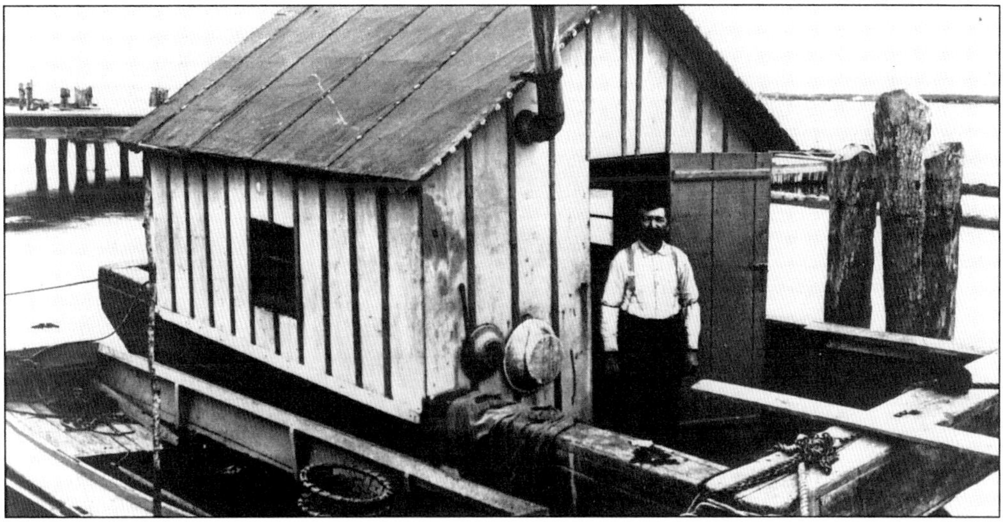

Bob Anderson print, oysterman with boat and float, also possibly in Mariner's Harbor. In *Made on Staten Island*, Charles Sachs reports that by 1900, Staten Island waters were producing 200,000 bushels of oysters. Once the island was no longer the province of independent watermen, most oystermen worked for wealthy planters. Oystering, an industry that had constituted a significant part of the island's economy, became a vanishing way of life when typhoid fever was linked to island oysters. The oyster beds were closed by the department of health in 1916. The beds were re-opened around 1940, only to be closed again during World War II. (Collection of the Staten Island Historical Society.)

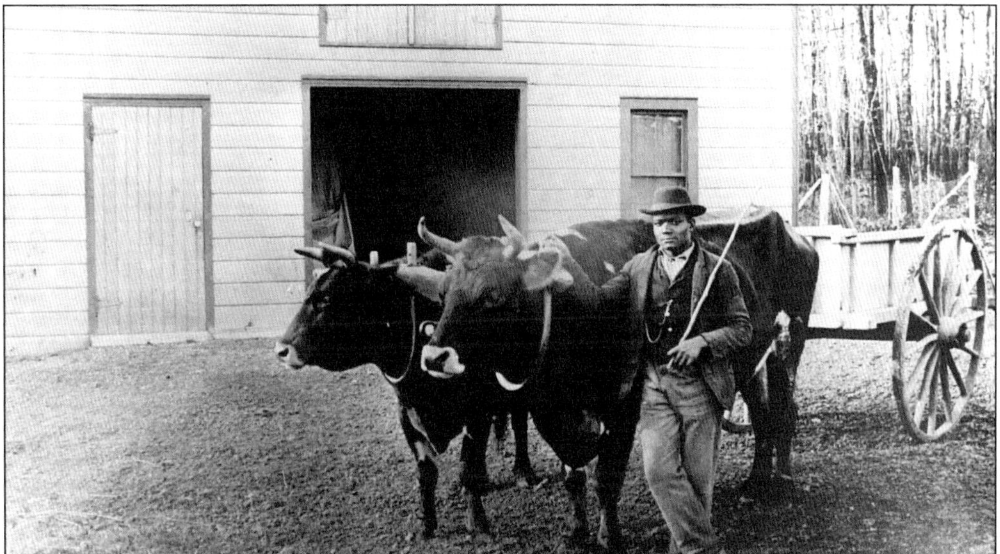

Farmer with oxen from Sandy Ground, around the turn of the century. The Sandy Ground community was founded in the 1830s by free African-Americans, and many residents engaged in agricultural pursuits. This photograph captures much of Staten Island's rural and agrarian past. Staten Island historian Edna Holden notes that in 1886 there were more than three hundred farms on the island, producing crops such as potatoes, corn, oats, and wheat. At the turn of the century, truck farms in Graniteville, New Springville, and Bull's Head provided food for Manhattan and Jersey City. (Collection of the Staten Island Historical Society.)

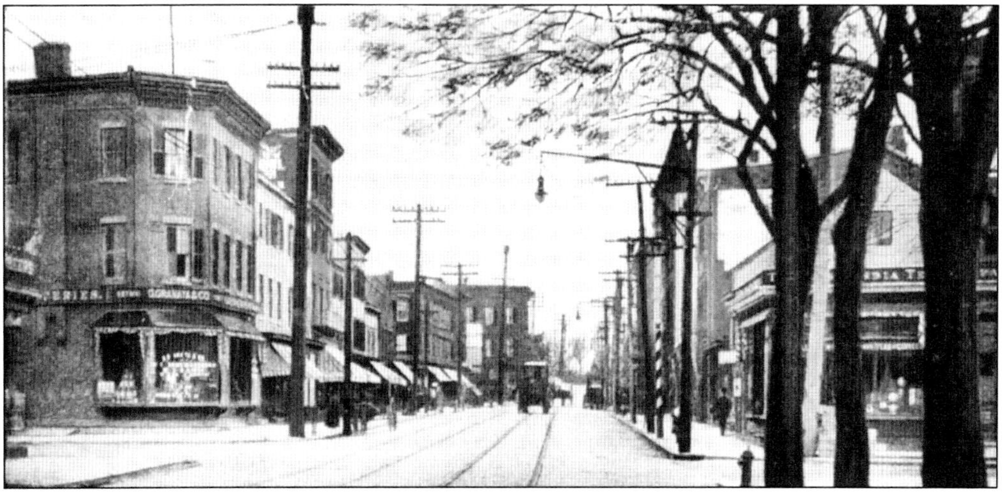

Postcard dated January 27, 1901, Bay Street looking south from the park. To the immediate left is the G. Granata Grocery Store. As Staten Island historian Marjorie Johnson says, in the days before telephone and the Internet, the postcard was a much relied upon form of communication dealing with both the important and the mundane. The message on the card reads, "Nan, Just wondering how you are? Rudman." (Collection of Randall Gabrielan.)

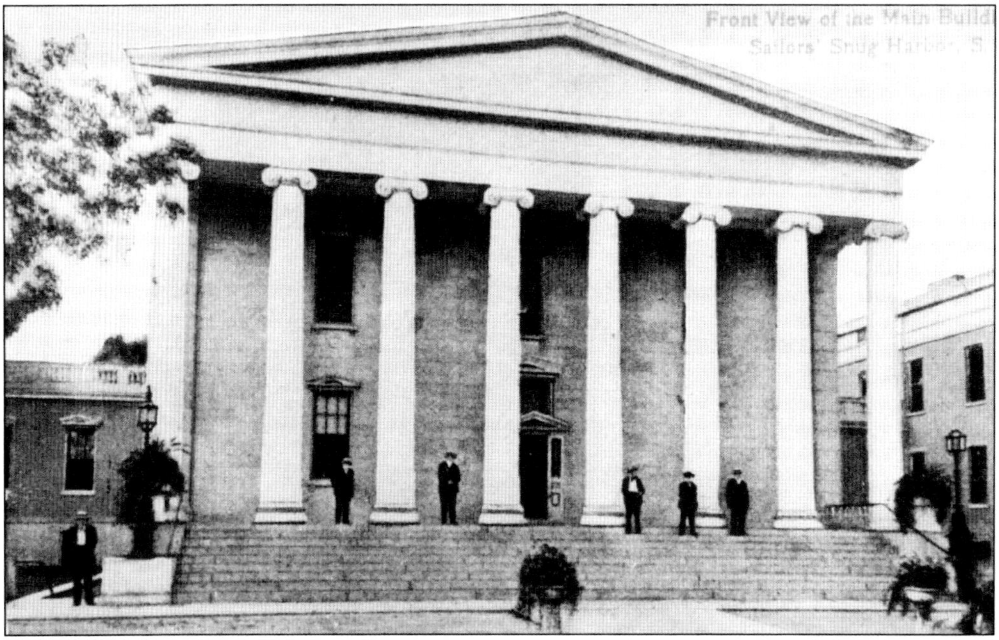

The front view of the Main Building Sailors' Snug Harbor, c.1900. Sailors' Snug Harbor is touted not only for its nobility of purpose, but also for the beauty of its surroundings. The design of the building is the work of several renowned architects and is recognized as containing some of the finest examples of Greek Revival architecture in the country. What Sailors' Snug Harbor accomplished on a humanitarian level is reflected in the oft-quoted statement of a resident, "I went high an' I went low looking fur a helpin', but no one would give me a lift. ...is goin' to take care of a middle-aged crippled seamun? Try the Snug 'Arbor, sez he. They took me in...put me in a new suit of clothes, stuck a pipe in my mouth, an' sez, 'There, you're safe an' sound forever, an' God bless you soul!' " (*Harpers Weekly*, August 12, 1882, collection of Randall Gabrielan.)

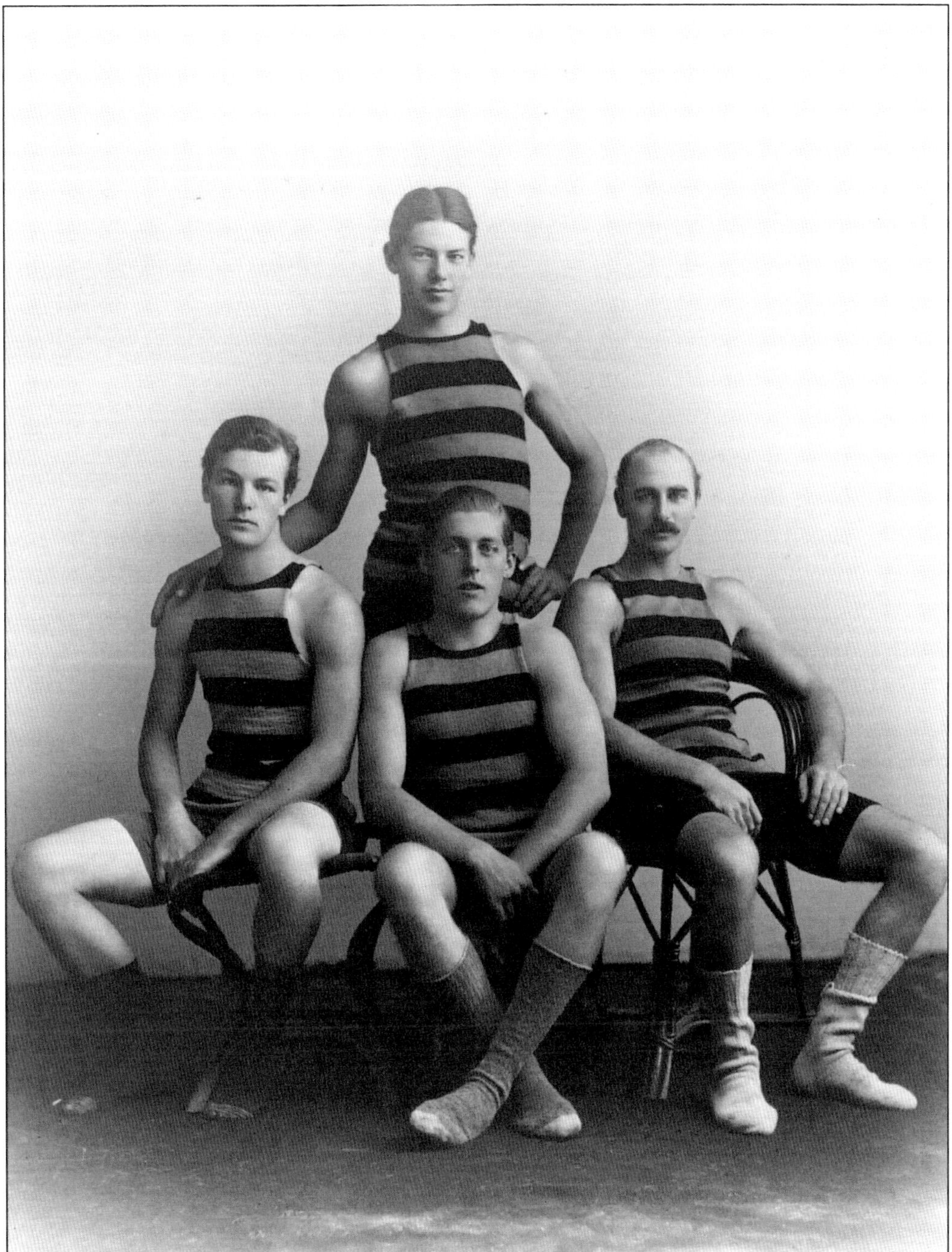

Staten Island Boat Club, 1904–1905. Sitting from left to right are William H. Konald, Harold Serymer, and A. Davey, with Victor Garrett standing. During this time some of the other boat clubs included the New York Yacht Club in Rosebank, the Corinthian Yacht Club in Stapleton, and the Staten Island Yacht Club at the Kill Van Kull. (Collection of the Staten Island Historical Society.)

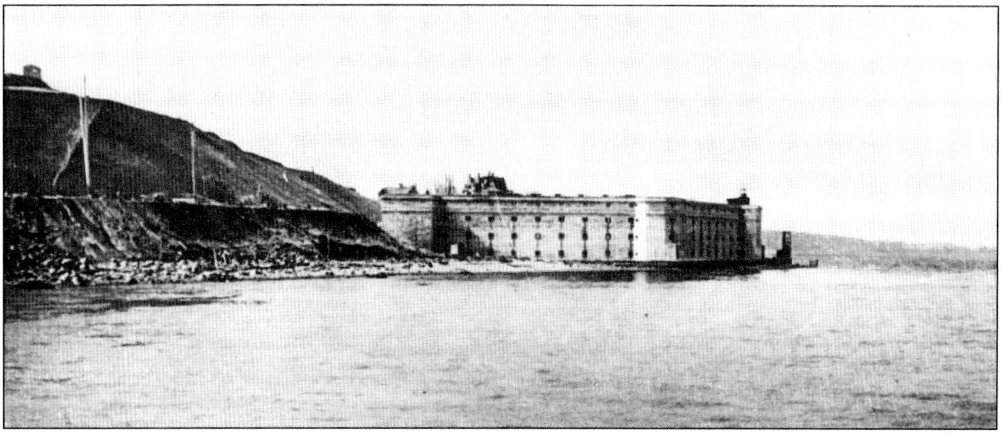

Fort Wadsworth in 1903. Part of the Gateway National Recreation Area, Fort Wadsworth is the oldest continually staffed military reservation in the United States. The fort's location at the entrance to the harbor makes it strategically important in the defense of the area. It was renamed in 1865 to honor Brigadier General James W. Wadsworth, who was killed in the Battle of The Wilderness. By 1901, the fort had expanded to include 226 acres. (Collection of Randall Gabrielan.)

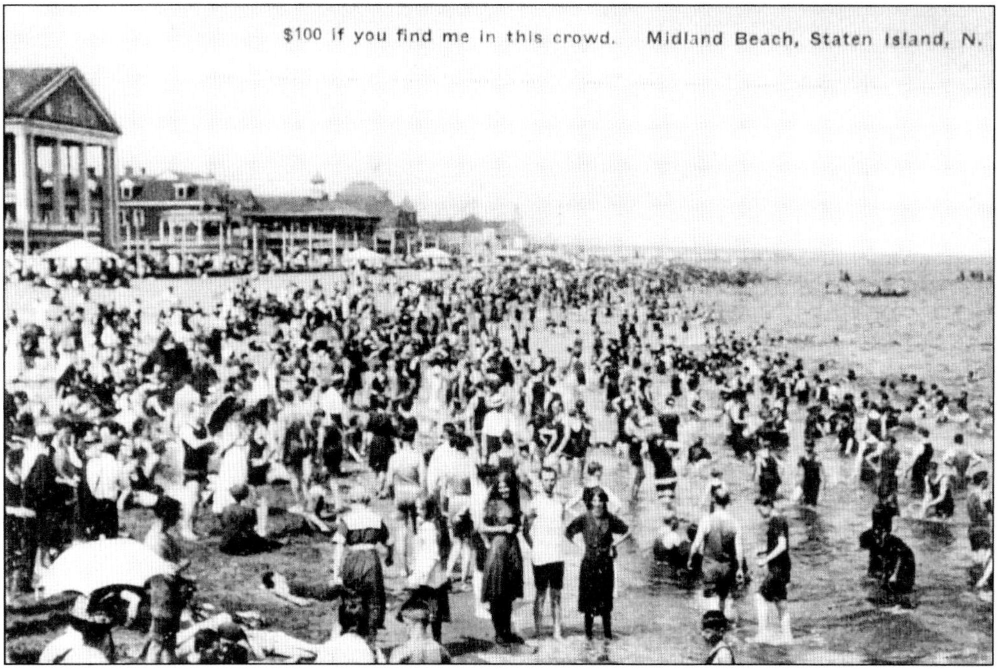

This crowded Midland Beach scene announces "$100 if you find me in this crowd." Midland Beach opened about the turn of the century with a large casino in addition to two bandstands. Excursion boats ran directly from Newark and Manhattan. (Collection of Randall Gabrielan.)

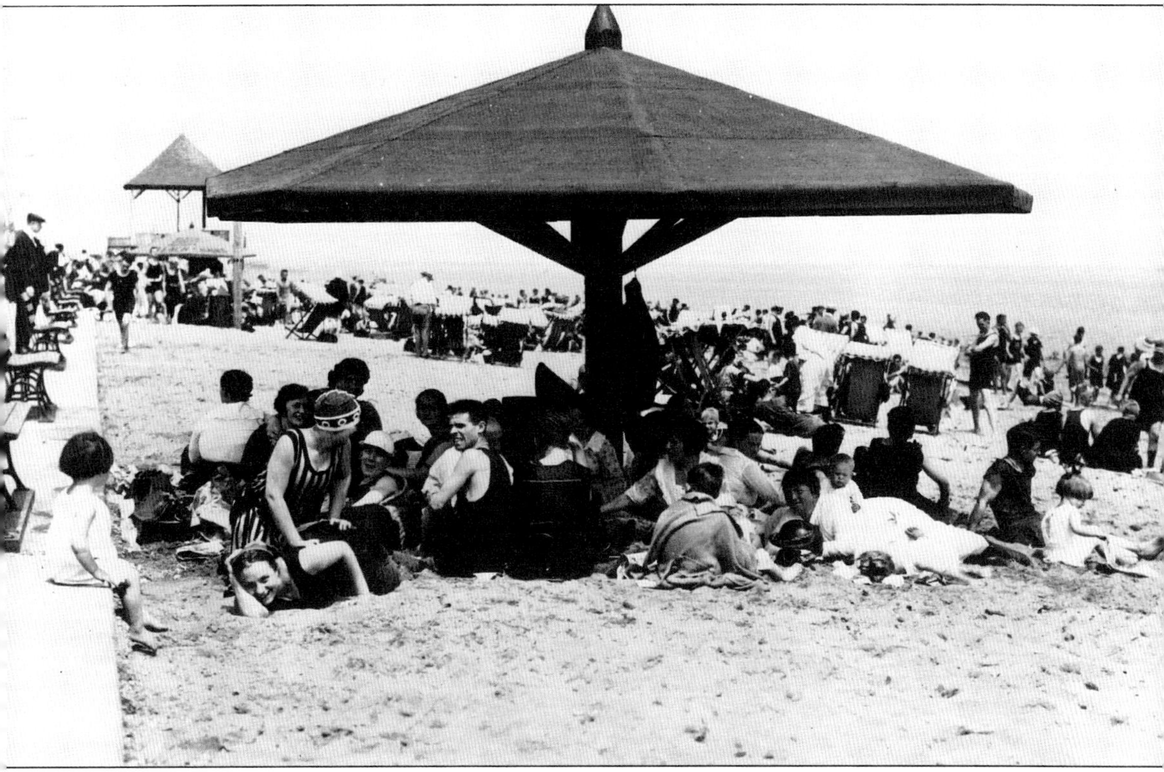

A "mushroom party" at Midland Beach. It was probably so named because of the mushroom-shaped sun shield. (Collection of Staten Island Historical Society.)

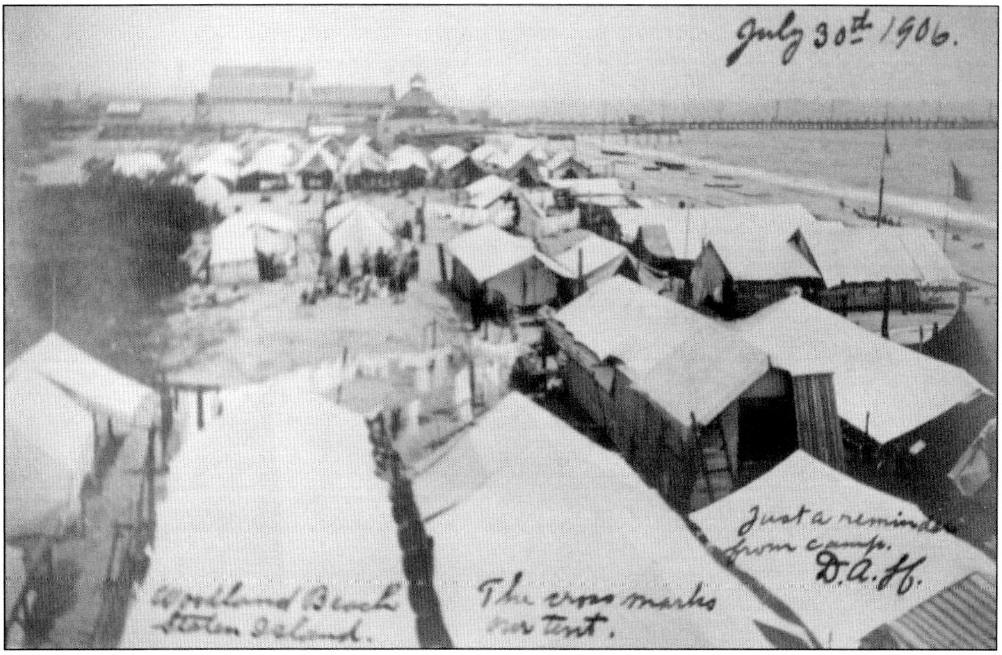

July 30, 1906, the tents of Woodland Beach. (Collection of William and Judith McMillen.)

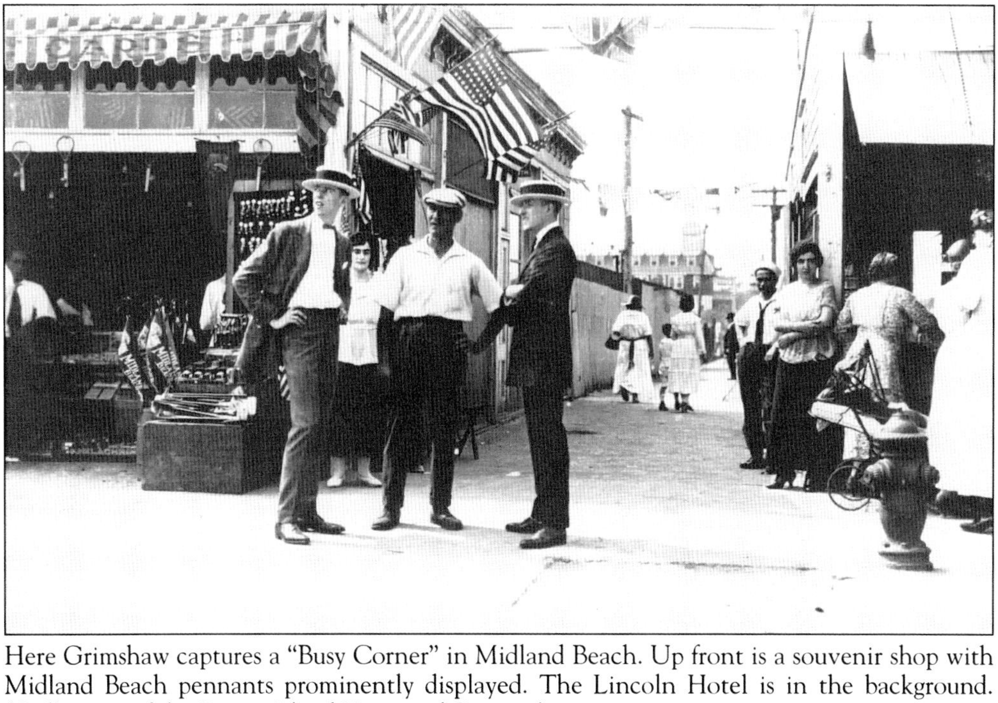

Here Grimshaw captures a "Busy Corner" in Midland Beach. Up front is a souvenir shop with Midland Beach pennants prominently displayed. The Lincoln Hotel is in the background. (Collection of the Staten Island Historical Society.)

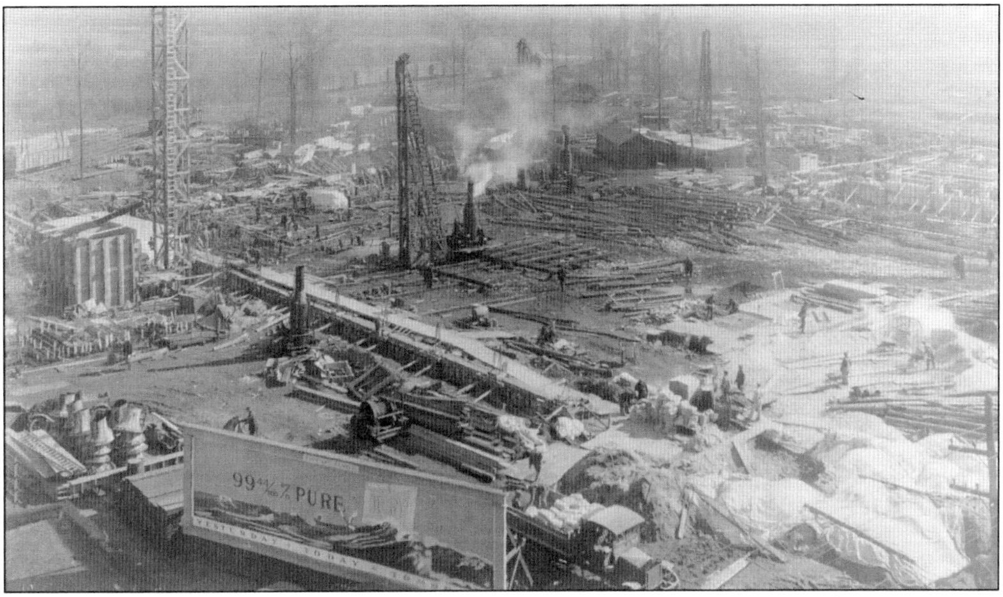

Construction of Port Ivory at Howland Hook. The plant which began production in 1907 was the third Procter and Gamble plant to be opened following Ivorydale in Cincinnati and Kansas City. The company was founded in 1834 by William Procter, a candle maker, and his brother-in-law, James Gamble, a soap maker. The plant was named for the company's premier product, Ivory soap, developed in 1879 and known to be 99 and 44/100 percent pure. The plant was constructed by the Milliken Brothers of Howland Hook and opened with four hundred employees. (Used with permission of Procter and Gamble.)

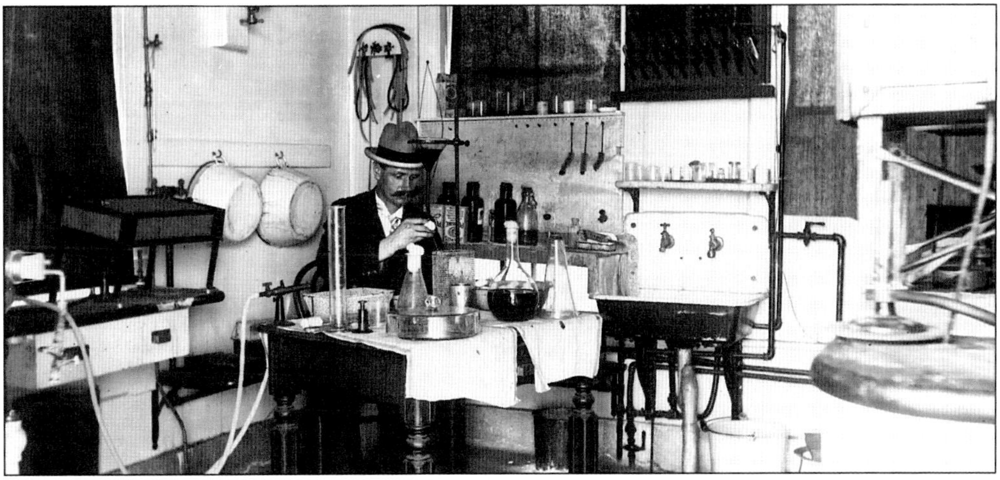

Chemist at work at the Quarantine Station. The Quarantine Station served as an inspection facility for ships entering New York Harbor. Health officers inspected for carriers of diseases such as smallpox, cholera, typhoid, and yellow fever. The hospitals for those quarantined had been removed to Swinburn and Hoffman Island in 1858 following riots by Staten Islanders. At the request of Dr. Doty, Alice Austen photographed many of the activities at the Station over a period of years. In this photograph, a chemist is working with bacterial cultures in the "media room." (Austen's notation: "Quarantine. 'Fred' at work. Bright day. 11.10 a.m. Mon., April 29, 1901. Cramer Crown, Waterbury lense, 10 ft., counted 18." (Collection of the Staten Island Historical Society.)

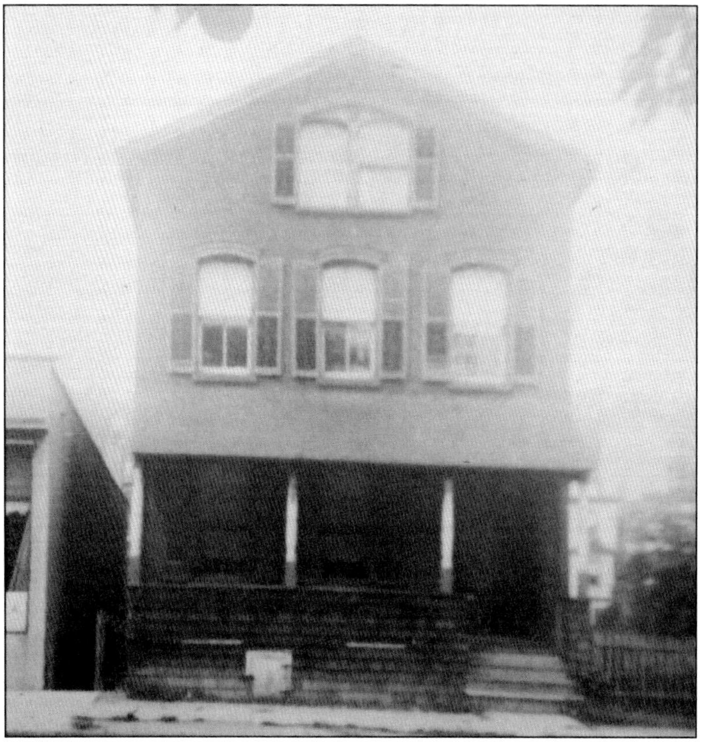

First Casey Funeral Home on Victory Boulevard. The company was founded by Mary Casey, grandmother of the present owners. Mrs. Casey, who was married to William Casey, had a background in nursing and was the first woman to be licensed as an undertaker in the state of New York. Today, the Casey Funeral Home is still operated at two locations, one on Slosson Avenue. (Courtesy of Jack Casey, Casey Funeral Homes.)

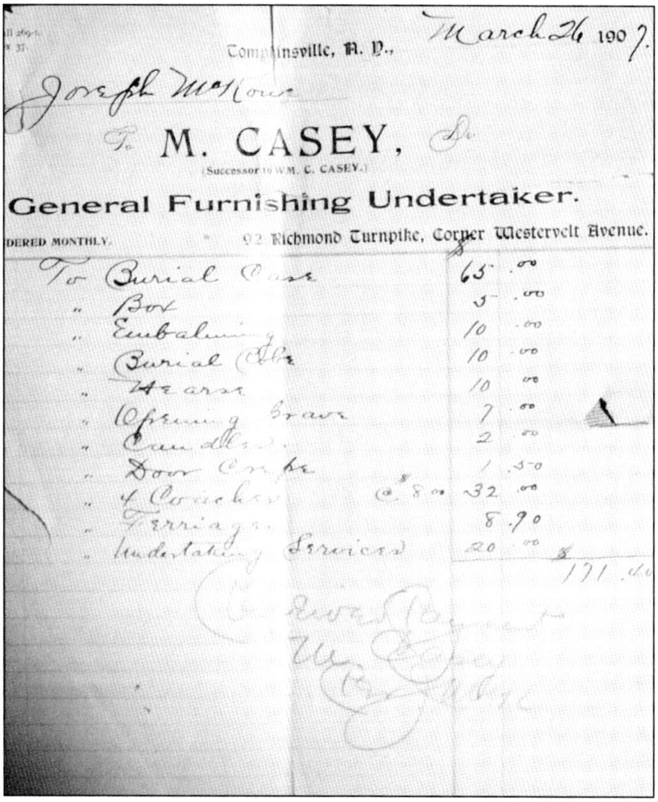

Tompkinsville, N. Y., March 26 1907.

Joseph McHowe

To M. CASEY, Dr.

(Successor to WM. C. CASEY.)

General Furnishing Undertaker.

DERED MONTHLY. 92 Richmond Turnpike, Corner Westervelt Avenue.

		$
To Burial Case		65.00
" Box		5.00
" Embalming		10.00
" Burial Robe		10.00
" Hearse		10.00
" Opening Grave		7.00
" Candles		2.00
" Door Crape		1.50
" 4 Coaches	@ $8.00	32.00
" Ferriage		8.90
" Undertaking Services		20.00
		$171.40

Received Payment M. Casey

This bill dated March 7, 1907, is from Mary Casey for funeral services.

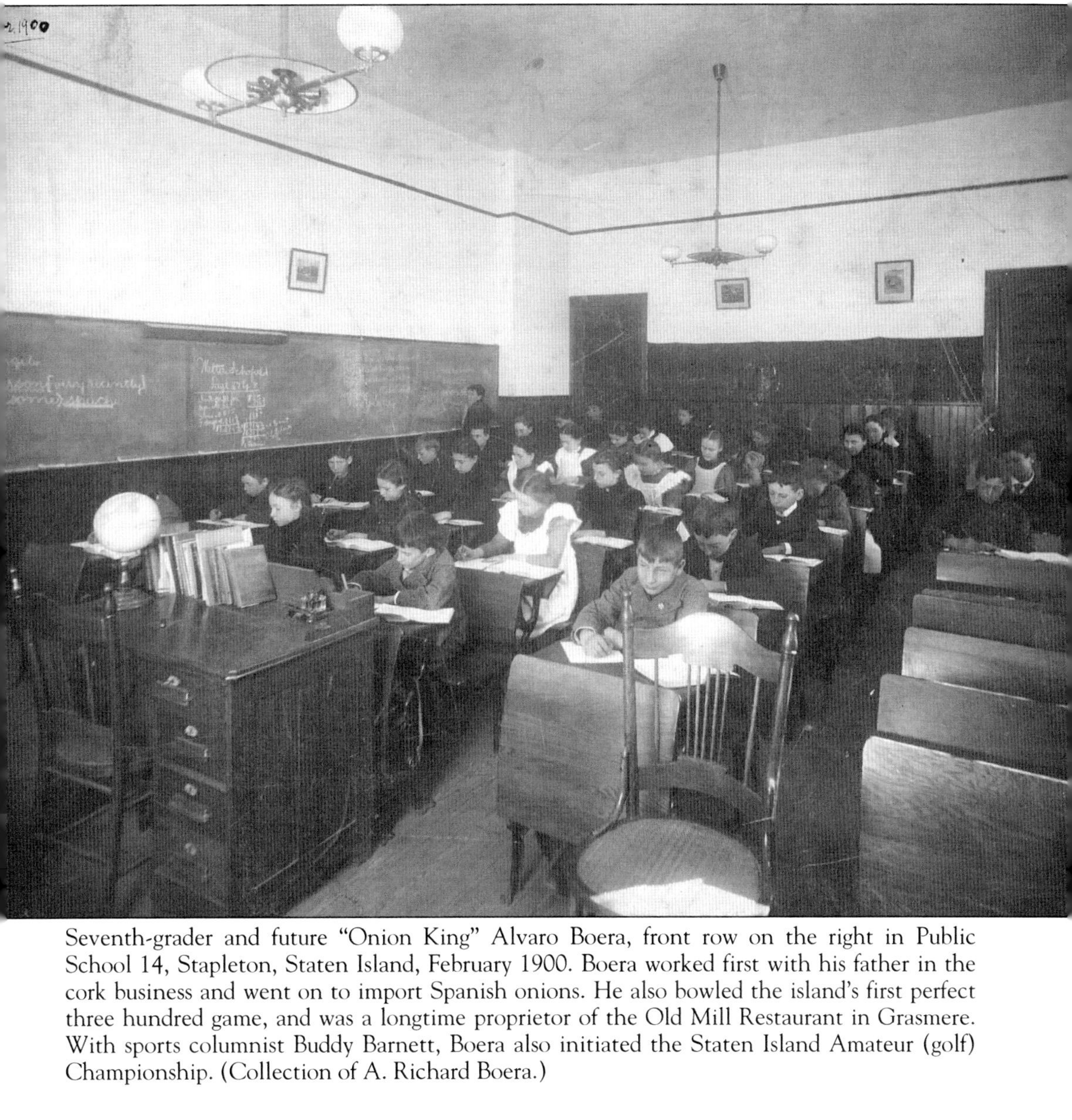

Seventh-grader and future "Onion King" Alvaro Boera, front row on the right in Public School 14, Stapleton, Staten Island, February 1900. Boera worked first with his father in the cork business and went on to import Spanish onions. He also bowled the island's first perfect three hundred game, and was a longtime proprietor of the Old Mill Restaurant in Grasmere. With sports columnist Buddy Barnett, Boera also initiated the Staten Island Amateur (golf) Championship. (Collection of A. Richard Boera.)

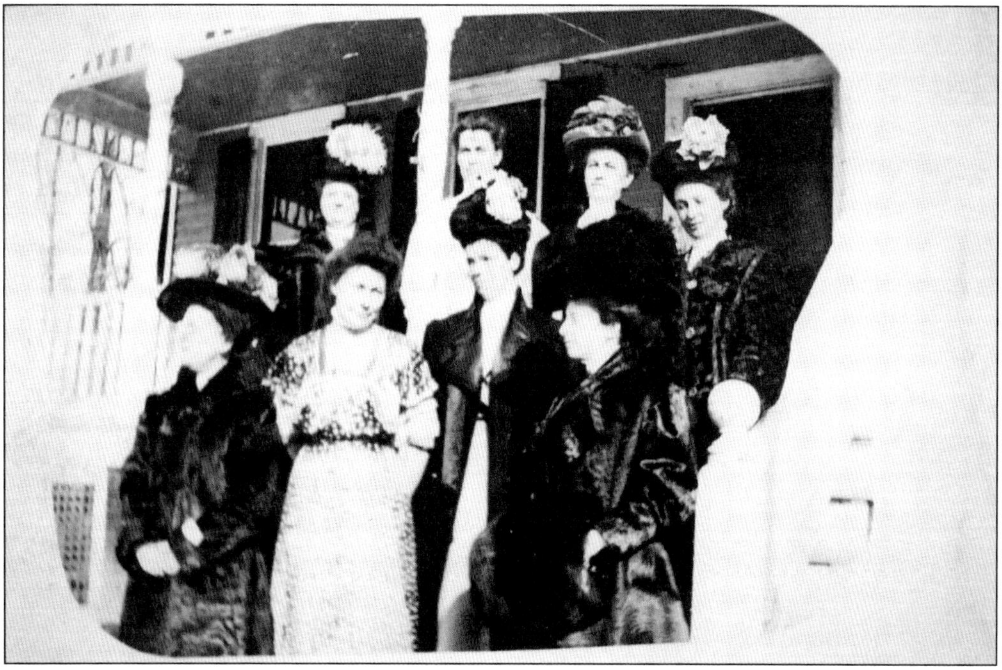

Ladies on a porch in 1909. Pictured in the first row, on the far left, is Louise Stephens; third and center is Frances Pitts. (Collection of Claire and Bill Drinnan.)

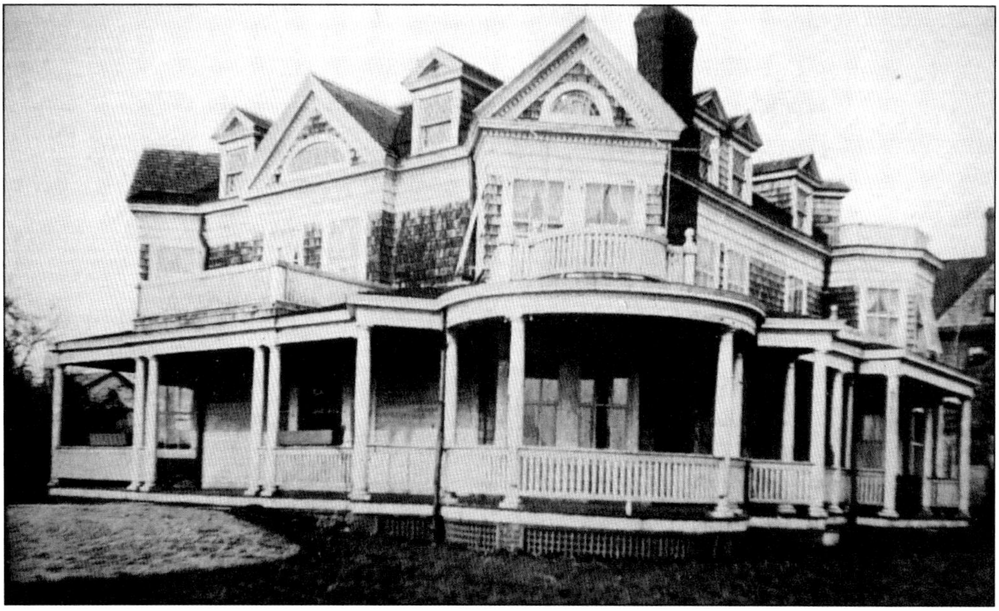

Residence of Judge Marsh, Clifton, Staten Island, 1905. The architect was E.A. Sargent and Henry Spruck and Sons were the builders. In *Rambling Through Rosebank: A Guided Walking Tour of Alice Austen's Neighborhood*, Marjorie Johnson describes this home: "English-born and trained architect Edward Alfred Sargent (1842–1914) designed a Colonial-Revival style house with wrap-around porches in 1902 for Nathaniel Marsh Jr., a supervisor of the township of Southfield, S.I., and the brother of Miss Austen's close friend Julia." (Collection of Marjorie Johnson.)

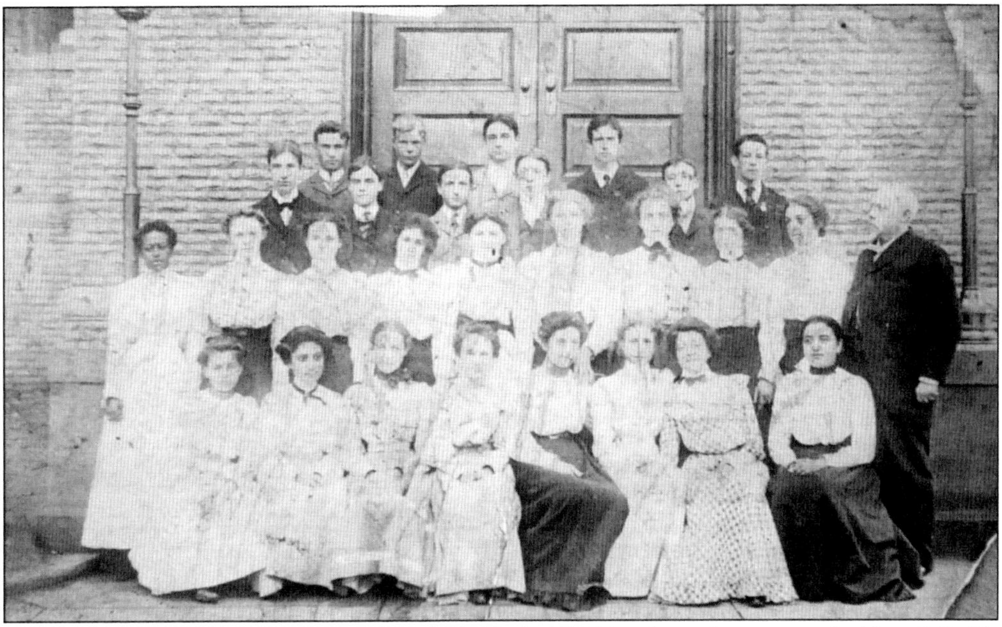

Graduating class of Port Richmond High School in 1901, when classes were held at P.S. 20. Walter Stephens is in the last row, third from left. He later married Frances Pitts, second row, second from the left. (Collection of Claire and Bill Drinnan.)

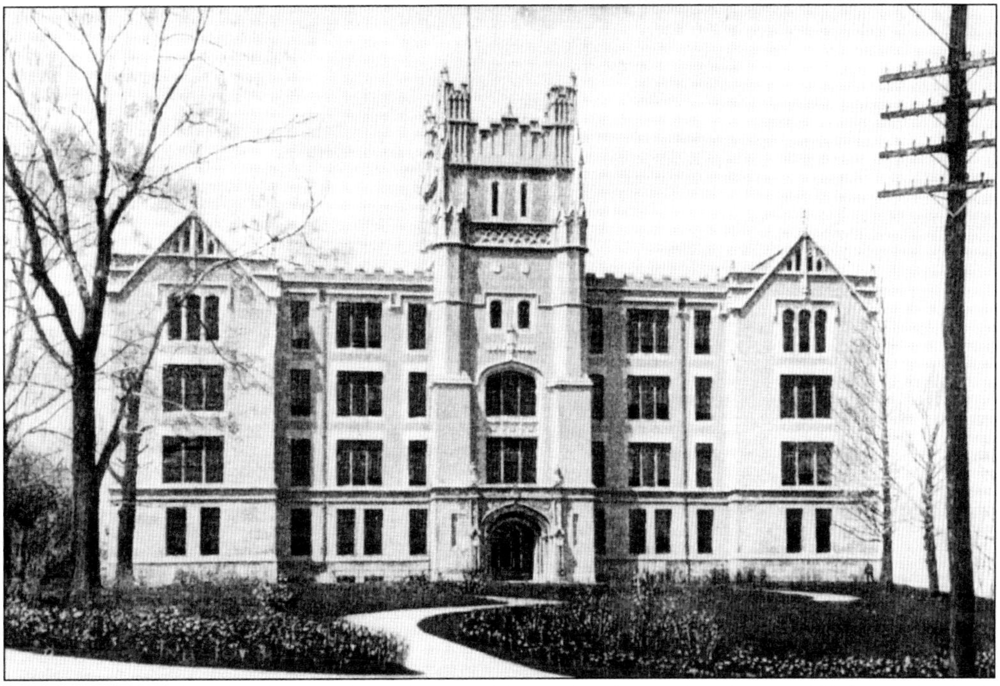

Curtis High School. Built in 1904 and named for author/journalist George William Curtis, it was the first high school on Staten Island. The beautiful Gothic Revival building complete with gargoyles was built opposite the Hotel Castleton that was destroyed by fire in 1907. Curtis said, "God may have made a prettier spot than Staten Island, but He never did." (Collection of Randall Gabrielan.)

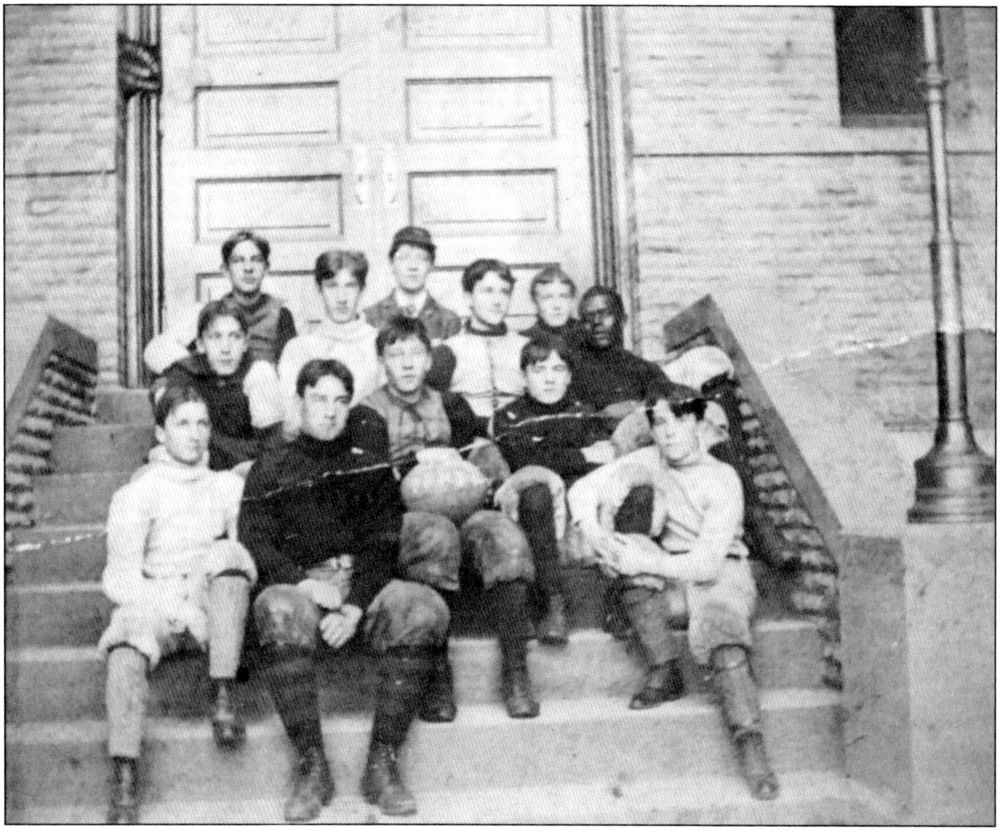

Port Richmond High School football team in 1901. (Collection of Claire and Bill Drinnan.)

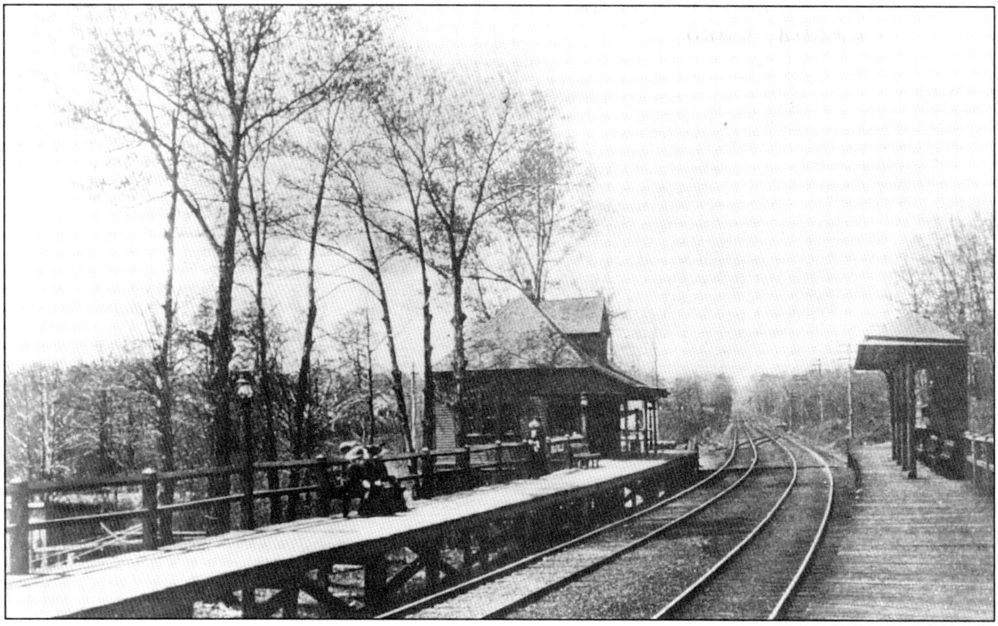

Staten Island Rapid Transit Station at Great Kills, *c.* 1905, possibly by W.J. Grimshaw. (Collection of the Staten Island Historical Society.)

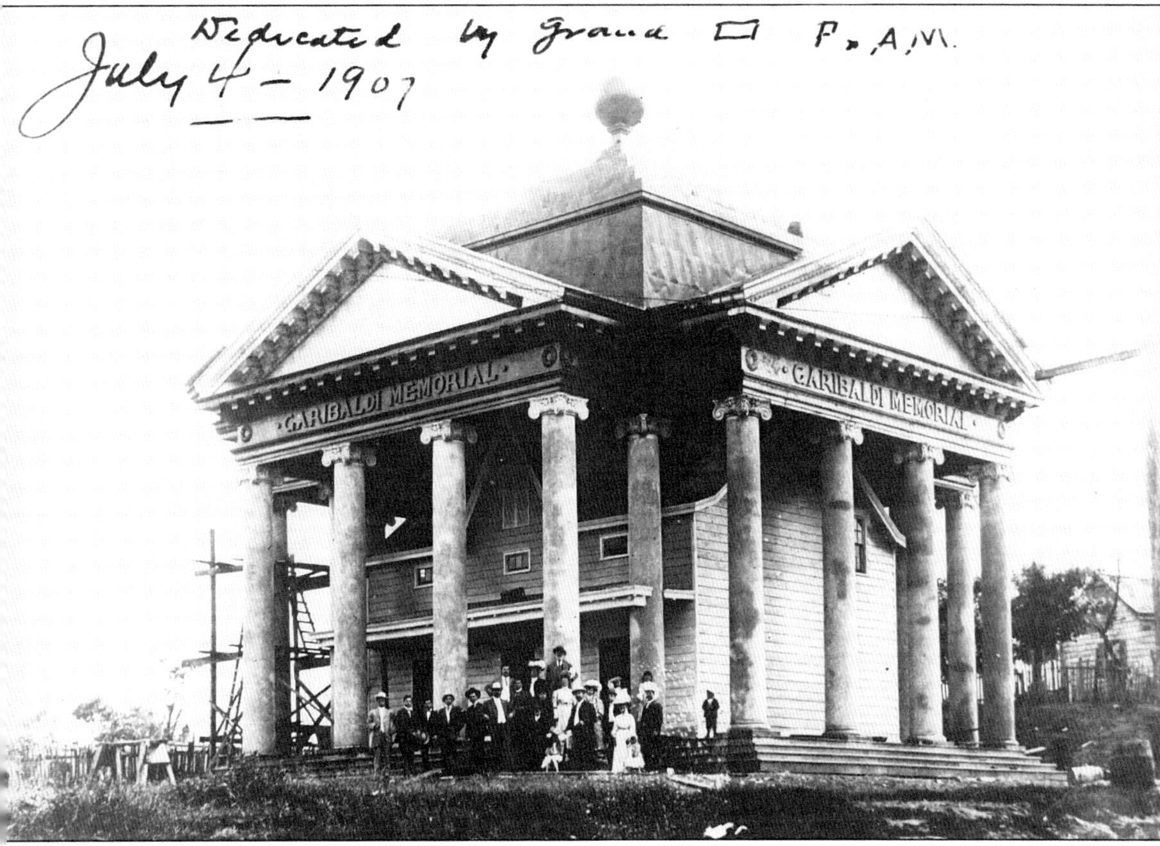

July 4, 1907 dedication of Garibaldi Memorial. The elaborate pantheon that encloses the Rosebank house of Antonio Meucci is a tribute to the memories of patriot Giuseppe Garibaldi and inventor Meucci. Garibaldi spent a year on Staten Island in the company of his friend, but returned to life as a sailor when he was unable to get work. Meucci, who had a candlemaking factory and brewery, is thought to be the first to develop a working telephone but did not acquire a patent. The pantheon was built by Rocco Scocco, the building contractor who also built the Notre Dame Convent and the Linden apartments in Rosebank. The Garibaldi Memorial is open to visitors. (Collection of the Staten Island Historical Society.)

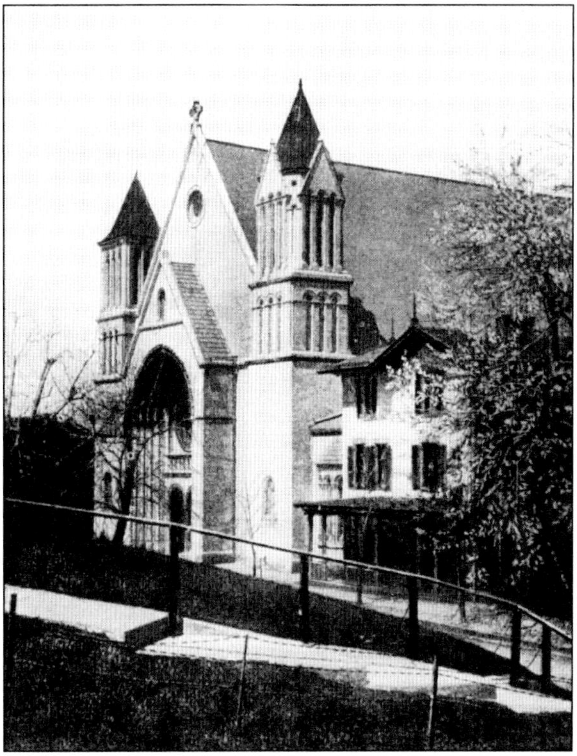

St. Peter's Church. The cornerstone for the Romanesque church on St. Mark's Place in New Brighton was laid in 1903. St. Peter's was the first Roman Catholic parish organized. At one point the congregation met in a gun factory on Richmond Terrace and Lafayette Avenue. The Reverend Ildefonso Medrano was pastor until 1845. The Cardinal's Tower, built at a later date, was named for John Cardinal Farley, who had been a curate at St. Peter's. The church is a New York City landmark. (Collection of Randall Gabrielan.)

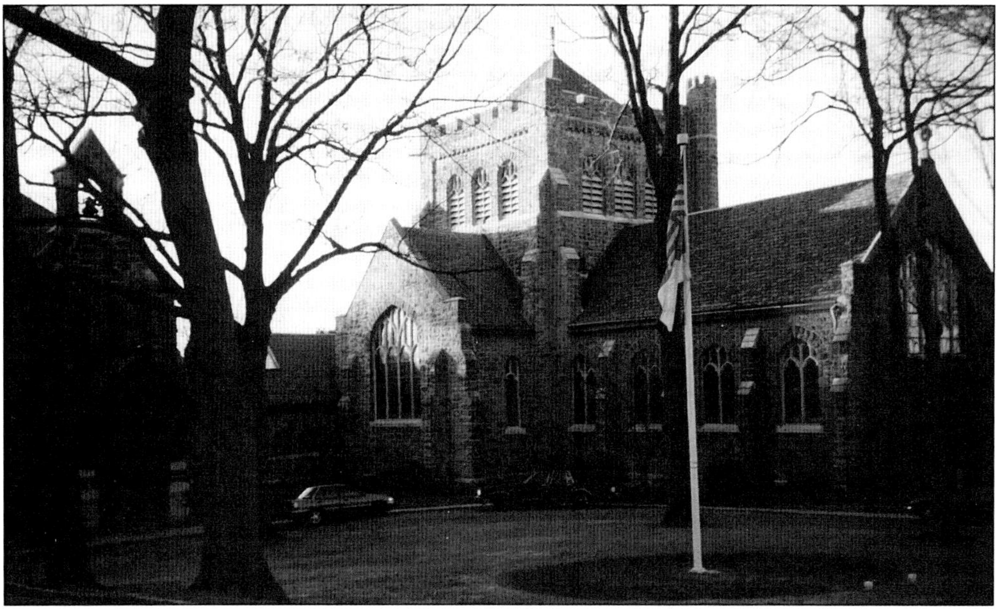

Christ Church. Built on the site of a previous church this building was designed by Philadelphia architect Isaac Pursell. It was dedicated in 1905. The church contains beautiful stained-glass windows made by Louis Comfort Tiffany, and Lamb, D'Ascenzo, Valentine D'Ogries, Gorham, and Leuchs. The chancel window of 1904 made by Tiffany depicts "The Resurrection" and is dedicated to the memory of Anita Ludlum DeBost, whose death at the age of 24 saddened the community. (Photograph by Margaret Lundrigan.)

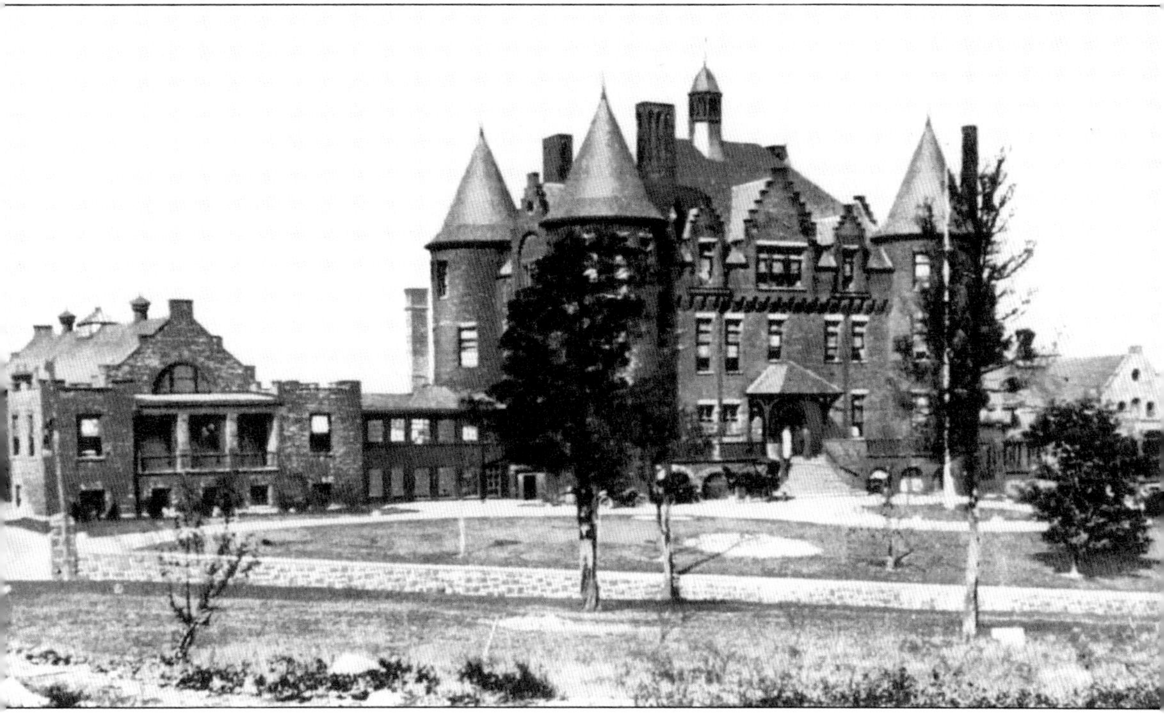

Smith's Infirmary, Tompkinsville, March 26, 1907. This was the first voluntary hospital on Staten Island. The Tower building, designed by Alfred E. Barlow, was built in 1889, following the gift of 6 acres of land on Castleton Avenue. Originally located at Bay Street and Union Place in Stapleton, the infirmary, named for much-loved local physician Samuel R. Smith, was founded in 1861 to care for the indigent ill. In 1870 the infirmary moved to Dr. Smith's former residence at the corner of Hannah and Van Duzer Streets in Tompkinsville. Ralph Waldo Emerson is said to be one the speakers at the infirmary's opening. Mrs. Thomas Melville, sister-in-law of novelist Herman Melville and wife of the superintendent of Sailors' Snug Harbor, was active in the Women's Auxiliary, an organization responsible for fund-raising. Around 1919, the name was officially changed to Staten Island Hospital. (Collection of Randall Gabrielan.)

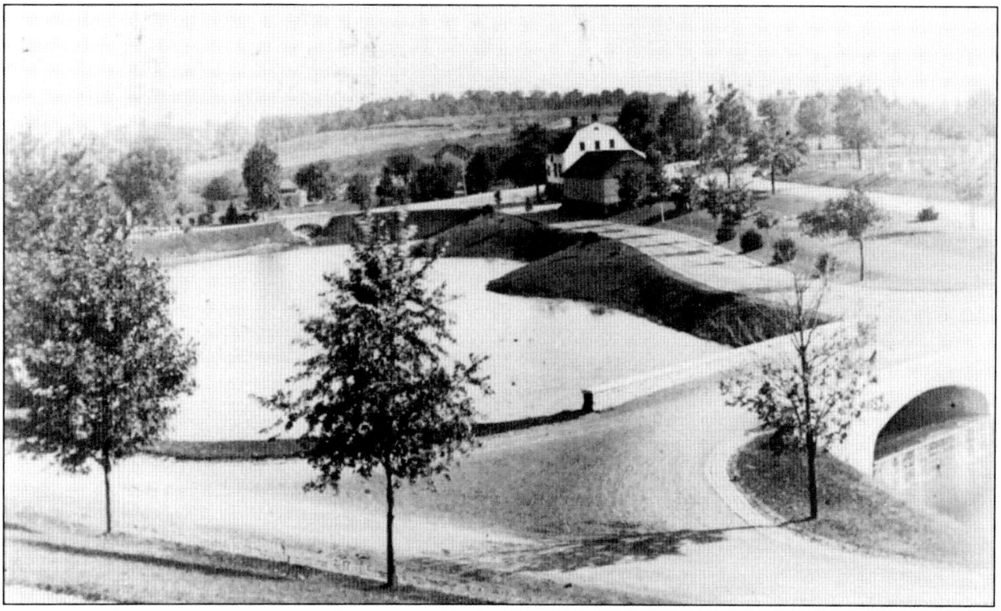

Moravian Cemetery, 1906. The building that is presently the cemetery office served as meeting place for the congregation. The original cemetery was approximately 5 acres and was enlarged to 40 primarily through gifts, many from the Vanderbilt family, which has long been associated with the Moravian church. (Collection of Randall Gabrielan.)

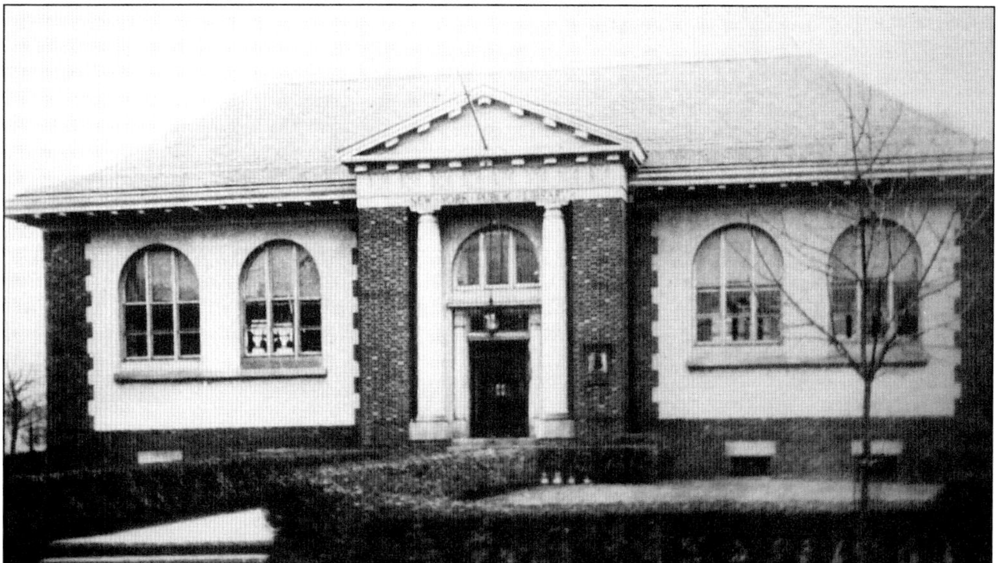

The Tottenville Library. This was the first branch of the New York City Public Library to open on Staten Island in 1904. In 1901, Andrew Carnegie made $5.2 million available for communities that wished to construct local libraries, and several local organizations including the Philemon Society applied for these funds. Edna Holden wrote that in 1899 there had been a public library on Johnson Avenue in Tottenville with a stock of 230 books. The Port Richmond library opened in 1905, followed in 1907 by the St. George and Stapleton branches. Between 1902 and 1914, 37 branches of the New York City Public libraries were erected in Manhattan, the Bronx, and Staten Island. (Collection of the Bedell/Pizzo Funeral Home.)

Two

1910–1919

Into and Beyond World War I

*Authors Mark Twain and Leo Tolstoi, and nursing pioneer Florence Nightingale die, 1910.
*The first "Father's Day" celebrated in Spokane, Washington, 1910.
*Leonardo da Vinci's *Mona Lisa* stolen from Louvre, 1911; found 1913 in Italy.
*Scientist Marie Curie wins Nobel Prize for Chemistry, 1911.
*Mexican Civil War ends by armistice, 1911.
*The S.S. *Titanic* hits iceberg and sinks on her maiden voyage, 1912; 1,513 people drown.
*Woodrow Wilson elected U.S. president, 1912.
*Carl Jung writes *The Theory of Psychoanalysis*, 1912.
*F.W. Woolworth Company founded, 1912.
*The Armory Show introduces Cubism and Post-Impressionism in New York City, 1913.
*Grand Central Terminal in New York opened, 1913.
*Bela Schick discovers immunity test for diphtheria, 1913.
*World War I declared after June 28 assassination of Austrian Archduke Francis Ferdinand and his wife in Sarajevo, July 28, 1914.
*The Panama Canal opens, 1914
*U.S. Coast Guard established, 1915.
*The *Lusitania* is sunk by Germany, 1915.
*W. Somerset Maugham writes *Of Human Bondage*, and Edgar Lee Masters writes *A Spoon River Anthology*, 1915
*American playwright Arthur Miller born, 1915.
*Classic New Orleans jazz gains popularity, 1915.
*Margaret Sanger jailed for producing *Family Limitation*, the first book on birth control, 1915.
*"Shell-shock" theory (today known as Post Traumatic Stress Disorder) introduced by F.W. Mott, 1916.

*President Woodrow Wilson reelected, 1916.

*"Buffalo Bill" (W.F. Cody) dies, 1916.

*Actress Sarah Bernhardt, 72, begins last tour of America, 1916.

*American industrialist Andrew Carnegie dies, 1919.

*"Bobbed" hair becomes a fad in Britain and the U.S., 1917.

*George M. Cohan writes popular American war song "Over There," 1917.

*Composer Leonard Bernstein and American evangelist Billy Graham born, 1918.

*United Lutheran Church established in U.S., 1918.

*Influenza epidemic, 1918; kills 22 million worldwide by 1920.

*Herbert Hoover appointed director-general of international organization for European relief, 1919.

*A.D. Juilliard bequeaths $20 million for Juilliard School of Music, 1919.

*Prohibition ratified as 18th amendment to U.S. Constitution, 1919.

*Walter Gropius founds Bauhaus, a revolutionized study of architecture, painting, sculpture, and industrial arts, 1919.

*Lady Astor elected first British woman member of Parliament, 1919.

*Theodore Roosevelt dies, 1919.

*President Woodrow Wilson wins Nobel Peace Prize, 1919.

*Babe Ruth hits 587-foot home run in game between Boston Red Sox and New York Giants, 1919, and is sold by Sox to New York Yankees, 1920, for $125,000.

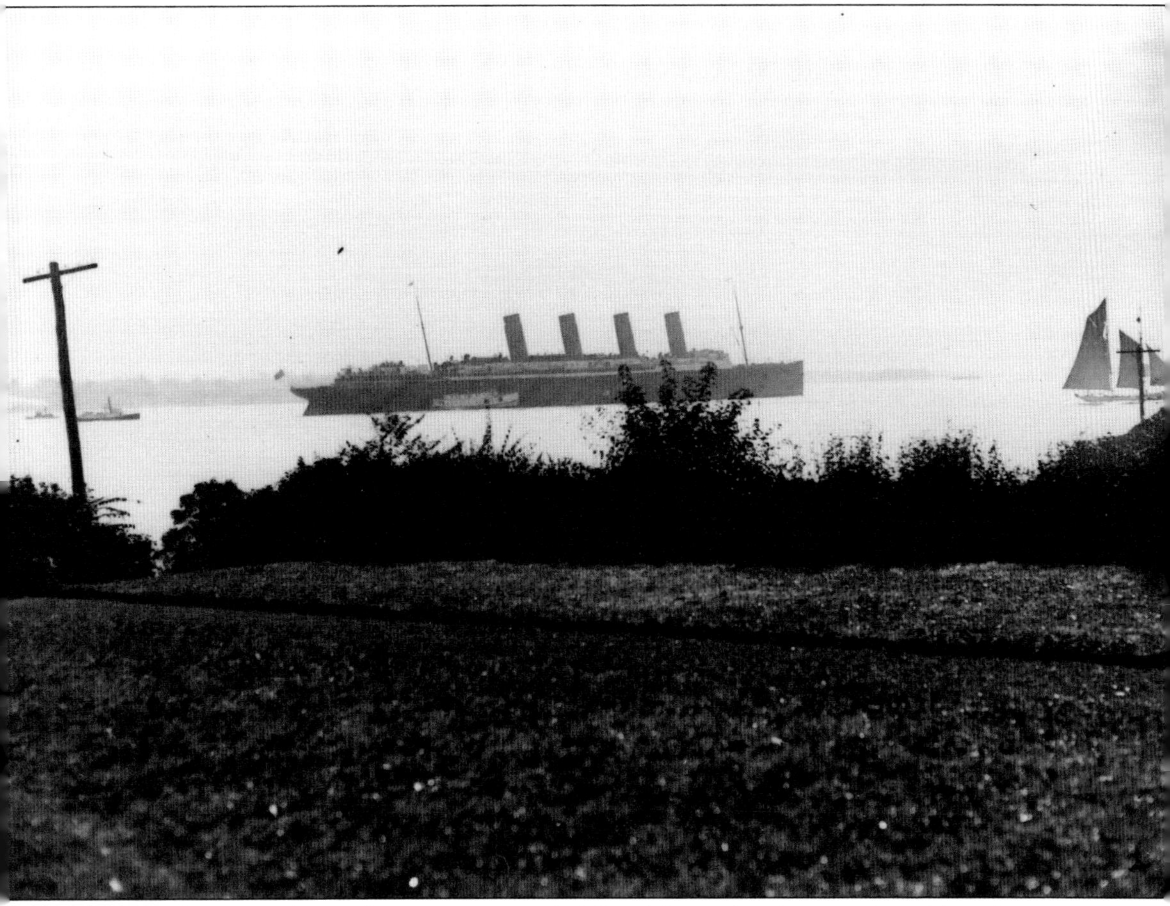

The S.S. *Lusitania*. A prophetic image entitled *Last Voyage* by photographer Alice Austen captures the Cunard liner as it leaves New York Harbor. The *Lusitania* was sunk a few miles off the coast of Ireland while on her normal run from New York to Liverpool. Because the vessel sank so quickly, the lifeboats could not be fully loaded and lowered. As a result, 1,198 of the passengers aboard died. The sinking of the British liner on May 7, 1915, by a German submarine contributed to the United States' entry into World War I. (Collection of the Staten Island Historical Society.)

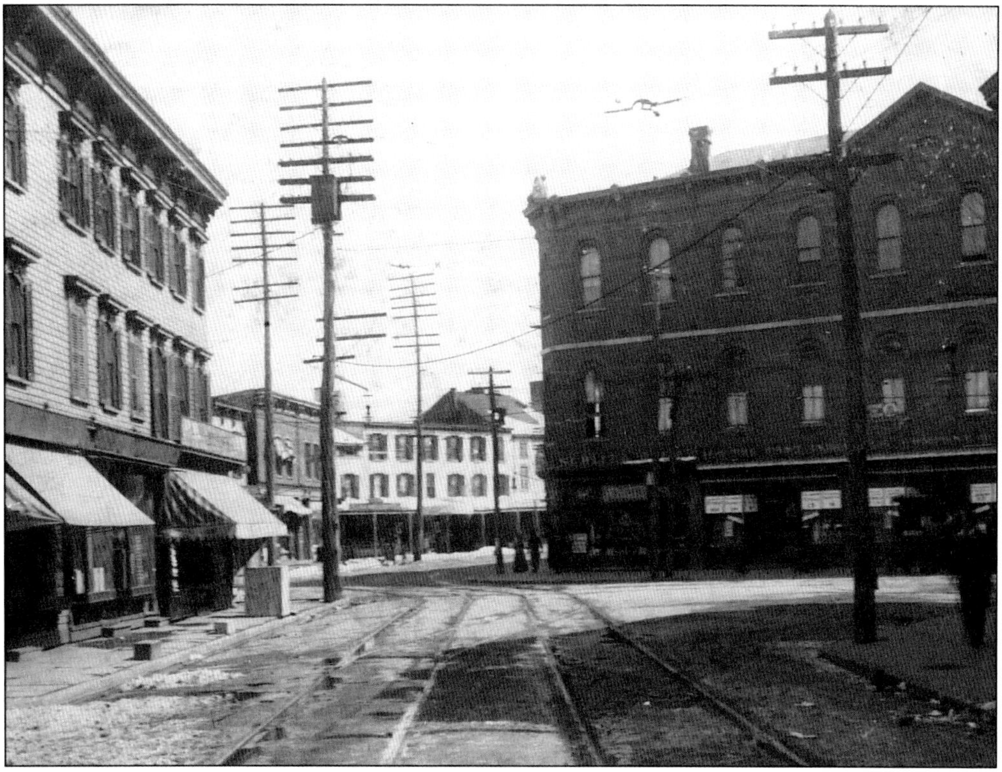

Port Richmond Square, c. 1910, featuring the Griffith Building. (Collection of the Staten Island Historical Society.)

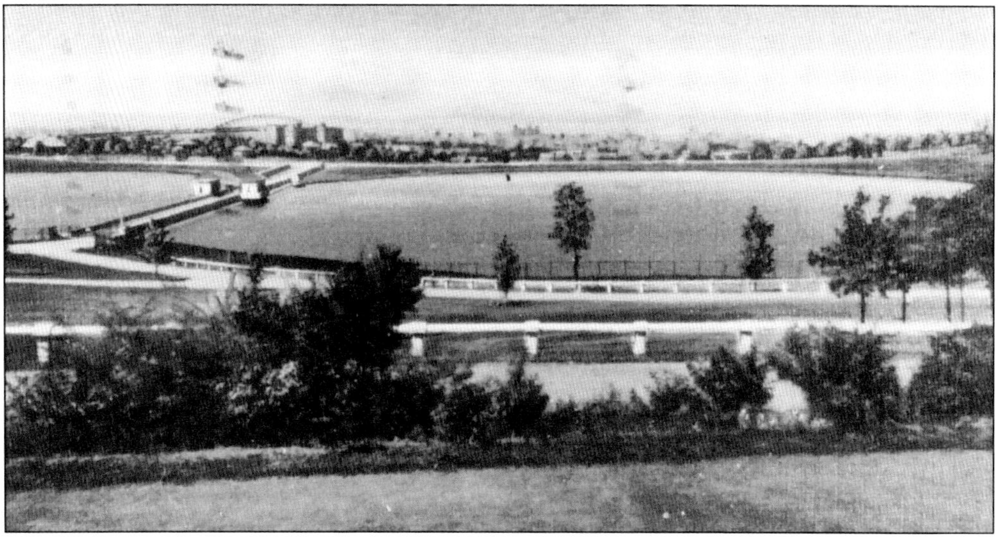

Silver Lake Reservoir and Park. Silver Lake was known as Fresh Pond until the 1850s. The Silver Lake Hotel was a popular summer resort with swimming, boating, and a dance pavilion. The Silver Lake Hotel became Raisch's Casino following the death of owner John Franzreb. The lake was also used for ice harvesting; the Hygeia Ice Company was owned by the Franzreb family. In 1917, the reservoir was built to bring in water from upstate New York. The golf course clubhouse was built in 1929. (Collection of Randall Gabrielan.)

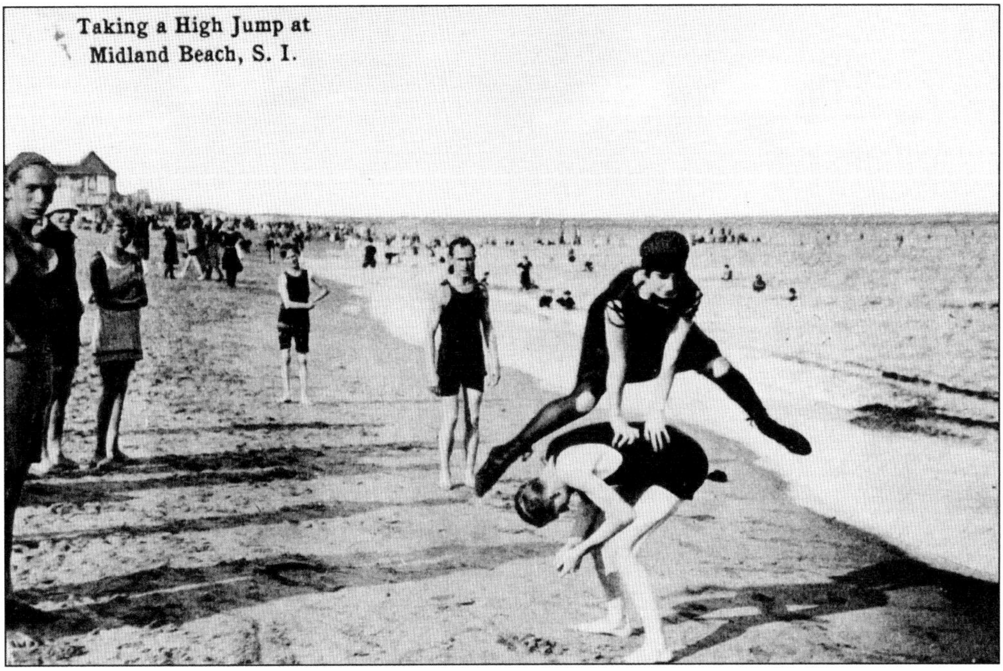

"Taking a High Jump at Midland Beach, S.I." (Collection of the Staten Island Historical Society.)

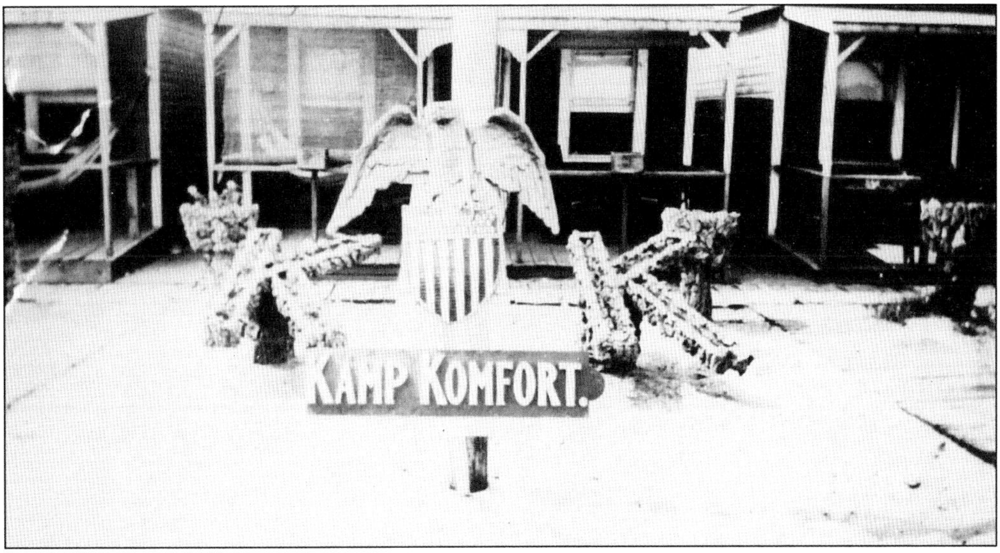

Kamp Komfort at South Beach, July 4, 1917. Kamp Komfort was the summer home of Senator Harry Palmer. Palmer was born in New Jersey, but was attracted to Staten Island because of pleasant memories of spending his childhood summers on the island. He was elected three times and officiated at the groundbreaking ceremonies for the Goethals and Outerbridge. South Beach, originally named Oude Dorp and later called Dover by the English, was the first Dutch settlement on Staten Island. (Collection of Marion and Richard Dutka.)

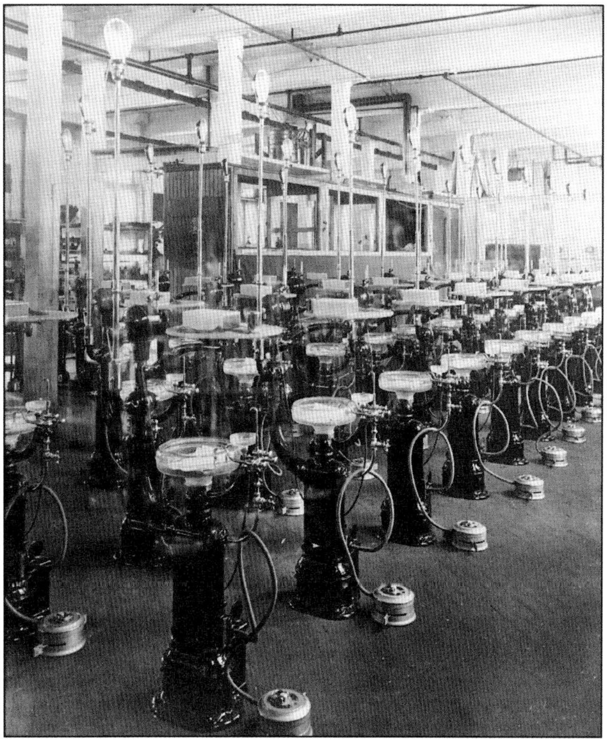

S.S. White Company assembly line. Copied from a print in the collection of Joseph Helmer, this photograph shows the fountain spittoon assembly area of the S.S. White Company. The company was founded in 1865 by Algernon Johnston and his brothers William and Melville on the site of a former candle factory. In 1881, the company merged with the firm created by Samuel Stockton White of Philadelphia to create the S.S. White Dental Manufacturing Company. S.S. White, affectionately known as the "Factory by the Sea," manufactured false teeth, dental instruments, and chairs. This picture, *c.* 1910, was taken by a company photographer. (Collection of the Staten Island Historical Society.)

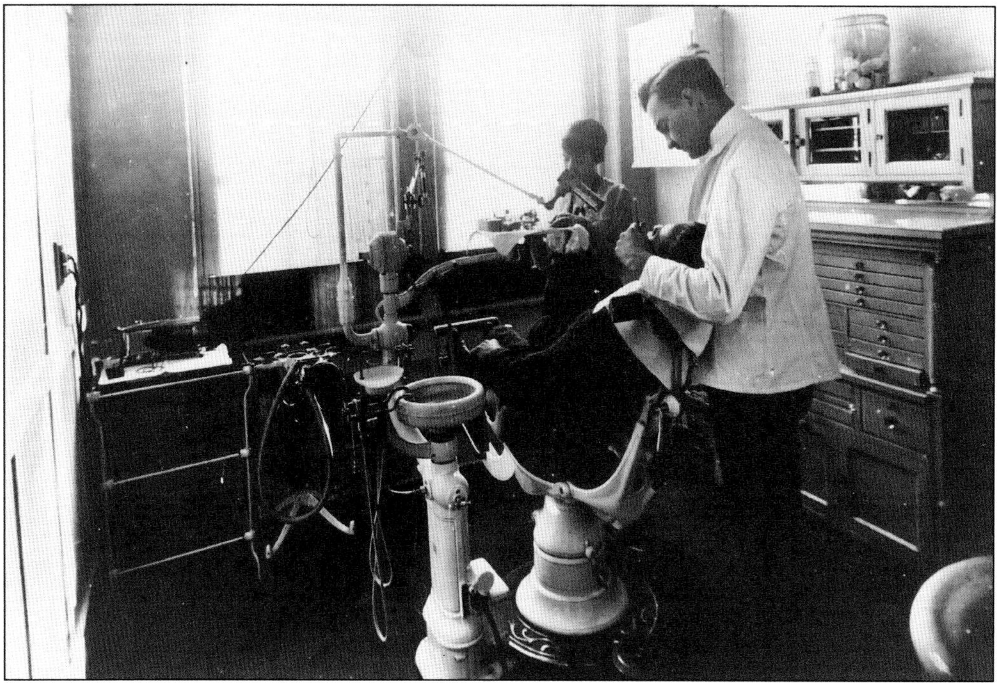

Another photograph, *c.* 1910, by a company photographer. It is of the employee dental clinic at the S.S. White Company, Princes Bay. By the 1890s the factory had become one of the largest industrial employers on Staten Island, with more than four hundred workers. (Collection of the Staten Island Historical Society.)

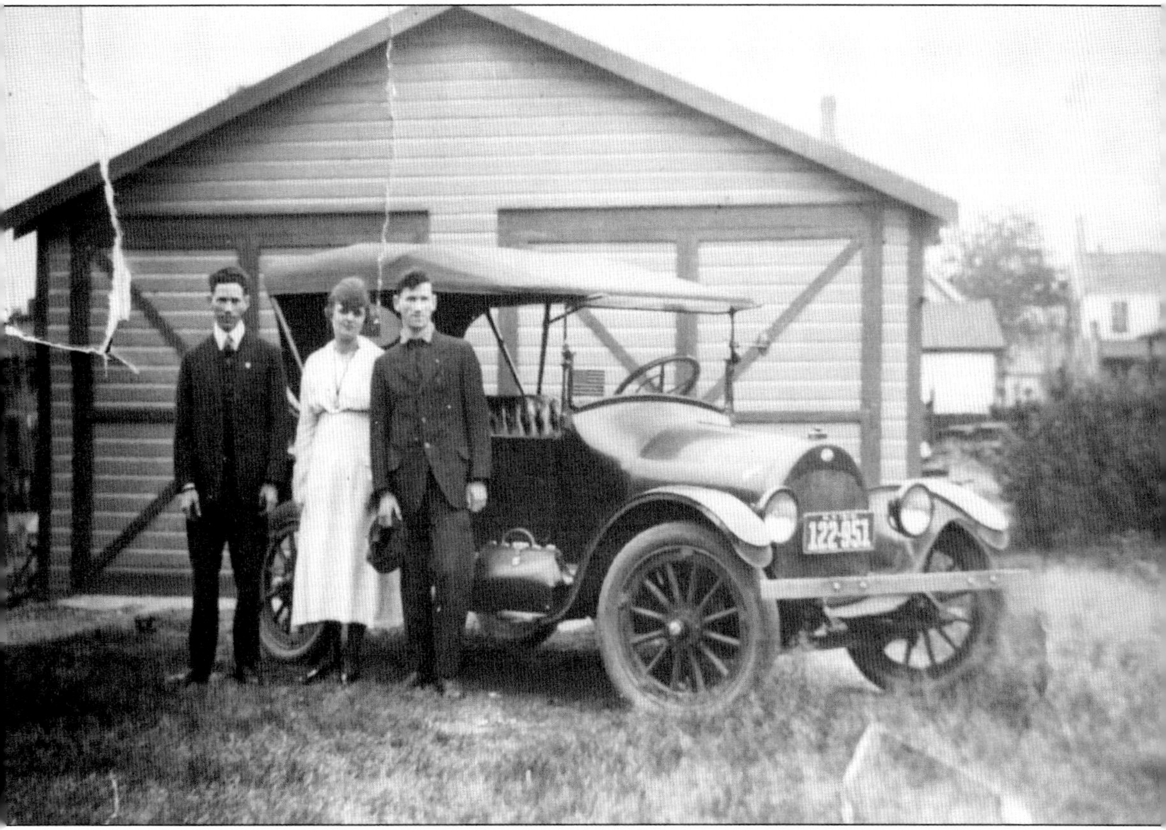

Ruth Martineau with fiancé, David Decker, and his brother Eugene prior to David's leaving to serve in World War I. David gave Eugene instructions to "take care of his car and girl." Ms. Martineau's diary records that she "went riding with Gene," indicating that Gene honored his promise. Ruth and David married upon his return from the war. Approximately five thousand Staten Islanders served in the war. (Collection of Marjorie Johnson.)

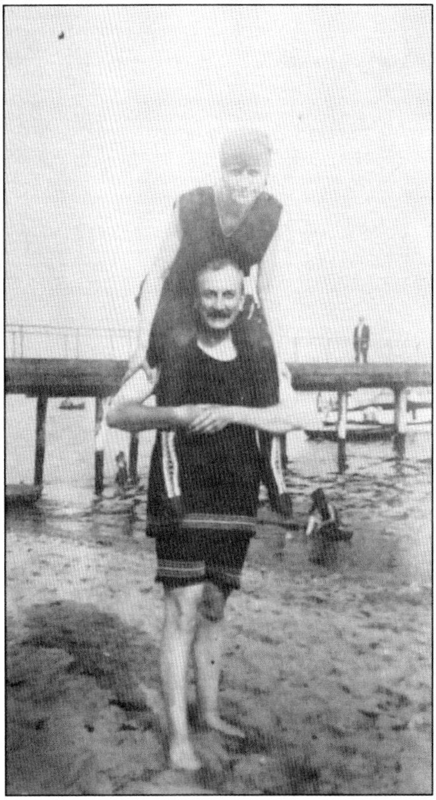

"Grampa and Auntie Mae at South Beach, 1917." The South Beach of the early 1900s was one of the premier resorts of the East Coast. Similar to Coney Island's Steeplechase and Luna Parks, South Beach's Happyland Amusement opened in 1906 to a crowd estimated at 30,000. Happyland had many arcades, a theater, and swimming pool. Severe fires swept through the area in 1917 and 1929. (Collection of Marion and Richard Dutka.)

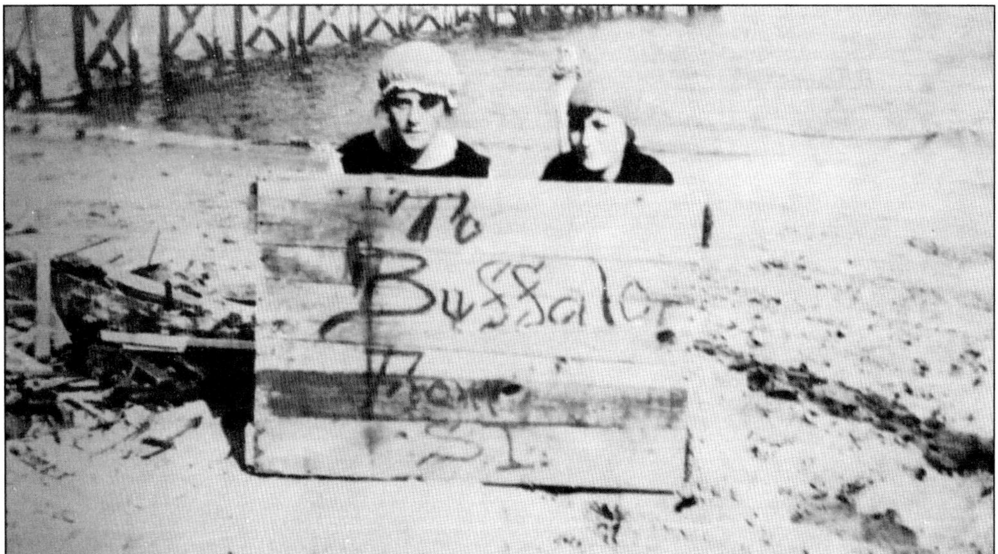

The sign announces "To Buffalo From S.I.," South Beach. (Collection of Marion and Richard Dutka.)

Pony picture, c. 1915. Many readers will fondly remember the popular pony picture taken by itinerant photographers. Edward Johnson is seated on the pony. (Collection of Marjorie Johnson.)

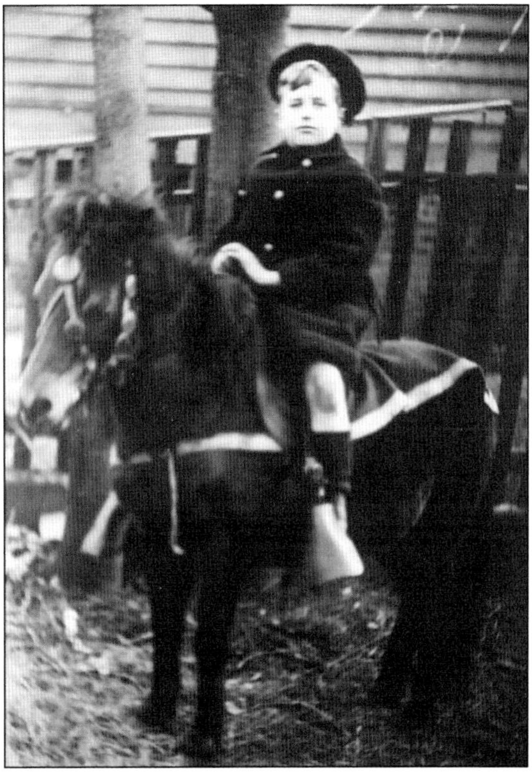

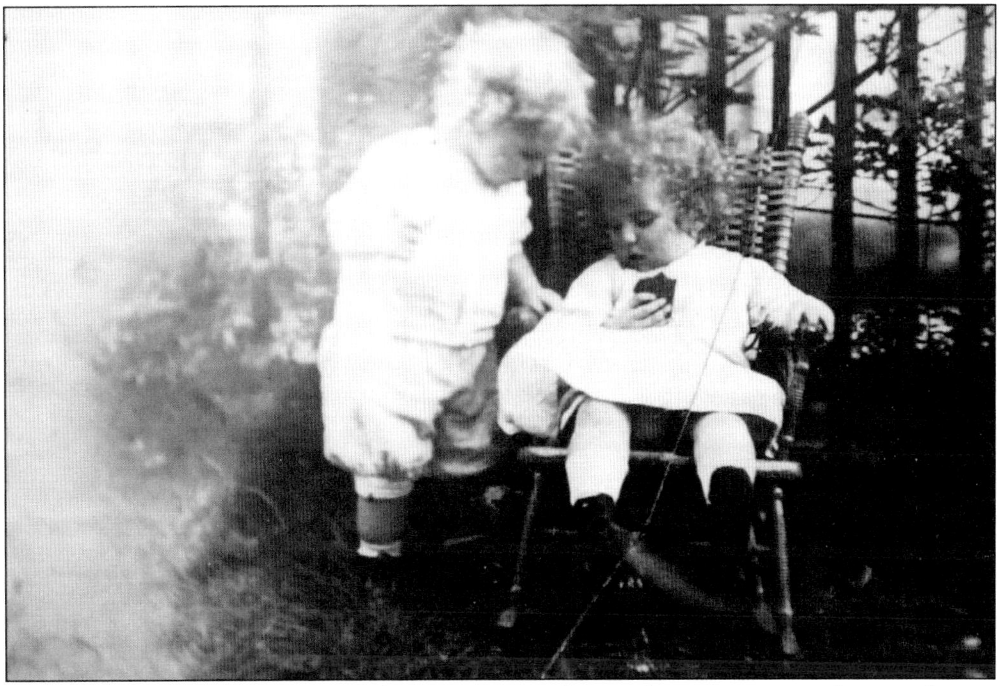

Edward Johnson and his cousin Jack Turner. Here the two boys are engrossed in watching a ladybug. This photograph served as a study for a lovely painting by Johnson's mother, Alice Sargent Johnson. (Collection of Marjorie Johnson.)

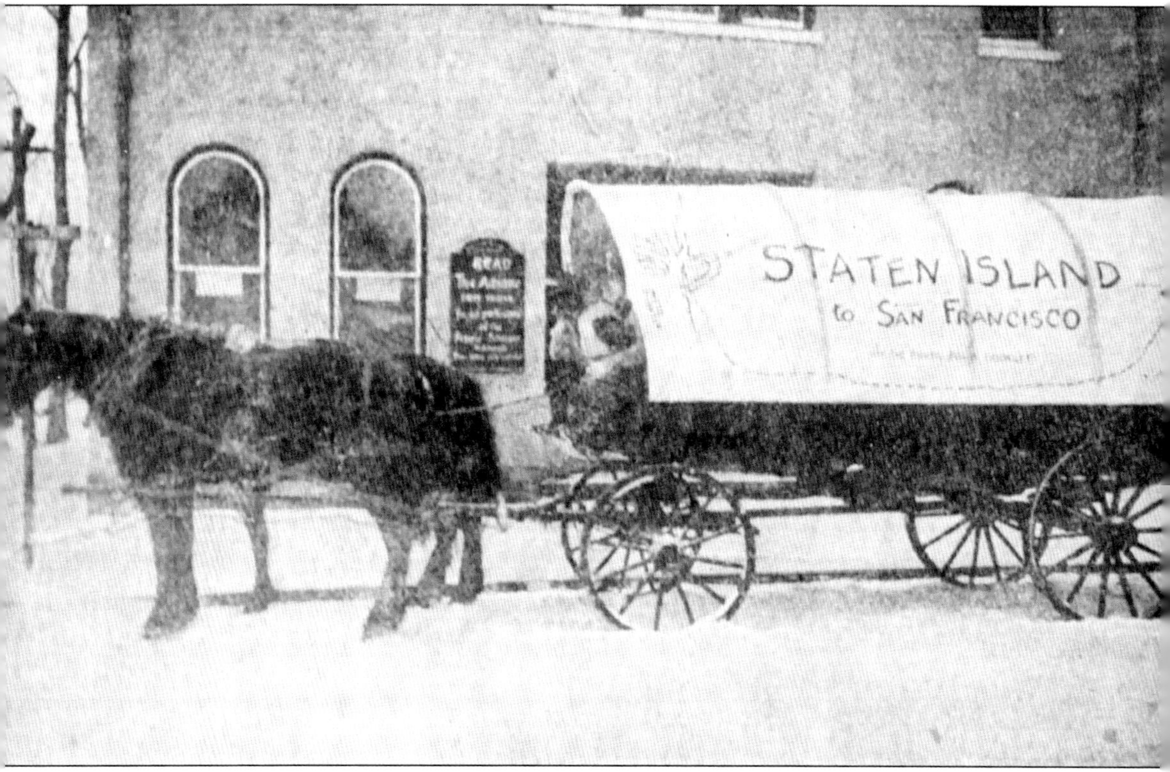

The Prairie Schooner. In a charming reversal of Horace Greeley's direction to "Go West, young man," the Prairie Schooner beckoned to "Come East"—namely to Staten Island. In an interesting public relations campaign, *Staten Island Advance* publisher William C. Wilcox sent a covered wagon west to distribute pamphlets extolling the virtues of living on Staten Island. Setting out on February 12, 1915, the itinerary was a 30-week trip to arrive at The Panama-Pacific Exposition in San Francisco. As the pamphlet noted, real estate was reasonably priced because there was not a subway connecting Staten Island to the other boroughs. Prospective "settlers" were encouraged to beat the rush and buy early. The crew of the schooner included *Advance* writer John Drebinger Jr. (a.k.a., Ten Flat), William Stephens, Edward Smith, a dog named Teddy, and flea-bitten Grey, the horse. Ten Flat kept a De Torquevillesque journal in which he recorded people's opinions on topics such as women's suffrage. After many colorful adventures, the journey was abandoned in Denver due to lack of funds. (Collection of Claire and Bill Drinnan.)

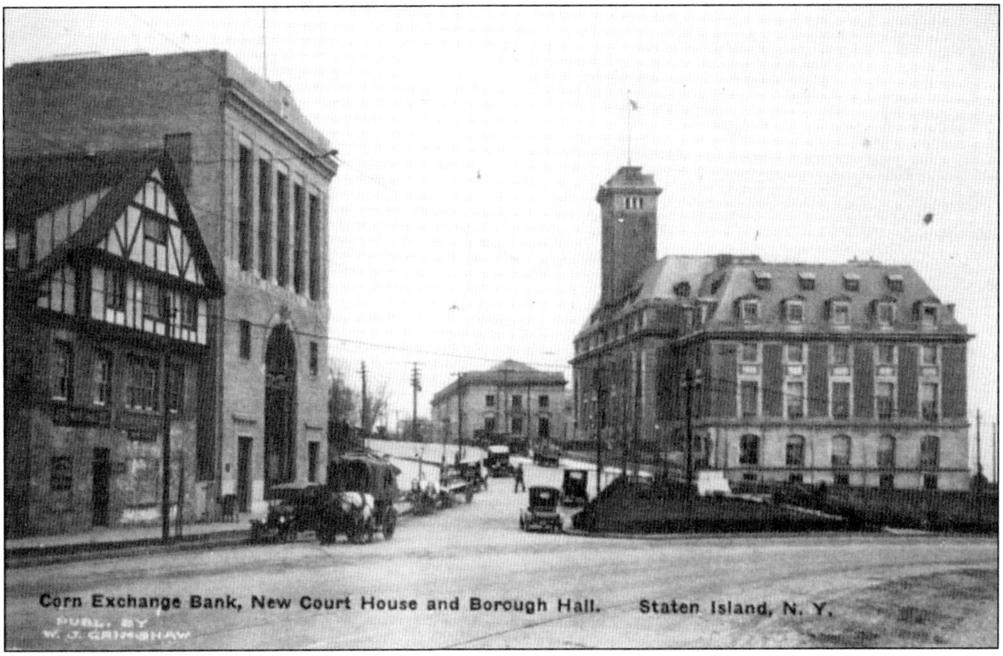

W.J. Grimshaw photographed the Corn Exchange Bank, New Court House, and Borough Hall. (Collection of William and Judith McMillen.)

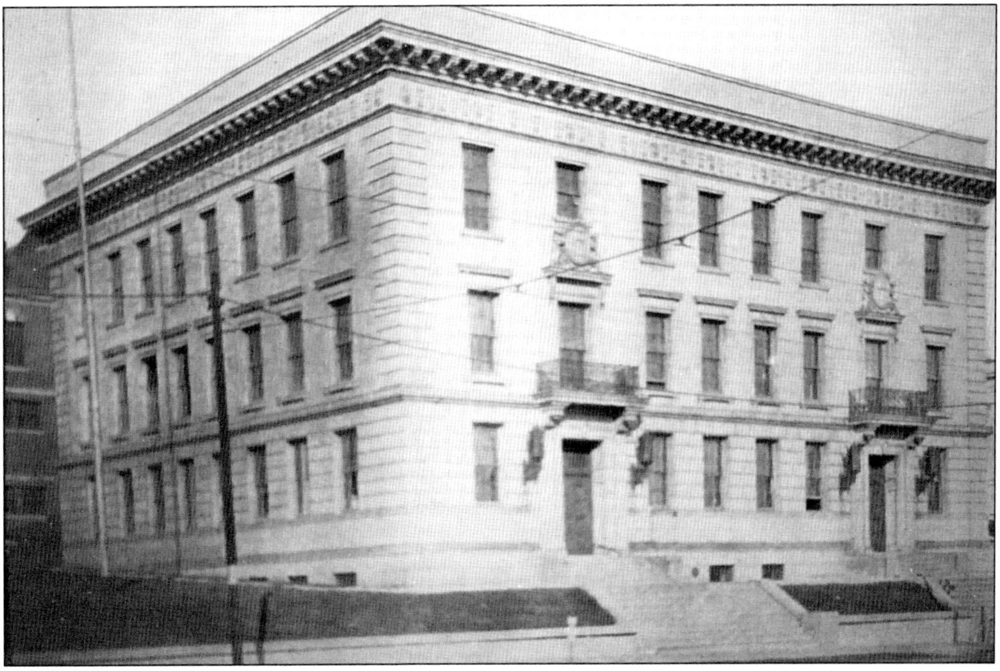

The 120th Precinct, Police Headquarters, St. George. James Whitford was the architect and Anderson Construction Co. were the builders for this building. In 1870, the police department had 50 officers and was headquartered on Beach Street in Stapleton. The building of the 120th Precinct in 1917 was part of the movement of civic functions to St. George. By the 1960s there were five hundred officers on Staten Island. (Collection of Marjorie Johnson.)

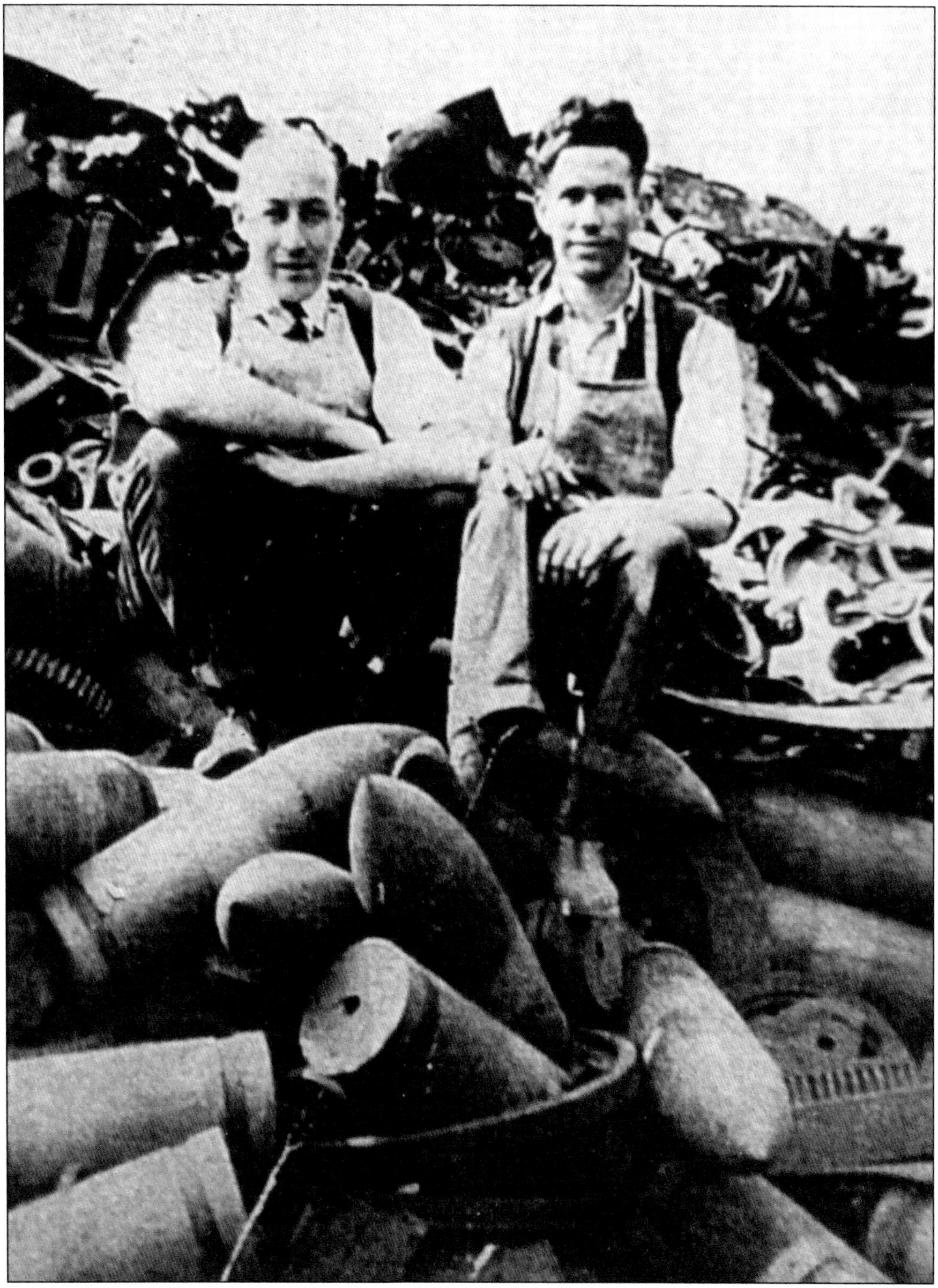

Gene Decker and a fellow worker at the foundry of the Staten Island Shipyard in 1917. The Staten Island Shipyard was later acquired by Bethlehem Steel. Shipbuilding, long an important industry on Staten Island, gained momentum during both world wars. Historians Davis and Leng noted that during World War I shipyard employees who were working too much overtime formed "The Disgruntled Millionaires Club" that met on a deserted barge in Mariners Harbor. (Collection of Marjorie Johnson.)

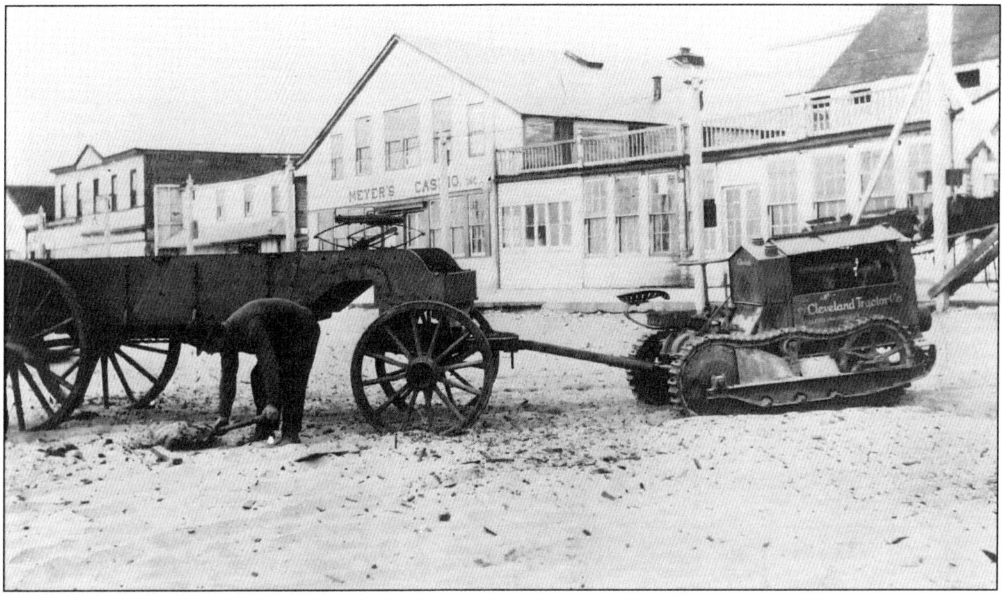

Beach cleaning photographed by Edwin Skinner, *c.* 1915. (Collection of the Staten Island Historical Society.)

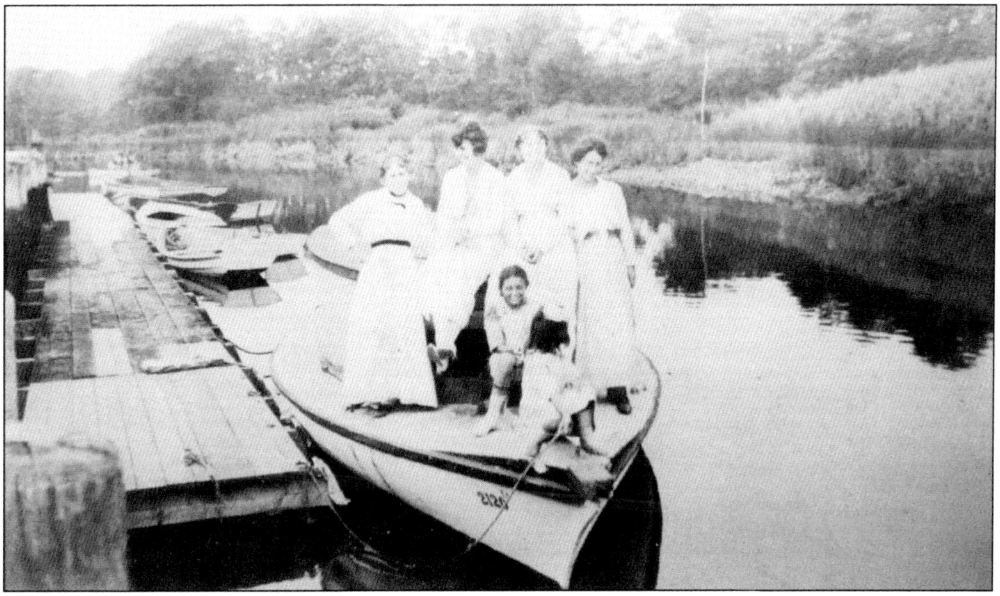
The Decker ladies on a boat, Friday, August 29, 1919. (Collection of Marjorie Johnson.)

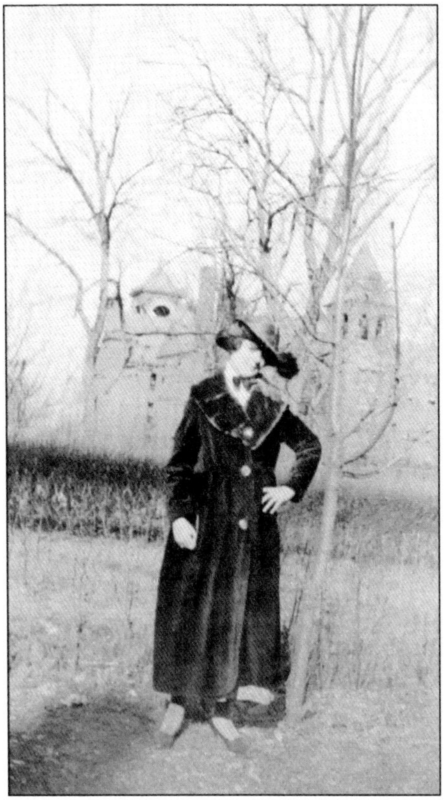

Ruth Martineau, all dressed up on Friday, March 21, 1919, with P.S. 20 in the background. (Collection of Marjorie Decker.)

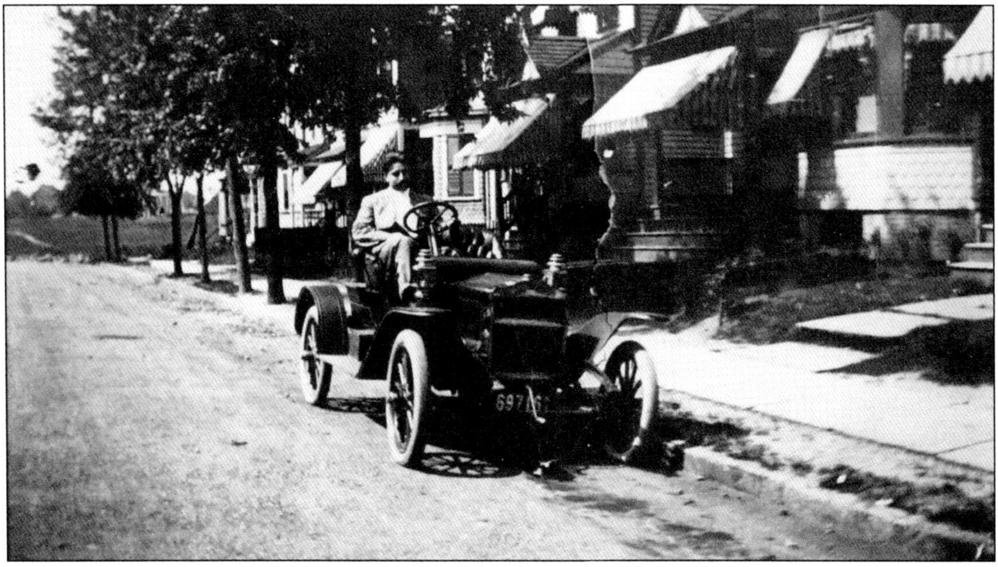

Walt Stephens in his automobile on Harrison Avenue in Port Richmond, September 1911. (Collection of Claire and Bill Drinnan.)

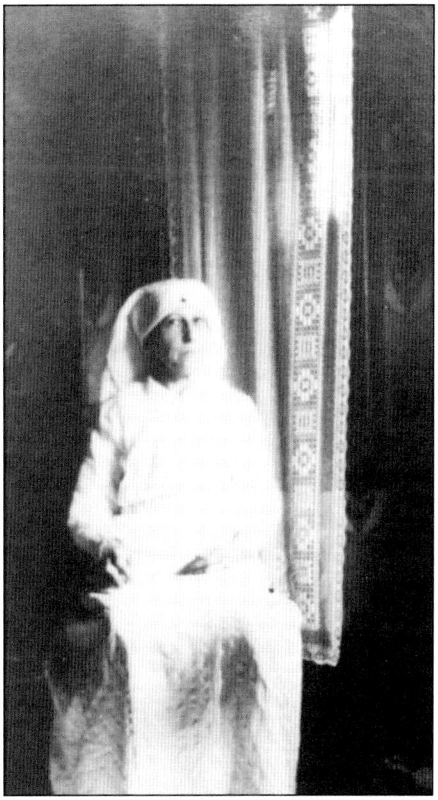

Sophie Van Name Decker as a Red Cross nurse, 1918. (Collection of Marjorie Johnson.)

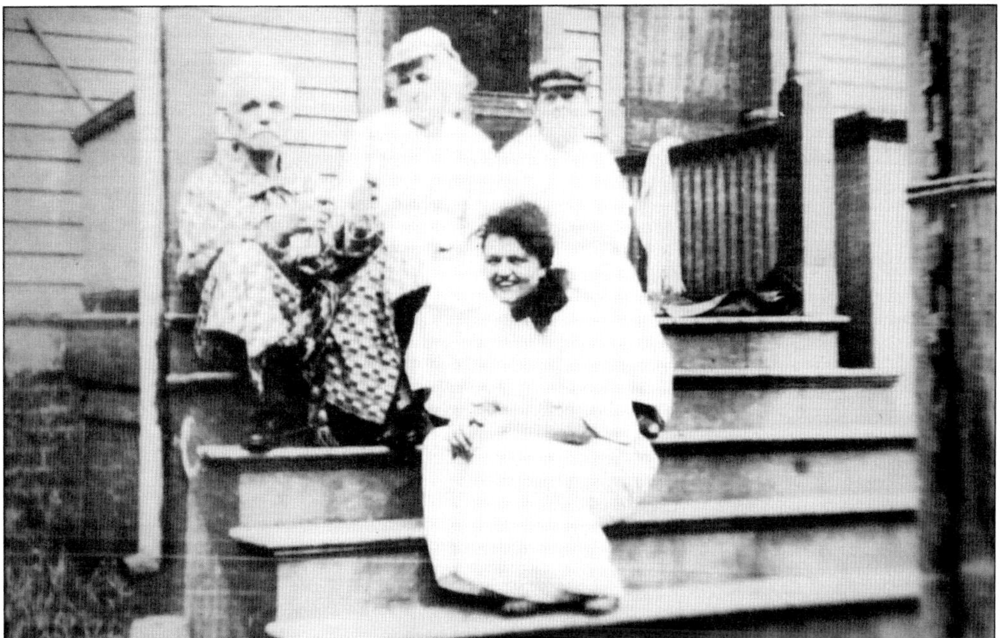

October 5, 1918, "The Day of the Morgan Explosion." The William Stephens family poses with their landlady on the steps of Albion Place, Port Richmond. (Collection of Claire and Bill Drinnan.)

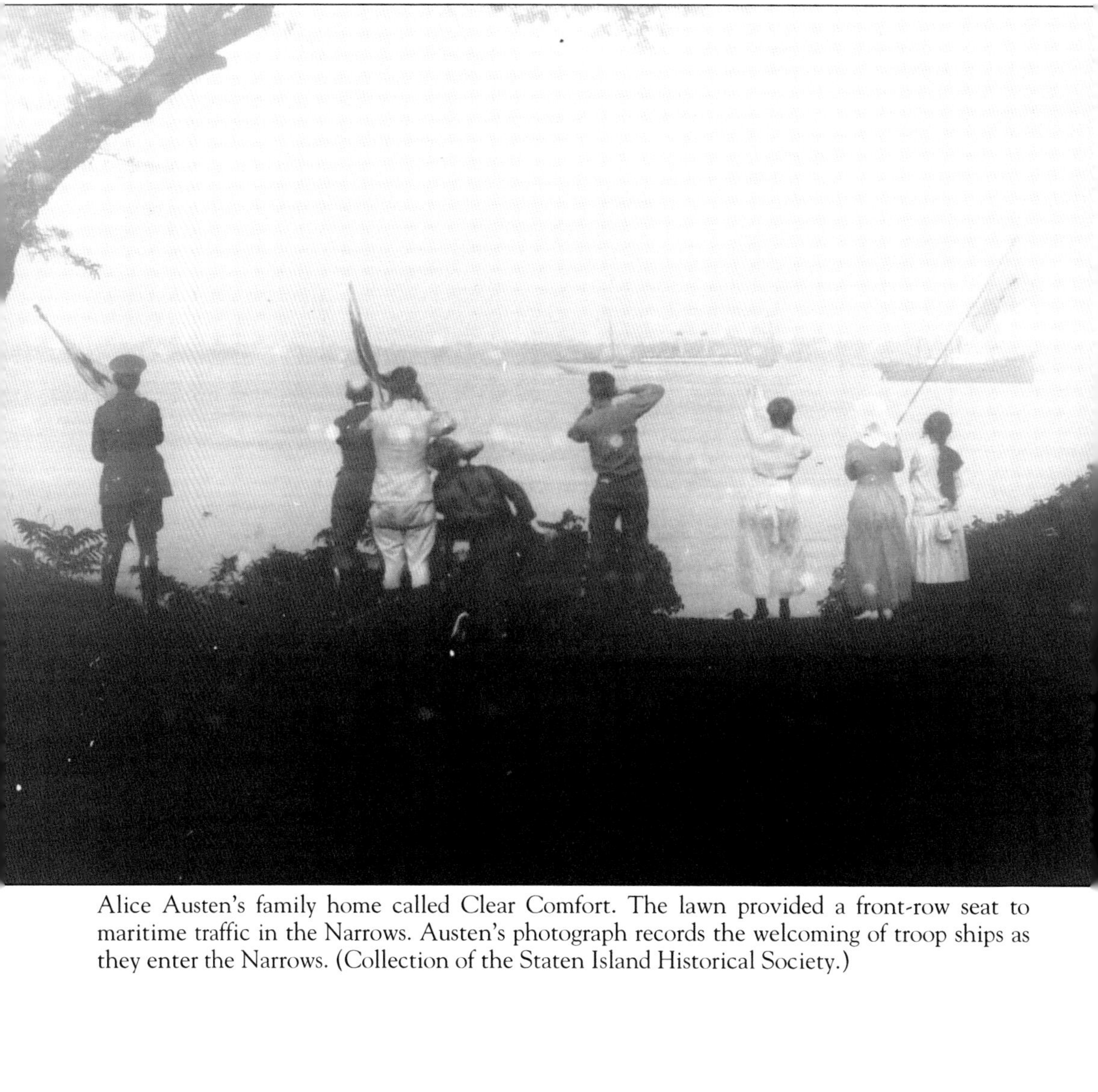

Alice Austen's family home called Clear Comfort. The lawn provided a front-row seat to maritime traffic in the Narrows. Austen's photograph records the welcoming of troop ships as they enter the Narrows. (Collection of the Staten Island Historical Society.)

Three

1920–1929

The Roaring Twenties

*Paris Peace Treaty signed, 1920.

*Warren G. Harding elected U.S. President, 1920.

*Sinclair Lewis writes *Main Street*,
and Eugene O'Neill writes Pulitzer Prize-winning *Beyond the Horizon*, 1920.

*American women get the right to vote in 19th Amendment, 1920.

*Joan of Arc (1412–1431) canonized by Pope Benedict XV, 1920.

*Nicola Sacco and Bartolomeo Vanzetti indicted for murder, 1920;
convicted, 1921; executed, 1927.

*Mohandas K. Gandhi, known as "The Mahatma" (Great Soul),
becomes leader of India's fight for independence from Britain, 1920.

*Earthquake in China kills two hundred thousand people, 1920.

*American surgeon Harvey Cushing develops new brain surgery techniques, 1920.

*Irish Free State established, 1921; officially proclaimed, 1922.

*D.H. Lawrence writes *Women in Love*,
and Albert Schweitzer writes *On the Edge of the Primeval Forest*, 1921.

*Camille Guerin and Albert Calmette develop the B-C-G vaccine for tuberculosis, 1921.

*Ku Klux Klan violence against blacks sweeps throughout southern U.S., 1921.

*Willa Cather writes *One of Ours*, 1922; wins Pulitzer Prize, 1923.

*James Joyce writes *Ulysses*, published in Paris;
five hundred copies burned on arrival in U.S. by post office, 1922.

*Louis Armstrong joins Joe "King" Oliver's band in Chicago, 1922.

*Irving Berlin's song "April Showers" popular, 1922.

*Insulin first prepared by Canadian physicians Banting, Best, and Macleod,
administered to patients with diabetes, 1922.

*George Gershwin writes "Rhapsody in Blue," Felis Salten writes *Bambi*, and William Butler Yeats wins Nobel Prize for Literature, 1923.

*Tutankhamen's tomb opened, 1923.

*"Yes, We Have No Bananas" among popular songs, 1923.

*Warren G. Harding dies, 1923, succeeded by Vice President Calvin Coolidge.

*Electric razor patented by Col. Jacob Schick, 1923.

*Lenin, founder of the U.S.S.R., and Woodrow Wilson die, 1924.

*Mah-Jongg card game becomes the rage, 1924.

*J. Edgar Hoover named director of FBI, 1924.

*Gandhi begins 21-day fast to protest feuds between Hindus and Moslems in India, 1924.

*Insecticides first used, 1924.

*Adolf Hitler reorganizes Nazi Party of 27,000 members, and first volume of *Mein Kampf* published, 1925.

*Nellie Tayloe Ross of Wyoming becomes first woman governor in America, 1925.

*The Scopes trial makes lawyer Clarence Darrow famous, 1925.

*Gene Tunney wins heavyweight boxing title from Jack Dempsey, 1926.

*Nineteen-year-old Gertrude Ederle swims the English Channel, breaking the men's record by two hours, 1926.

*Ernest Hemingway writes *The Sun Also Rises*, 1926.

*American artist Mary Cassatt, French artist Claude Monet, and actor Rudolph Valentino die, 1926.

*Lebanon proclaimed a republic, 1926.

*Talking pictures emerge with Al Jolson in *The Jazz Singer* and Greta Garbo in *Flesh and the Devil*, 1927.

*Charles Lindbergh flies non-stop from New York to Paris in *The Spirit of St. Louis*, 1927.

*Amelia Earhart flies over the Atlantic Ocean, 1928.

*Mickey Mouse makes his debut as "Steamboat Willie," 1928.

**Amos 'n' Andy* enjoy radio fame, 1928.

*"Black Friday," October 28, 1929; the U.S. Stock Exchange plummets into ruin, with $26 billion lost and a world economic crisis launched.

*The Museum of Modern Art opens in New York City with an Impressionist exhibit of works by Van Gogh, Cezanne, Gauguin, and Seurat, 1929.

*The "St. Valentine's Day Massacre" of 1929; six Chicago gangsters killed by machine gun fire.

*"Stardust" and "Tiptoe Through the Tulips" among popular songs, 1929.

*The Church of Scotland established by the unification of Presbyterian churches, 1929.

*The word "apartheid" coined, 1929.

*Herbert C. Hoover elected and inaugurated as 31st U.S. president, 1929.

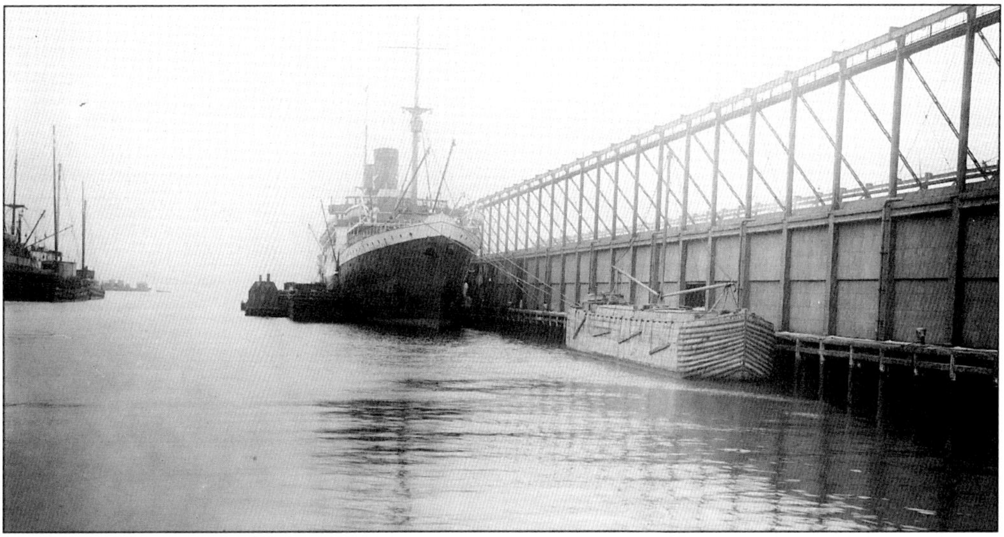

Spanish onions, the cargo on the S.S. *Guiseppe Verdi* at Thaten Terminal, January 1926. Importer Alvaro Boera persuaded the Italian Line to dock the passenger ship at the municipal terminal complex in Stapleton. Then passengers were taxied and ferried to midtown Manhattan in less time than it took to debark from the Hudson River piers. This experiment brought many more passenger liners to the island to boost the local economy. (International Newsreel photograph, collection of A. Richard Boera.)

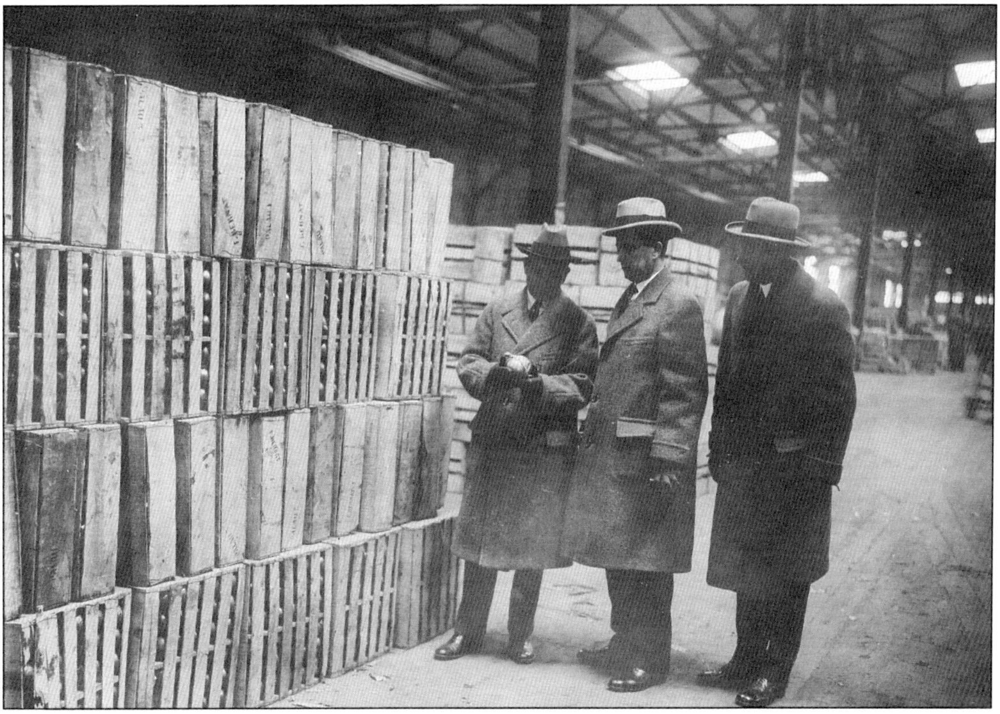

Unloading the onions, January 26, 1926. After the crates are unloaded inside Pier 12, Alvaro Boera shows Spanish onions to Borough President John A. Lynch and terminal developer/manager Max Thaten. (International Newsreel photograph, collection of A. Richard Boera.)

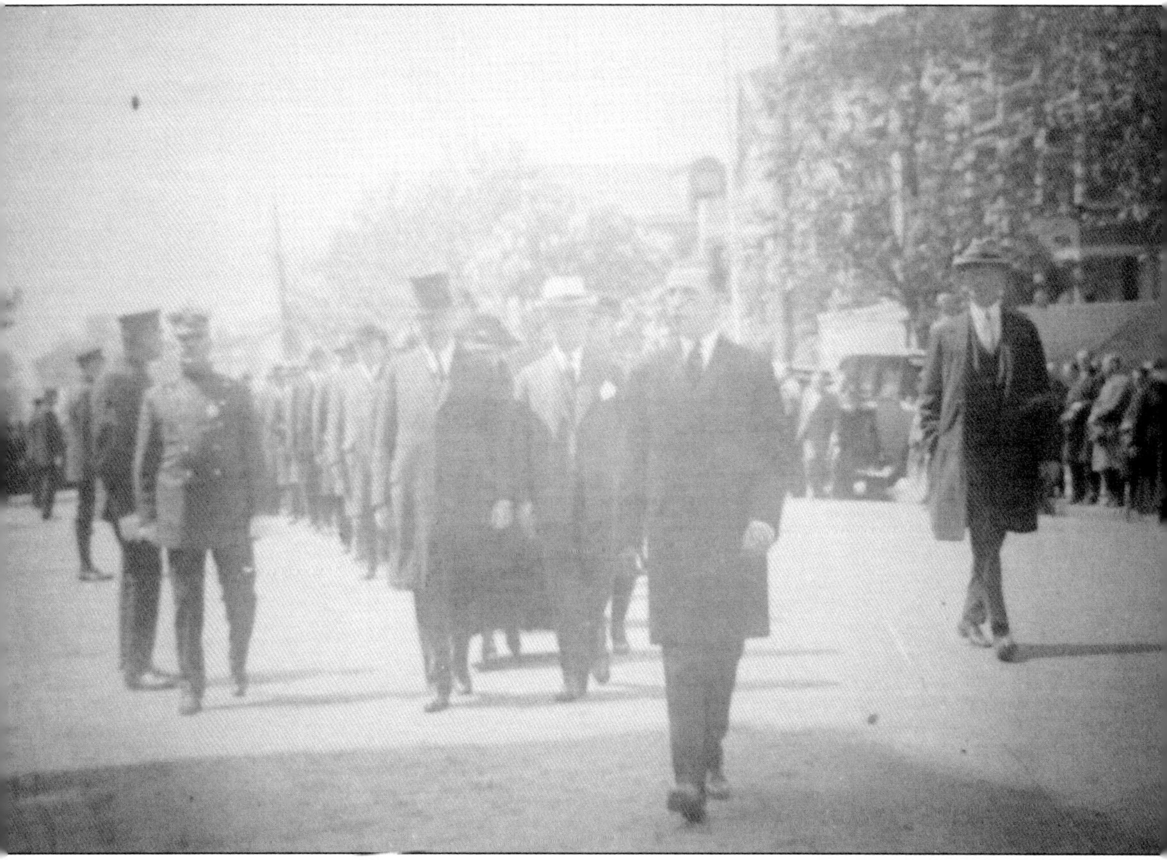

The funeral procession of Thomas R. McGinley in 1925. George D. Casey leads the affair and behind him are Mayor John F. Hylan and Gov. Al Smith. McGinley was active in Staten Island politics and held various posts including commissioner of parks and later, for taxes for the Borough of Richmond. He also owned McGinley Funeral Home. Mayor Hylan would later lose his seat to Jimmy Walker. Governor Smith went on to win the democratic nomination for president and become the first Catholic to run for this office. An *Advance* editorial wrote of McGinley "Courage was his outstanding quality and one that fitted him best for leadership.... He was always found fighting for what he considered best for his island home." (Collection of Jack Casey.)

The Carlough family. (Collection of Claire and Bill Drinnan.)

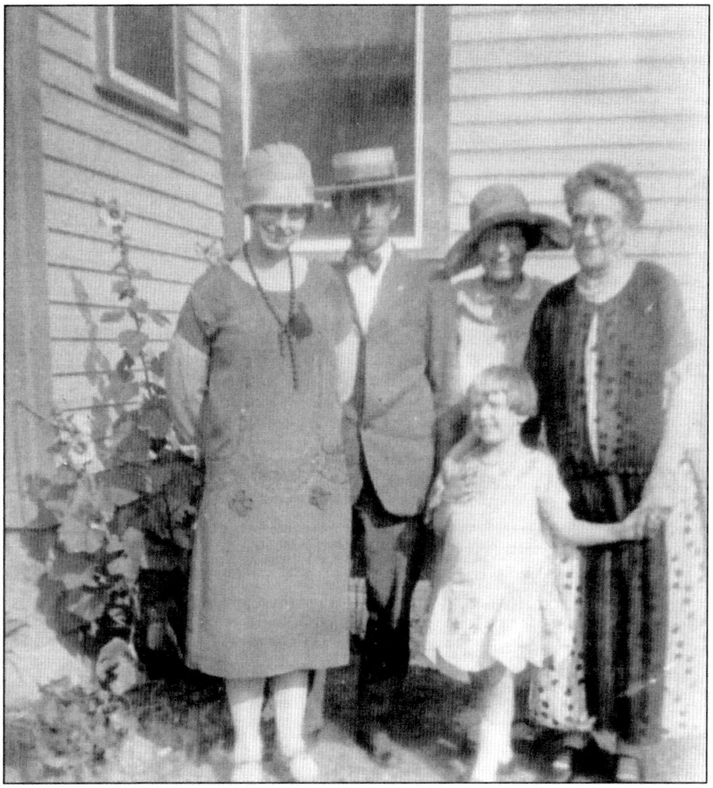

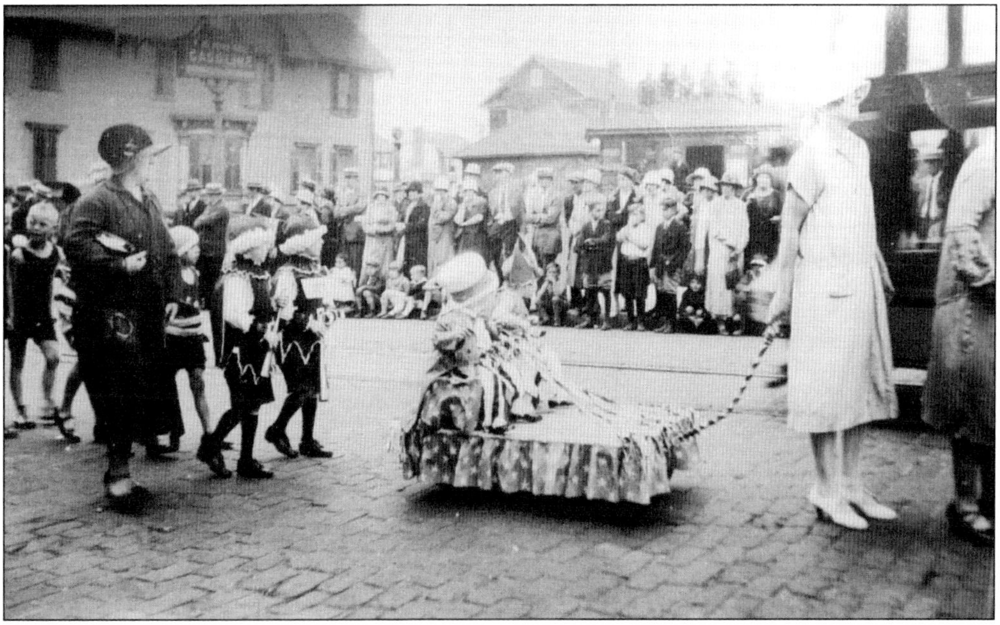

Baby parade, Port Richmond, 1926. One of the authors' all-time favorite shots is of this baby parade, one of the events of the sesquicentennial celebration of U.S. independence. Here are Marjorie and David Decker (a.k.a., Uncle Sam and Miss Liberty), pulled by proud mother Ruth Decker. (Collection of Marjorie Johnson.)

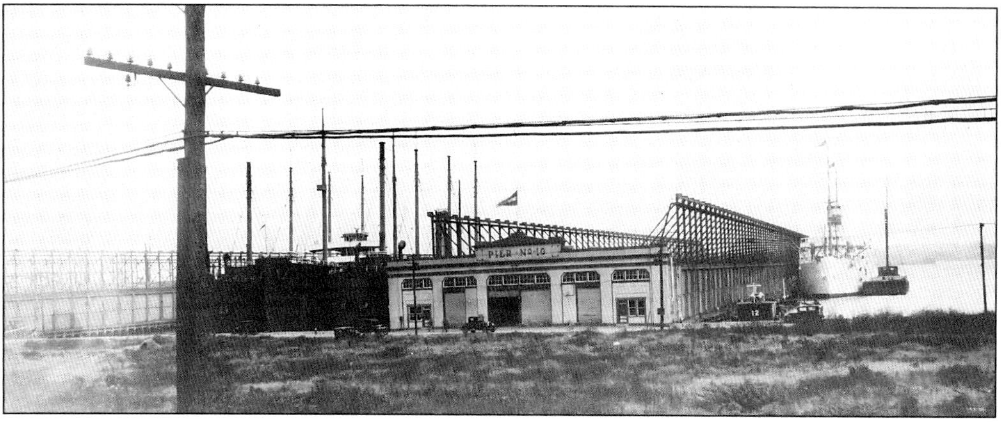

Pier 10, 1926. The 13 municipal piers between Stapleton and St. George, built for $28 million to meet demands of World War I, may well be a study in "pier pressure." They did not immediately fulfill the builders' expectations. When this photograph was taken, piers prospered at the hand of manager Max Thaten, former manager of the American Dock terminal at Tompkinsville and the Pouch Terminals at Clifton. Thaten developed the island's railroad traffic that made use of piers 12 and 13, which were equipped with electric cranes and railroad tracks. Later, these piers comprised the Free Port trade zone and, more recently, a major naval base. World War II troops and supplies to serve the Allied cause flowed through this embarkation port, which boasted the greatest volume of any U.S. gateway. Also, during the war, Winston Churchill disembarked here and boarded a night train on his way to a secret meeting with President Roosevelt. (International Newsreel photograph, collection of A. Richard Boera.)

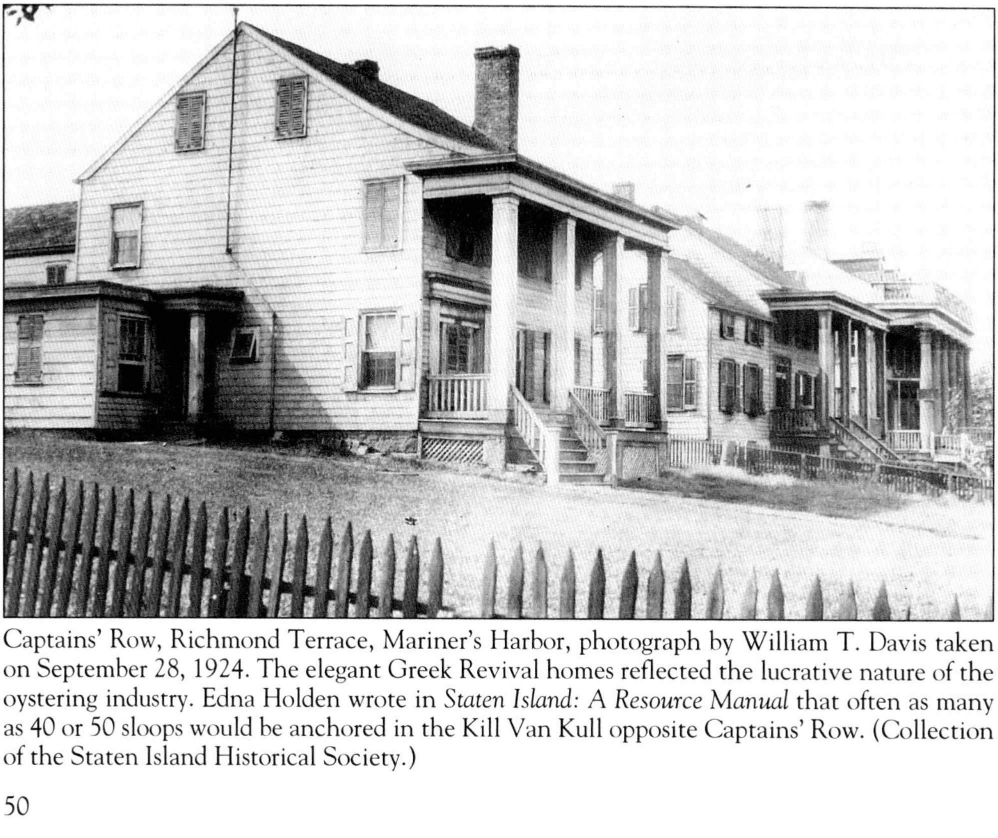

Captains' Row, Richmond Terrace, Mariner's Harbor, photograph by William T. Davis taken on September 28, 1924. The elegant Greek Revival homes reflected the lucrative nature of the oystering industry. Edna Holden wrote in *Staten Island: A Resource Manual* that often as many as 40 or 50 sloops would be anchored in the Kill Van Kull opposite Captains' Row. (Collection of the Staten Island Historical Society.)

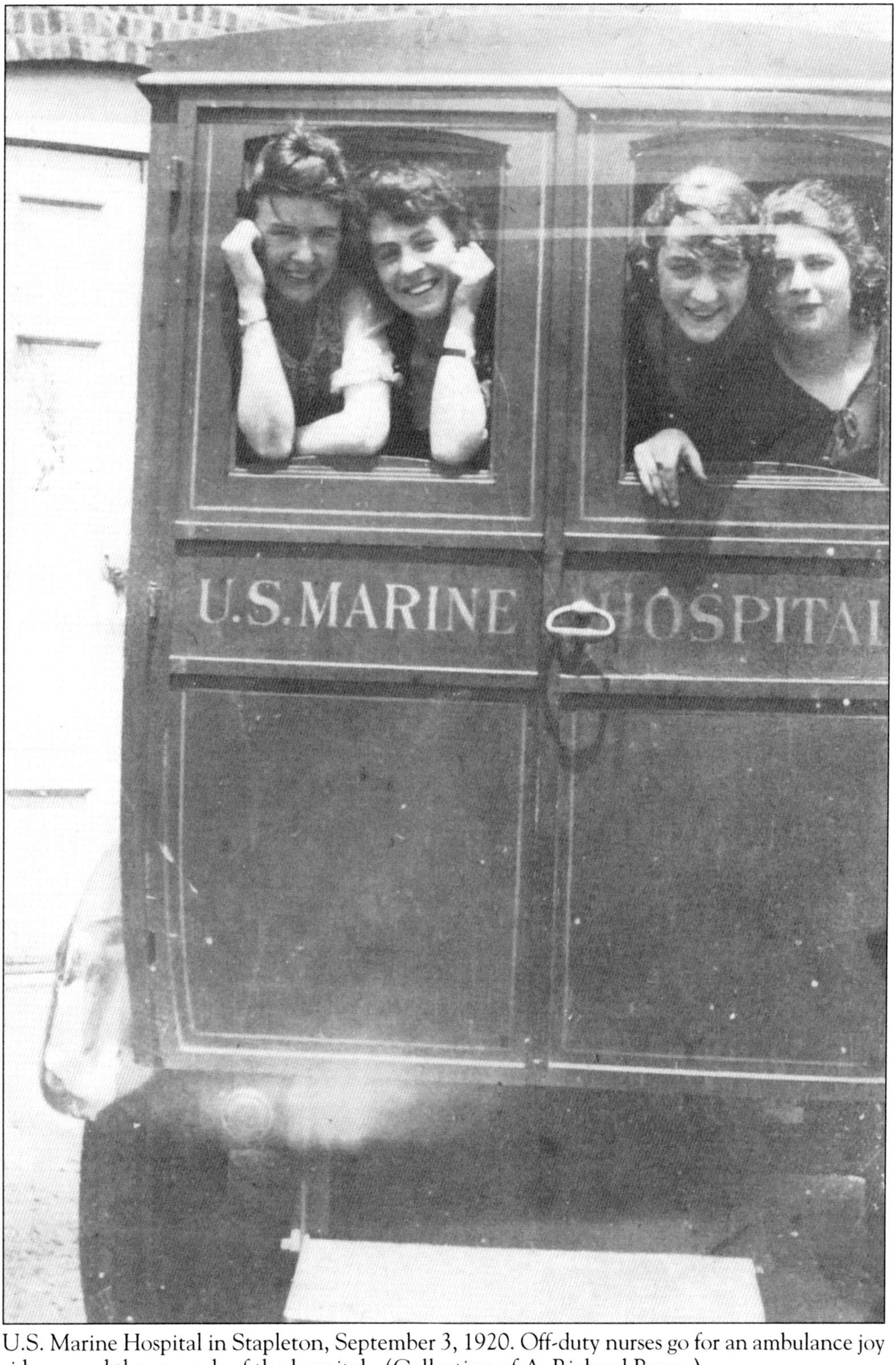

U.S. Marine Hospital in Stapleton, September 3, 1920. Off-duty nurses go for an ambulance joy ride around the grounds of the hospital. (Collection of A. Richard Boera.)

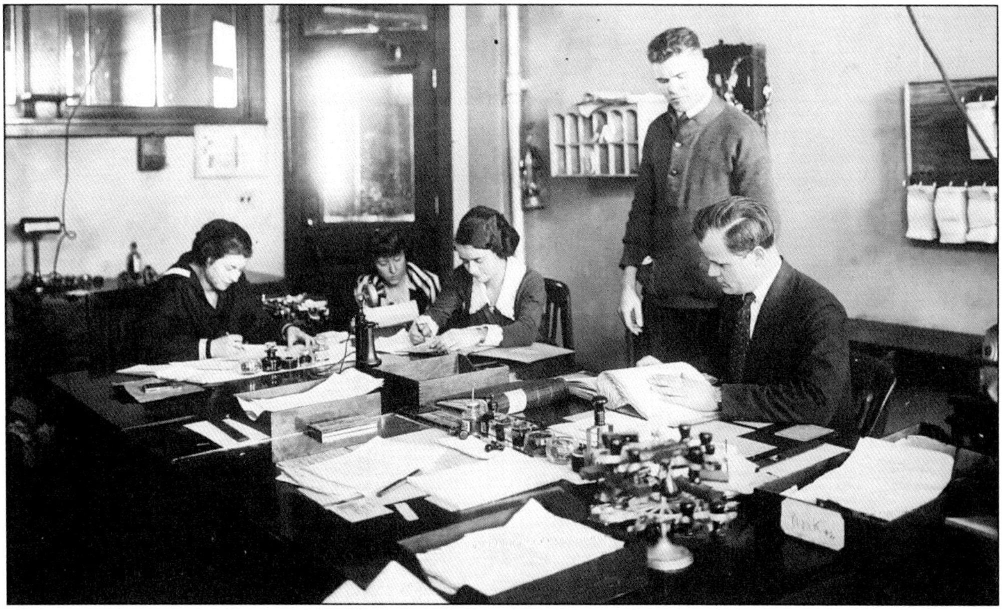

U.S. Marine Hospital, *c.* 1921. Sharing one telephone and a lantern (used during power failures), the entire administrative staff of the U.S. Marine Hospital, except CEO Dr. Walter H. Keen, pose for the camera. A Public Health Service yeoman (left) works with civilian colleagues including Clara Manz (middle), a graduate of the Baker Business School in Tompkinsville. An avid golfer and bowler, she married Al Boera in 1924 and worked with him in their restaurant, the Old Mill. In 1989, at the age of 89, Clara received her Curtis High School diploma! (Collection of A. Richard Boera.)

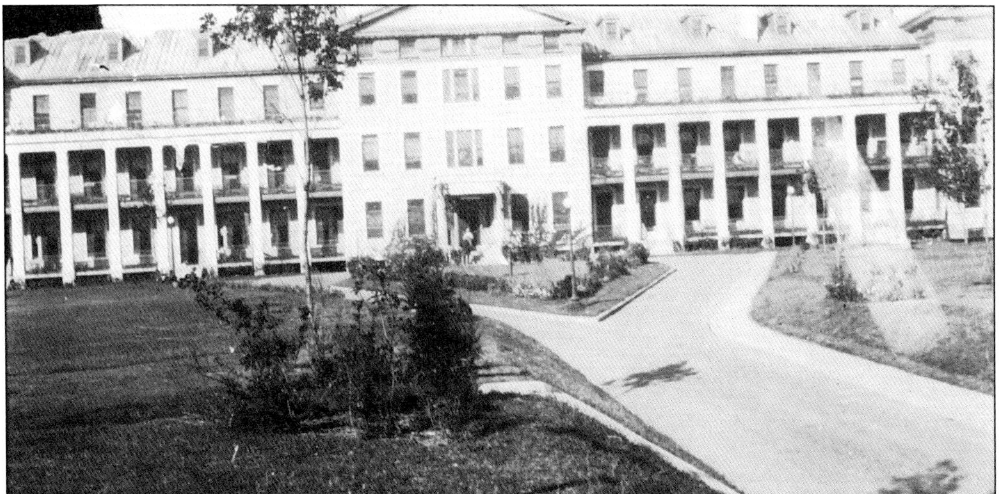

U.S. Marine Hospital, No. 21, on Bay Street (near Vanderbuilt Avenue) in Stapleton, September 3, 1921. The hospital was originally built in 1837 with fees paid to a state treasury account known as the Seamen's Retreat and Hospital Fund by foreign sailors upon entering the port of New York. Later the fund was voluntarily supported by ship owners. In 1903, the hospital (operated for 20 years by the Marine Society) was sold to become the U.S. Marine Hospital, operated by the U.S. Public Health Service. The building pictured here is the original Seamen's retreat building. (Collection of A. Richard Boera.)

One of Staten Island's oldest families. The DeHart family can trace their ancestors back seven generations to the times of slavery. Susie DeHart, mother of Evelyn Morris King, was a student of local history and shared this passion with her children. One of the most interesting stories concerns the Gay and Willcox families, prominent abolitionists whose home at 115 Davis Avenue was a station of the Underground Railroad. Nicholas Claus DeHart, Susie's grandfather, was born into slavery on May 7, 1800, two months before the law freeing all children born of slaves went into effect. "Claus," as he was affectionately known, was in the Mersereau family household until July 4, 1825, when all slaves on Staten Island were emancipated. Highly respected, his funeral was attended by Erastus Brookes, among other prominent islanders. Nicholas had been a gardener for the Wilcox family. Susie DeHart married William A. Morris. (Collection of Evelyn Morris King.)

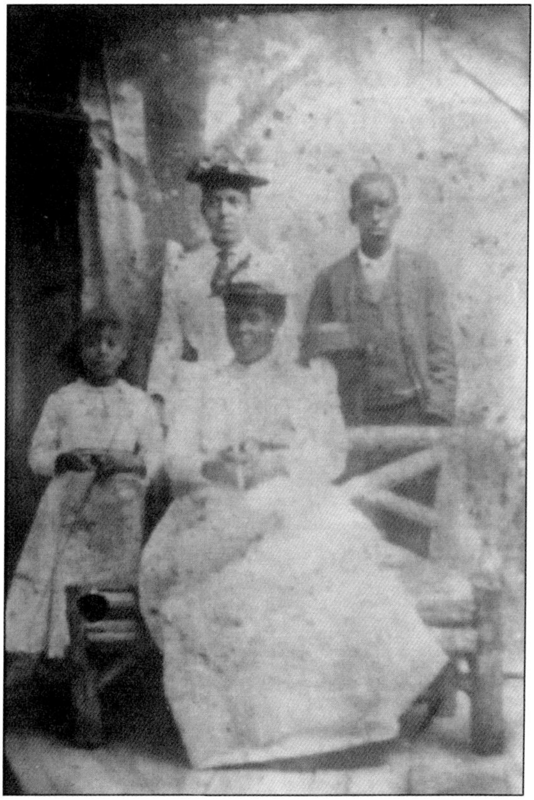

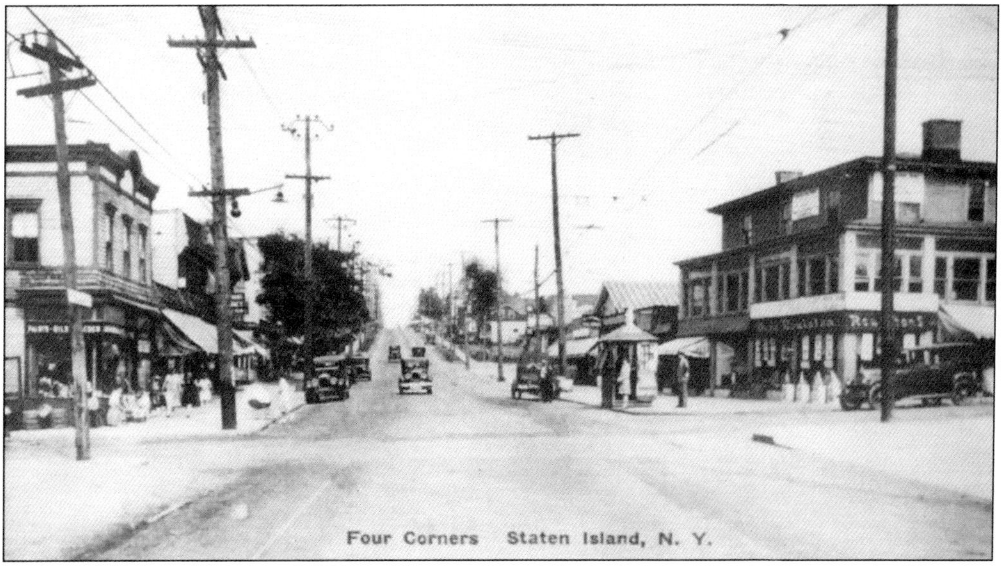

Four Corners, the intersection of Victory Boulevard and Manor Road, *c.* 1927. To the right is Thomas Ralston's grocery store, a precursor of the modern chain supermarket. To the left is Reiman's Hardware store, a fixture on the corner for many years until it moved up Victory Boulevard to larger quarters. Jerry's was originally a soda fountain and candy store located in what is today a pork store. In 1939, Jerry's moved to its present location and did away with its fountain service. (Collection of Rudolph Ayoub.)

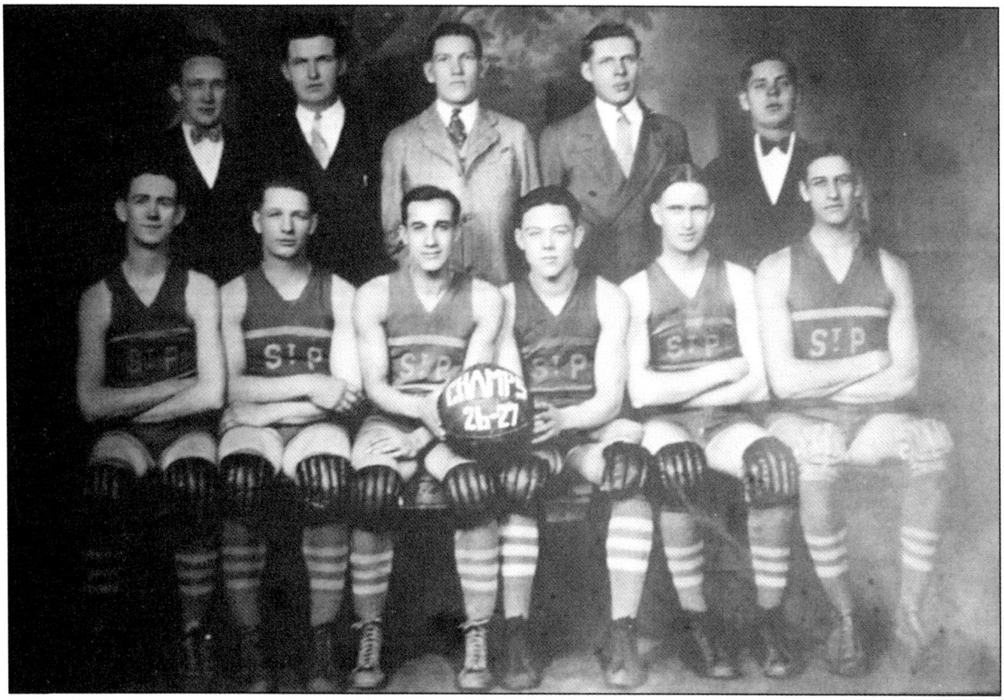

Basketball champions, 1926–27. They include Buddy Harris, Joe Byrne, and Oscar Michaud, called St. Peter's "Big Five." (Collection of Ted and Noreen Harris.)

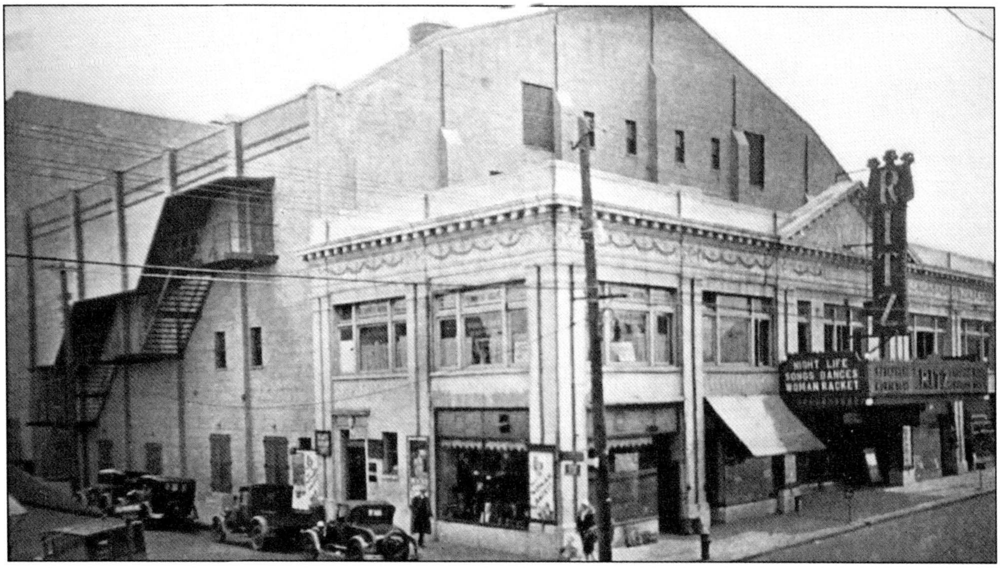

The Ritz Theatre, Port Richmond, designed by Staten Island architect James Whitford. The Staten Island Resource Manual reports that in the 1920s Charles Lewis and Eliza Moses organized the Isle Theatrical Company and built a chain of theaters. In addition to the Ritz, these theaters included the Lane in New Dorp, the Paramount in Stapleton, the Victory in Tompkinsville, the Strand in Great Kills, the Stadium in Tottenville, and the Capital in New Brighton. The Ritz held rock concerts in the 1960s and 1970s. (Collection of Marjorie Johnson.)

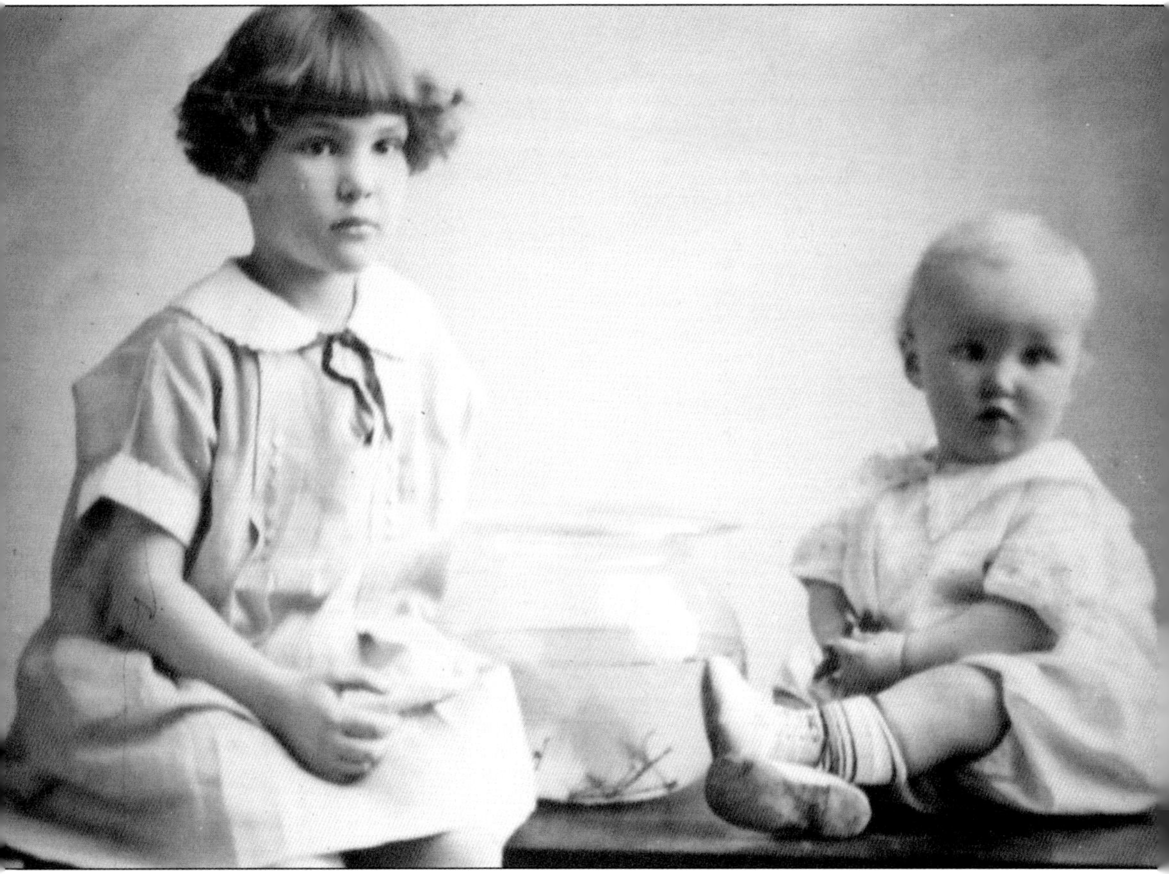
Al and Edna Holtermann with a goldfish bowl. (Collection of Edith and Al Holtermann.)

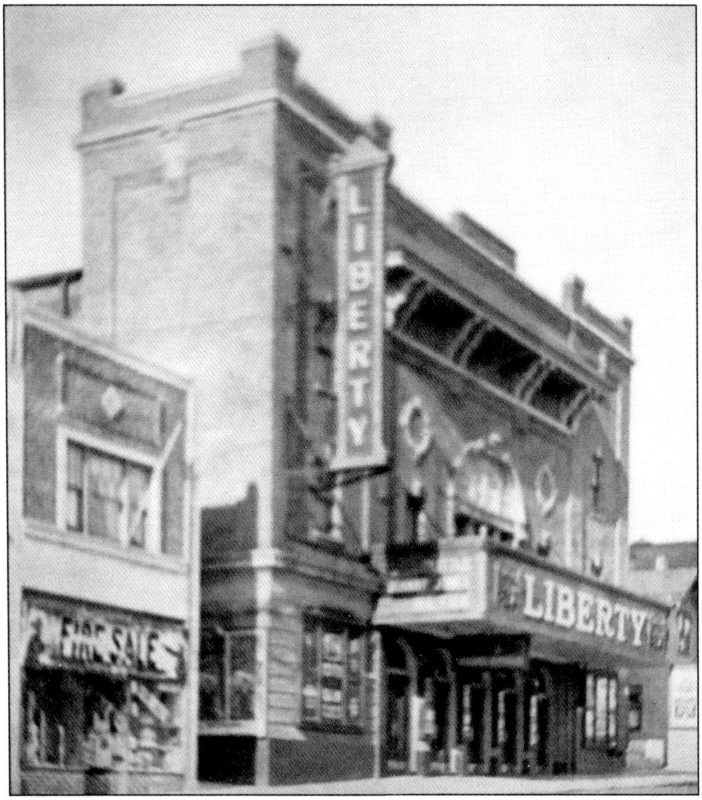

Liberty Theater, Stapleton, also designed by James Whitford. The theater held stock-company performances in the 1920s. It later became a bowling alley. (Collection of Marjorie Johnson.)

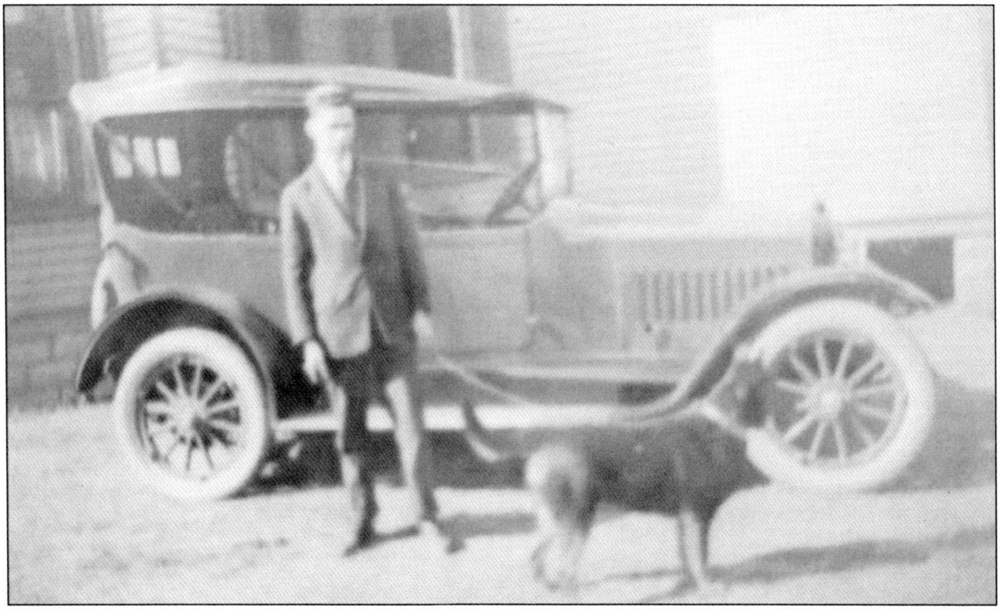

Liberty. This photograph, taken on Sunday, March 21, 1920, is of Gene Decker posing in front of his car with his dog Liberty. (Collection of Marjorie Johnson.)

Four

1930–1939

The Jazz Years and the Depression

*Constantinople renamed Istanbul, 1930.

*Premier Hamaguchi of Japan assassinated, 1930.

*Sinclair Lewis wins Nobel Prize for Literature with *Babbitt*, and William Faulkner writes *As I Lay Dying*, 1930.

*English novelist D.H. Lawrence dies, 1930.

*Marlene Dietrich stars in the film *The Blue Angel*, 1930.

*The planet Pluto discovered by C.W. Tombaugh at the Lowell Observatory, 1930.

*Pearl S. Buck writes *The Good Earth*, 1931.

*Surrealist Salvador Dali paints the famous *Persistence of Memory*, 1931.

*Jehovah's Witnesses established, 1931.

*Russian ballerina Anna Pavlova and American inventor Thomas A. Edison die, 1931.

*"The Star-Spangled Banner," with lyrics by Francis Scott Key, established as the U.S. national anthem, 1931.

*The Empire State Building and the George Washington Bridge completed, 1931.

*Franklin D. Roosevelt elected 32nd U.S. president, 1932.

*The Depression, with 15,000,000 people out of work, 1932.

*Aldous Huxley writes *Brave New World*, 1932.

*The Lindbergh baby kidnapped and murdered, 1932.

*Adolf Hitler appointed German Chancellor, granted dictatorial powers; creates the first concentration camps, 1933.

**King Kong* among popular films released, 1933.

*Chicago World's Fair opens, 1933.

*Prohibition repealed in 21st Amendment to U.S. Constitution, 1933.

*Artist Louis Comfort Tiffany and humorist Ring Lardner die, 1933.

*French S.S. *Normandie* and S.S. *Queen Mary* launched, 1934.

*Ocean liner *Morro Castle* sinks off Asbury Park, New Jersey, with 130 deaths, 1934.

*Robert Graves writes *I, Claudius*, and Cole Porter writes *Anything Goes*, 1934.

*Italian actress Sophia Loren born, 1934.

*American jurist Oliver Wendell Holmes dies, 1935.

*"Public Enemy No.1," John Dillinger, shot by FBI, 1934.

*Alcoholics Anonymous founded in New York City, 1935.

*Chiang Kai-shek named President of China, 1935.

*George Gershwin's opera *Porgy and Bess* opens in New York City, 1935.

*U.S. Social Security Act signed by President Franklin Roosevelt, 1935.

*Persia changes its name to Iran, 1935.

*FDR reelected U.S. president, 1936.

*Spanish Civil War begins, Abyssinian War ends, 1936.

*King Edward VIII abdicates his throne to wed American divorcee Wallis Simpson; the two become the Duke and Duchess of Windsor, 1936.

*King Farouk succeeds his father, King Fuad of Egypt, 1936.

*War on Japan declared by Chiang Kai-shek, 1936.

*Margaret Mitchell wins Pulitzer Prize for *Gone with the Wind*, and Eugene O'Neill wins Nobel Prize for Literature, 1936.

*Mussolini's son-in-law, Count Ciano, appointed Italian Foreign Minister, 1936.

*Baseball Hall of Fame founded at Cooperstown, New York, 1936.

Amelia Earhart lost on Pacific flight, 1937.

The dirigible *Hindenburg* crashes in Lakehurst, New Jersey, 1937.

*John Steinbeck writes *Of Mice and Men*, 1937.

*John D. Rockefeller dies, 1937.

*Picasso's *Guernica* mural displayed at Paris World Exhibition, 1937.

*The first jet engine is built by Frank Whittle, 1937.

*Insulin first used as treatment of diabetes, 1937.

*Minimum wage law for women set forth by U.S. Supreme Court, 1937.

*Public panic caused by Orson Welles' radio broadcast of H.G. Wells' *War of the Worlds*, 1938.

*Lewis Mumford writes *The Culture of Cities*, and Daphne du Maurier writes *Rebecca*, 1938.

*American lawyer Clarence Darrow dies, 1938.

*The 40-hour work week established in America, 1938.

*Popular songs include "Flat Foot Floogie with a Floy Floy" and "September Song," 1938.

*Nylon stockings become popular, and polyethylene invented, 1939.

*John Steinbeck writes Pulitzer Prize-winning novel *The Grapes of Wrath*, 1939.

*"Father of Psychiatry" Dr. Sigmund Freud, Irish poet William Butler Yeats Jr., and American actor Douglas Fairbanks die, 1939.

Germany invades Poland, triggers World War II, 1939.

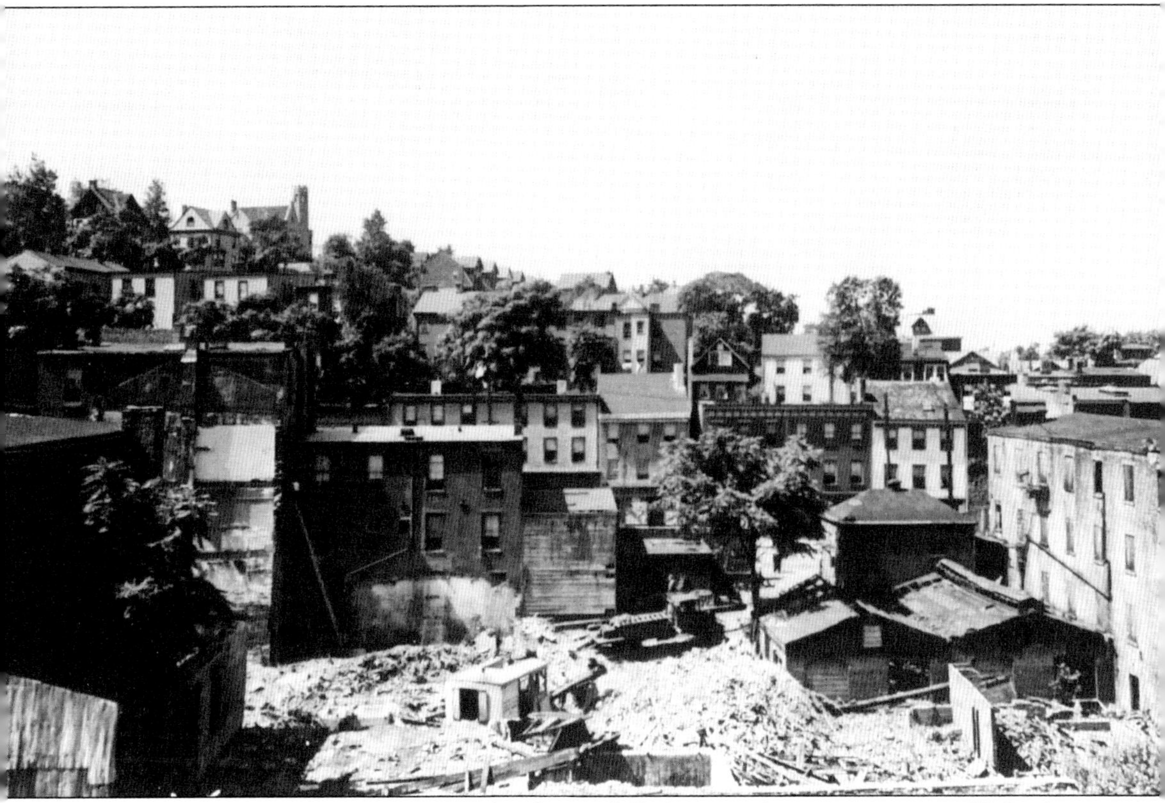

Collapse of the New Street tenement. This disaster killed 19 people on August 11, 1937. Little remains in this photograph to show the tragedy that occurred days before. The foundation of the apartments, located in a former factory, was undermined by water that pooled following the clearing of several nearby condemned buildings. Rosemary Bower, of the *Staten Island Advance*, wrote, "Patrolman Joseph J. McBreen, father of a nine-day-old son, died a hero's death last night, another man's child clasped tight in his arms—dead." The building collapsed as Officer McBreen was just feet from safety. The police officer was found hours later with four-year-old Virginia Dominick still clasped in his arms. Once located one block up on Jersey Street from Richmond Terrace, New Street no longer exists. The site is covered by the Richmond Terrace houses. (Collection of Marjorie Johnson.)

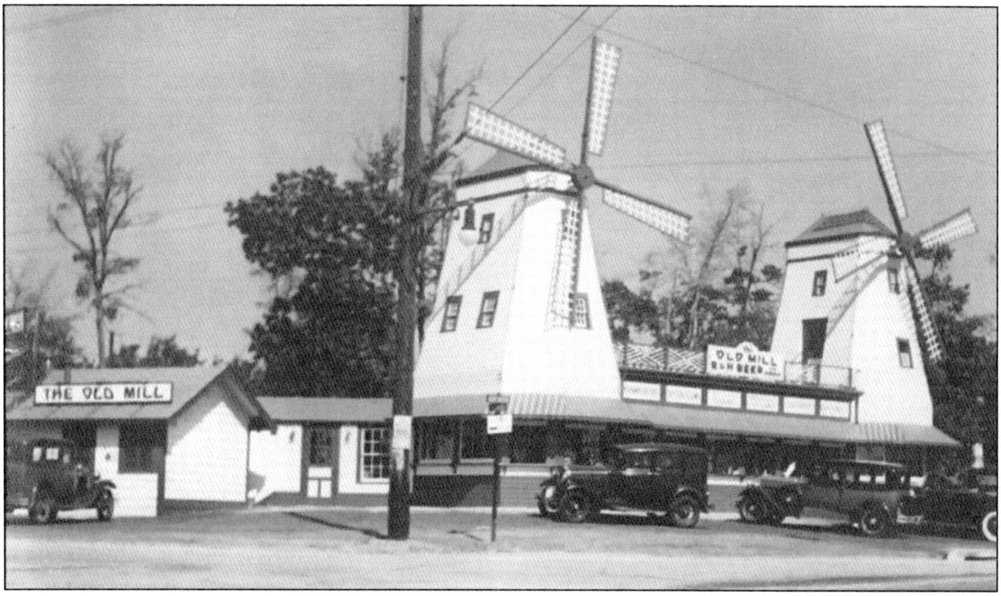

Old Mill. In 1934, this drive-in was a novelty that attracted families in Fords, Packards, Chevies and an occasional Cord to the Old Mill. Curb service included 5¢ cherry Cokes, a glass of local Rubsam & Hormann beer for a dime, 15¢ hamburgers, and soft-shell crabs for a quarter. The windmill vanes actually turned but needed to be braked in high winds. After they fell to a severe storm in November 1950, they were not replaced, though the Old Mill flourished. (Collection of A. Richard Boera.)

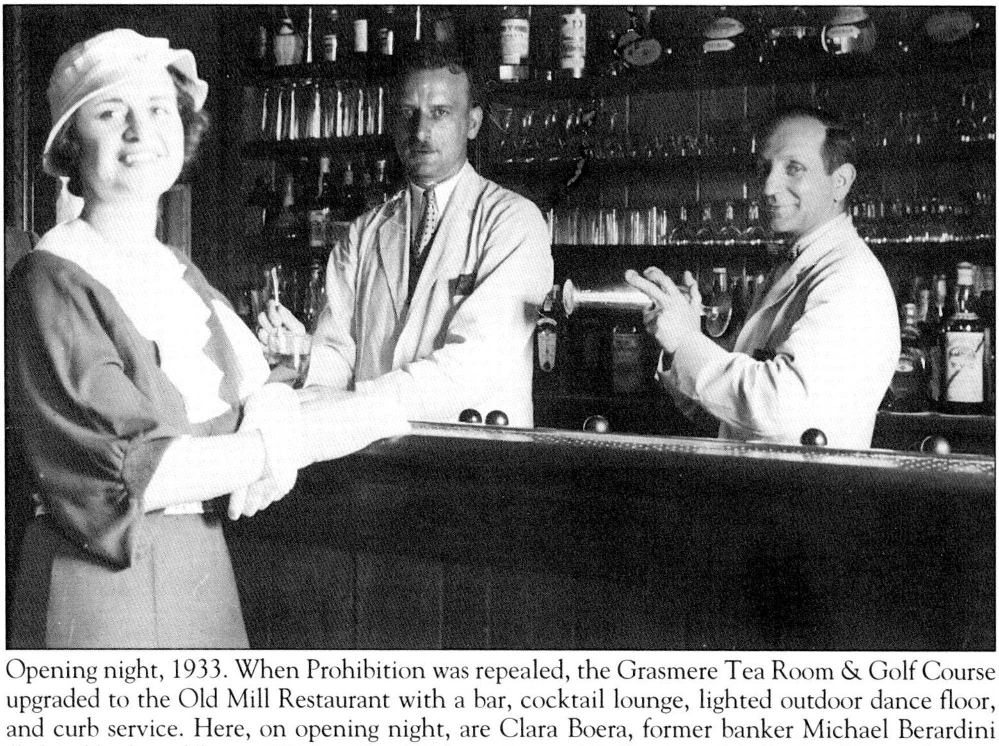

Opening night, 1933. When Prohibition was repealed, the Grasmere Tea Room & Golf Course upgraded to the Old Mill Restaurant with a bar, cocktail lounge, lighted outdoor dance floor, and curb service. Here, on opening night, are Clara Boera, former banker Michael Berardini (behind bar), and former "Onion King" Alvaro Boera. (Collection of A. Richard Boera.)

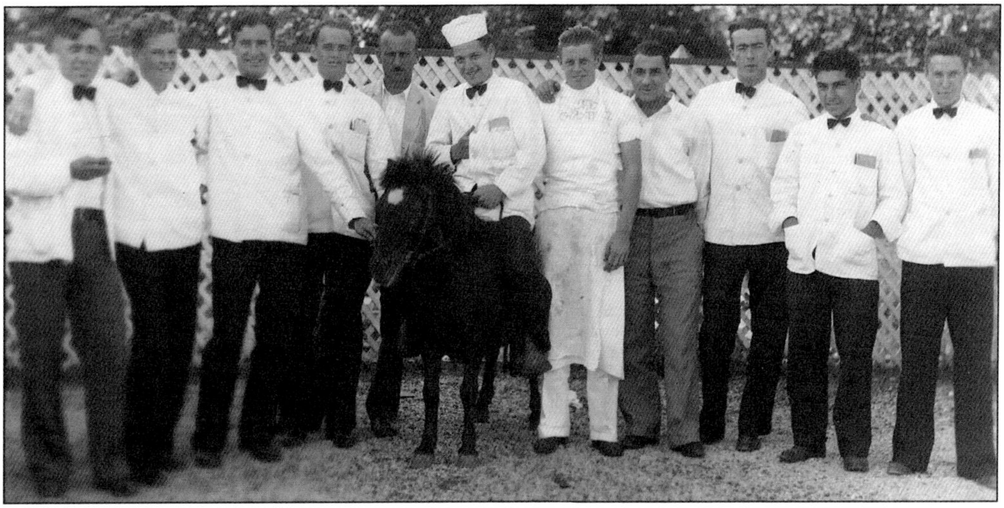

Old Mill Restaurant. An informal pose of the handsome service staff at the restaurant in Grasmere, *c.* 1936. One of the proprietors, Mike Berardini, is tieless and is standing next to the man on the pony. The car hops were college students recruited from Wagner and Manhattan College. Virtually all of the boys employed during the years 1933–1941 served in World War II and the owners corresponded with many of them; two of the boys never returned from the war. (Collection of A. Richard Boera.)

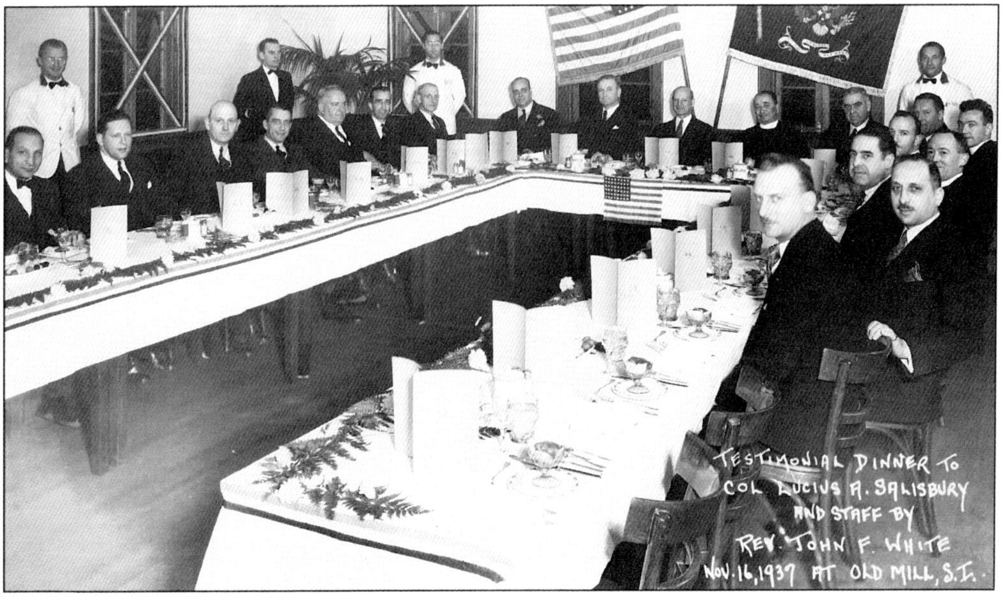

A November 16, 1937 testimonial dinner at the Old Mill Restaurant. The dinner was given for Col. Lucius R. Salisbury, commander of the 102nd Medical Regiment of the New York National Guard, by Rev. John F. White, pastor of Immaculate Conception Roman Catholic Church in Stapleton and buddy of celebrities George M. Cohan, Jimmy Cagney, Pat O'Brien, and Ray Bolger. Father White and Col. Salisbury were World War I comrades. Listed from left to right around the table are Alvaro Boera (wearing his trademark bow-tie), Bernard Berggren, Thomas Kiernan (with maitre d' Charles Gordon, standing), Harold Beves, unidentified, Col. Salisbury, Father White, unidentified, Howard Brown, Rev. John Crosson, unidentified, Adrian Sheiss, unidentified, and Michael Berardini. (Collection of A. Richard Boera.)

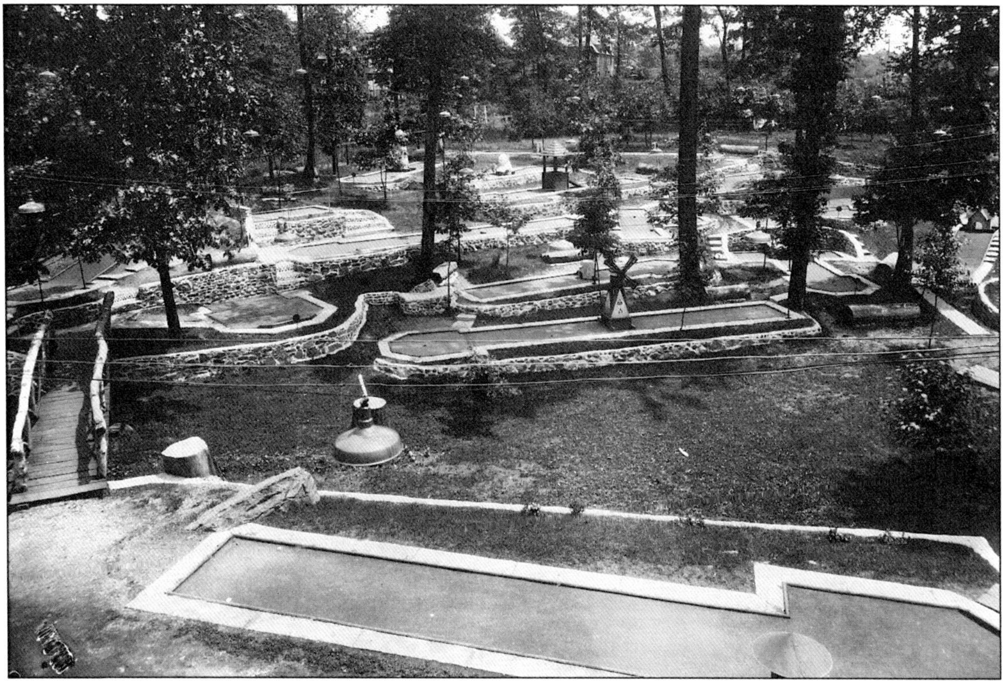

The miniature golf course behind the Grasmere Tea Room, which evolved into Grasmere's Old Mill Restaurant, *c.* 1931. At the depths of the Great Depression, Al Boera, in partnership with Thaddeus Wright, borrowed money to build this challenging, terraced miniature 18-hole course at the northeast corner of Clove Road and Hylan Boulevard. Al Deppe built another popular one on Richmond Avenue and a third sprang up at New Dorp Lane and Hylan. Boera later built a tea room alongside the golf course which evolved into the Old Mill Restaurant. (Collection of A. Richard Boera.)

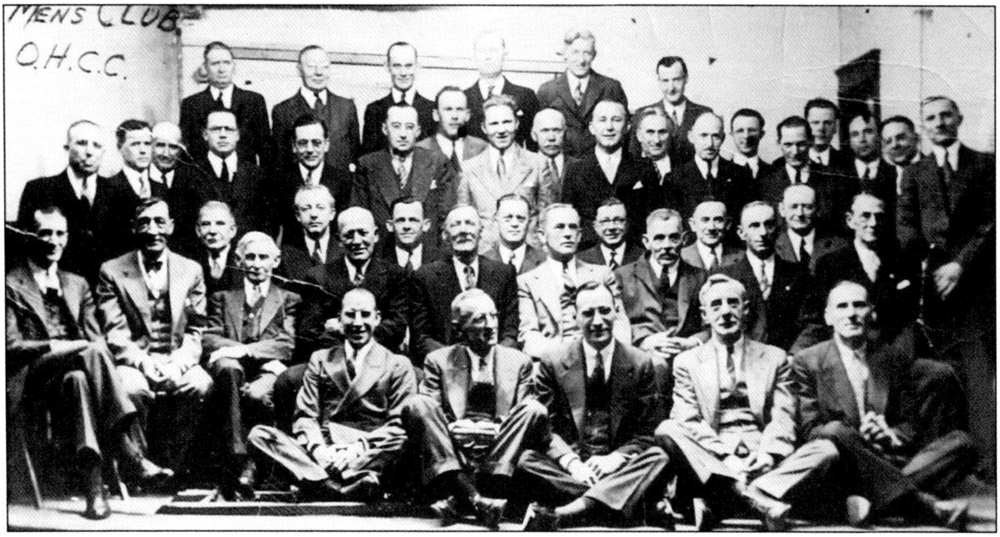

Oakwood Heights Community Men's Club in 1934. Some of the gentlemen included here are Bill Armend, Tom Harland, Ted Woerz, Bill Murray, Fred Boeniger, Howard Kratzenberg, Bill Fox, William Armendinger, Steve Kratzenberg, and Howard Powell. (Collection of Edith and Al Holtermann.)

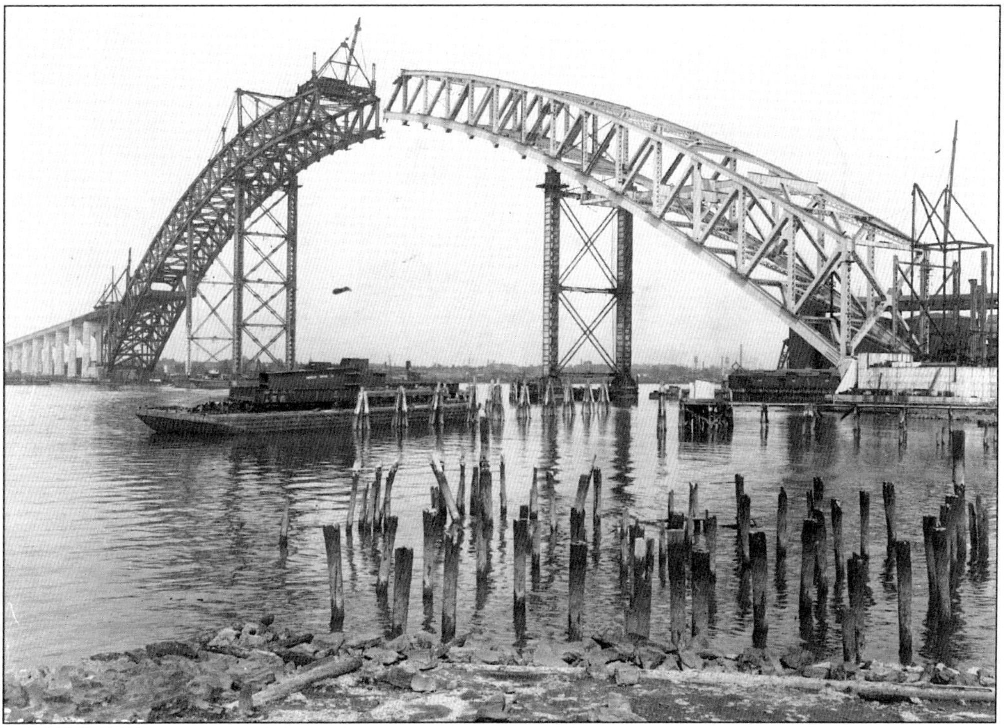

Bayonne Bridge under construction on September 21, 1930. The 1930s was a decade of bridge building with the completion of the Bayonne and Goethals bridges and the Outerbridge Crossing. (Collection of the Staten Island Historical Society.)

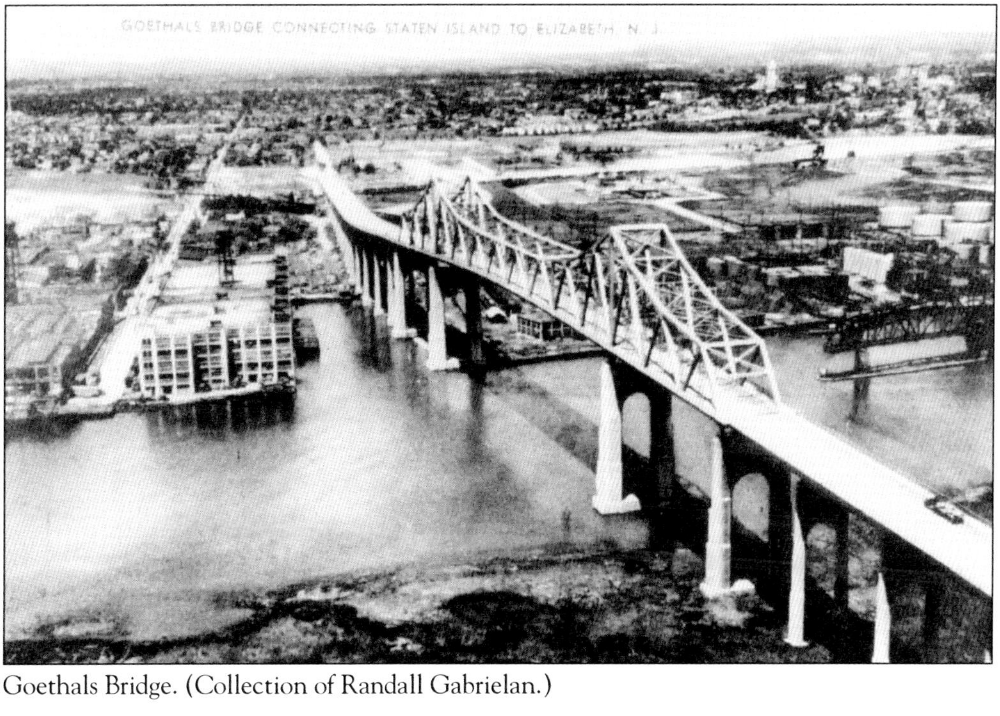

Goethals Bridge. (Collection of Randall Gabrielan.)

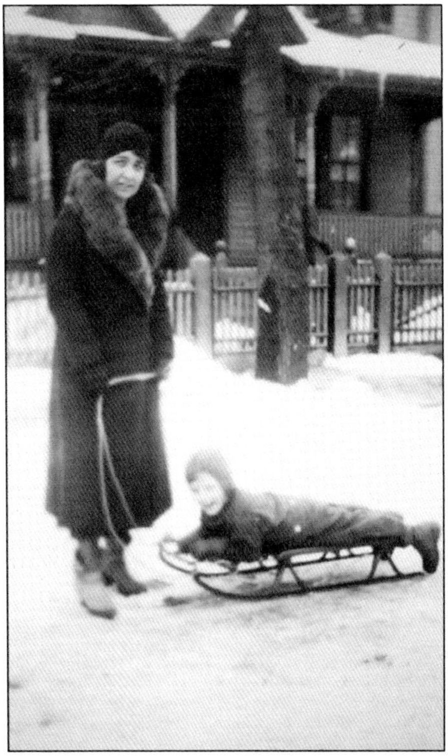

On Dongan Avenue, Bill Drinnan with his mother, Evelyn Cole Drinnan. The Drinnan family owned Drinnan's Garage at 1335 Castleton Avenue. The garage was a showroom for Pontiacs. (Collection of Claire and Bill Drinnan.)

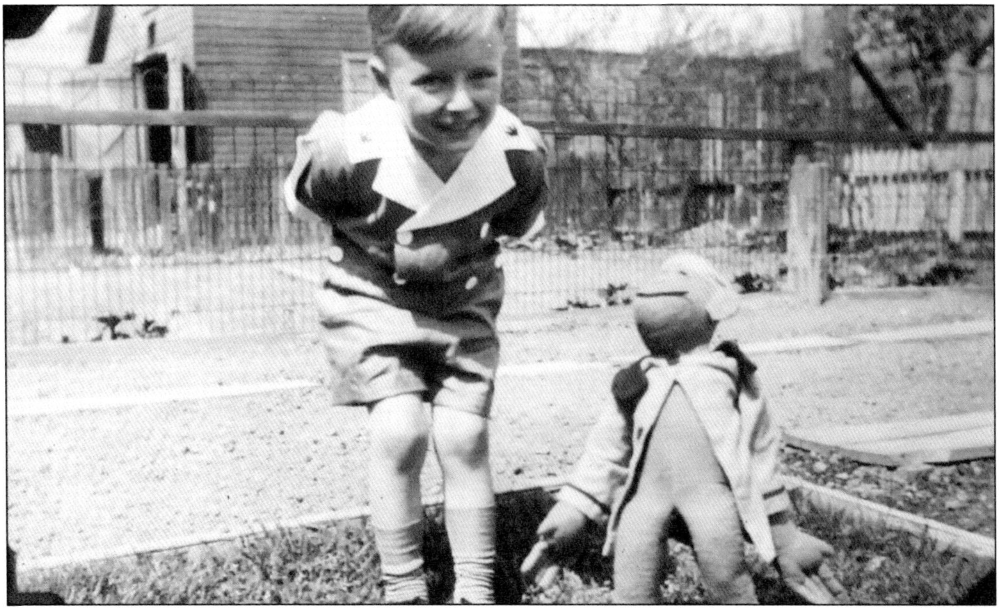

"A Tale of Two Monkeys," as Bill Drinnan calls it. This photograph was sent to Drinnan by the Staten Island Historical Society. A book of photographs of church members' children had been donated to the society and curator Maxine Friedman sent this charming 1932 photograph to the original "monkey." The photograph was taken at 175 Dongan Avenue. Elections were held in the rear of the R.W. Tompkins Department Store, which was in the vicinity. (Collection of Claire and Bill Drinnan.)

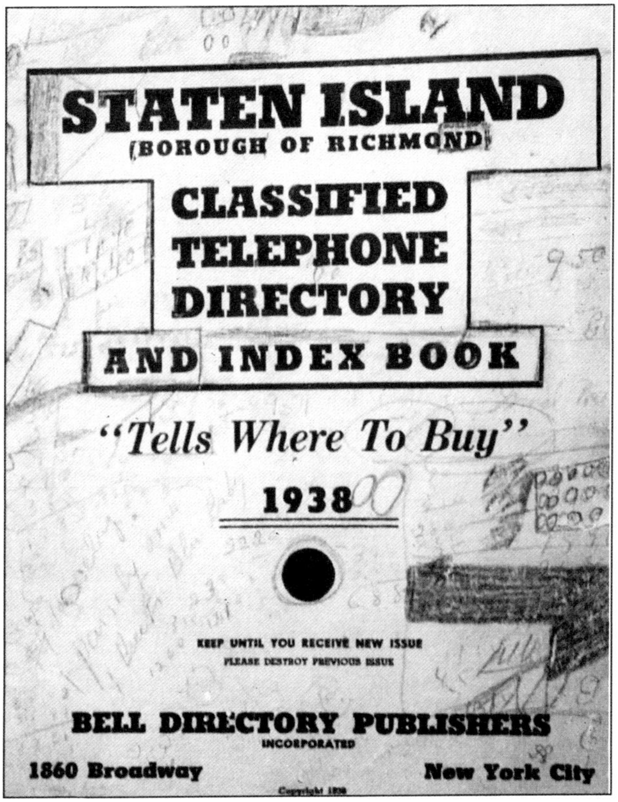

The Staten Island Telephone Directory cover. (Collection of Dorothy Cugini Nolan.)

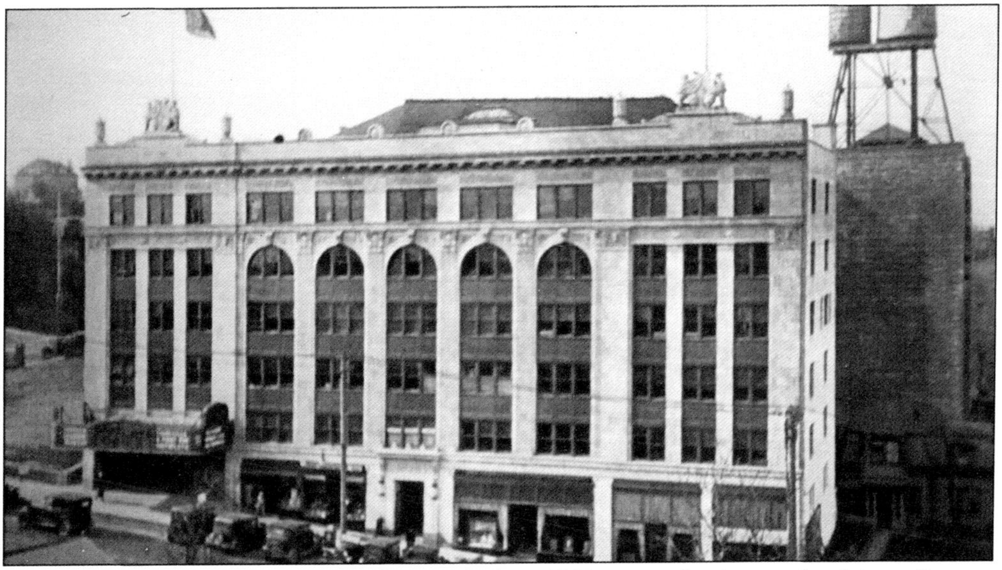

The beautifully ornate St. George Theatre. Built in 1930, it was the design of architects Eugene DeRosa and James Whitford with ornamentation by renowned sculptor John Skiba. Located at 27 Hyatt Street in St. George, the theater may well be considered the great lady of Staten Island's theaters. As "talking films" changed the face of entertainment forever, the sophisticated architecture of the theaters reflected the public's value of this form of entertainment. (Collection of Marjorie Johnson.)

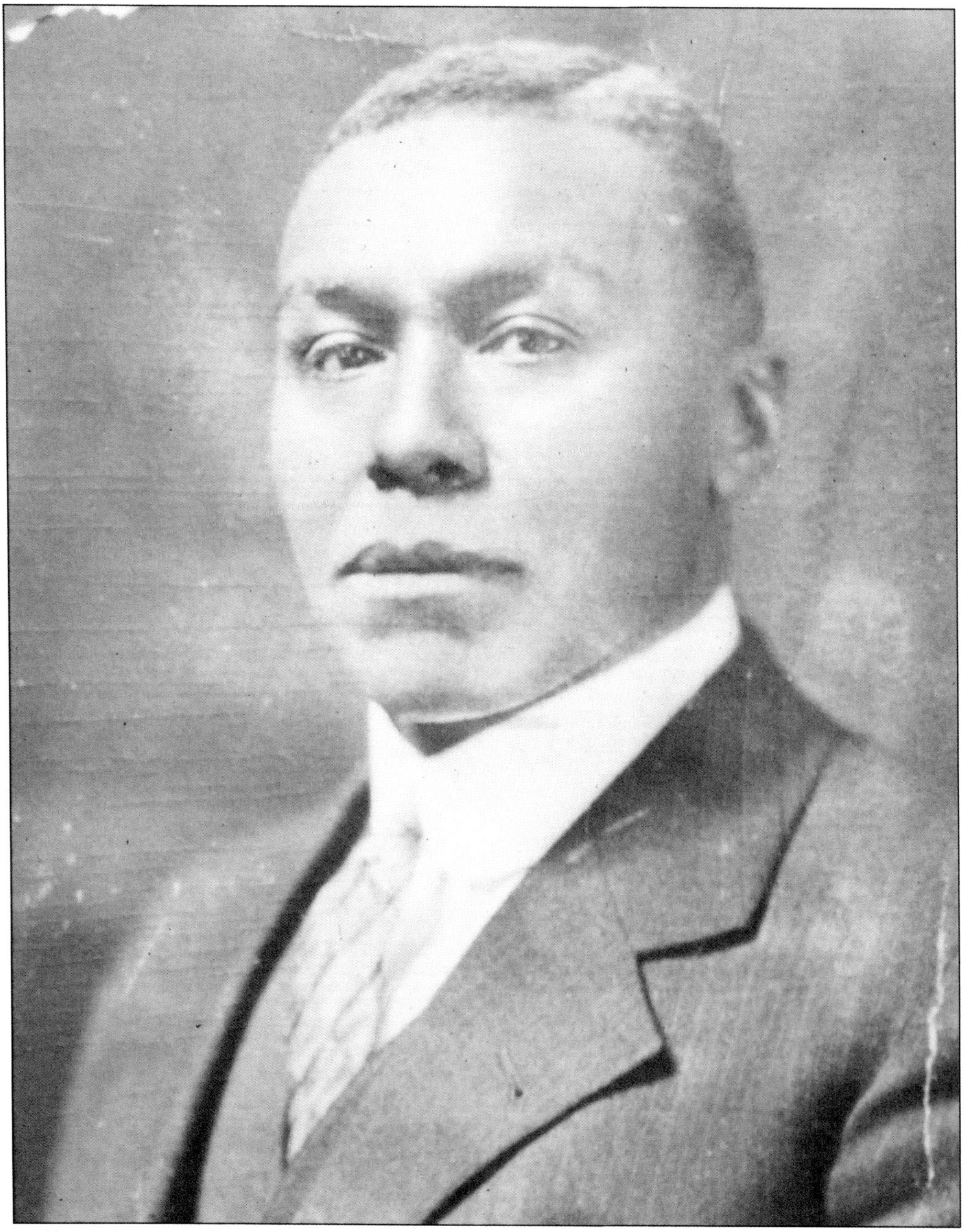

William A. Morris Moving & Storage Company founder William Morris. William was born in Elizabeth City, North Carolina, and came to Staten Island at age 18. He worked for the Richmond Storage Company before founding his own company. A man noted for his integrity, community spirit, and promotion of education, he became one of the founders of the Staten Island branch of the NAACP. Morris held many positions in his life, including first president of the local chapter of the NAACP, and the Staten Island Van Owners. He was also a Staten Island sheriff, a member of the Grand Jurors' Association, and one of the first organizers of the Shiloh Church, West Brighton. Intermediate School 61 was named for William Morris in recognition of his devotion to education. (Collection of Evelyn Morris King.)

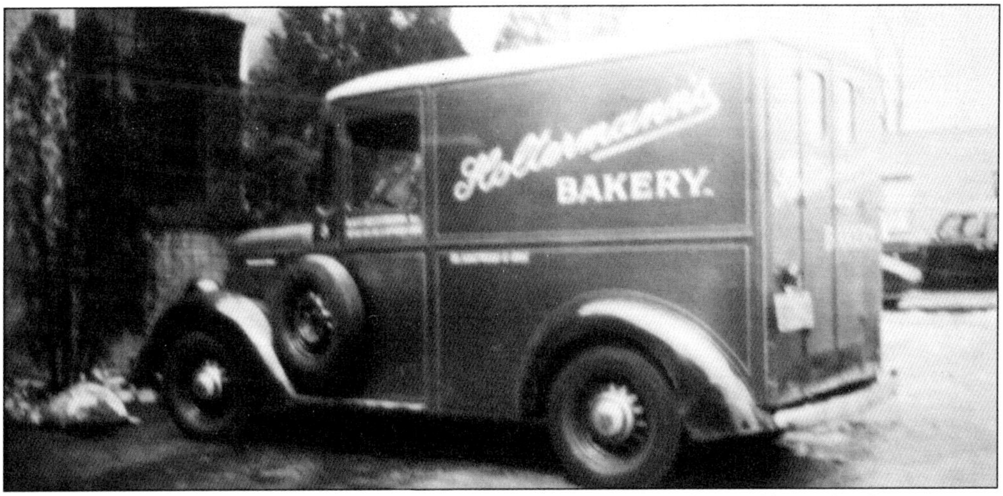

Holtermann's Bakery truck, 1938, at its present location on Arthur Kill Road. The company founded by Claus Holtermann in 1879 was originally located in the Treasure House, now part of Historic Richmondtown. Claus Holtermann became prominent in community and civic affairs. The Holtermann family home is now the rectory for St. Patrick's Church. Run for many years by Al and Cliff Holtermann, the bakery is operated by fourth-generation Holtermanns Billy and Jeff. (Collection of Edith and Al Holtermann.)

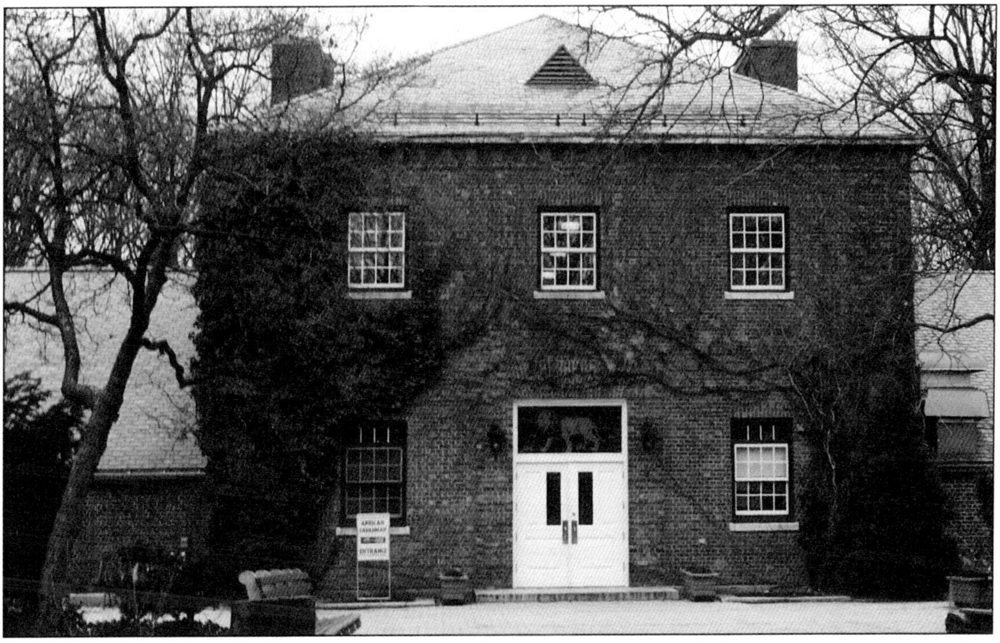

The Staten Island Zoo. Often referred to as a "Depression miracle," the zoo was opened in 1936 by WPA workers. It was the first educational zoo in America. Its first director was Carol Stryker, one of those interested in the natural sciences who were mentored by historian William Davis. For many years, Dr. Patricia O'Connor was director. The zoo has long been recognized for its outstanding reptile collection. (Photograph by Margaret Lundrigan.)

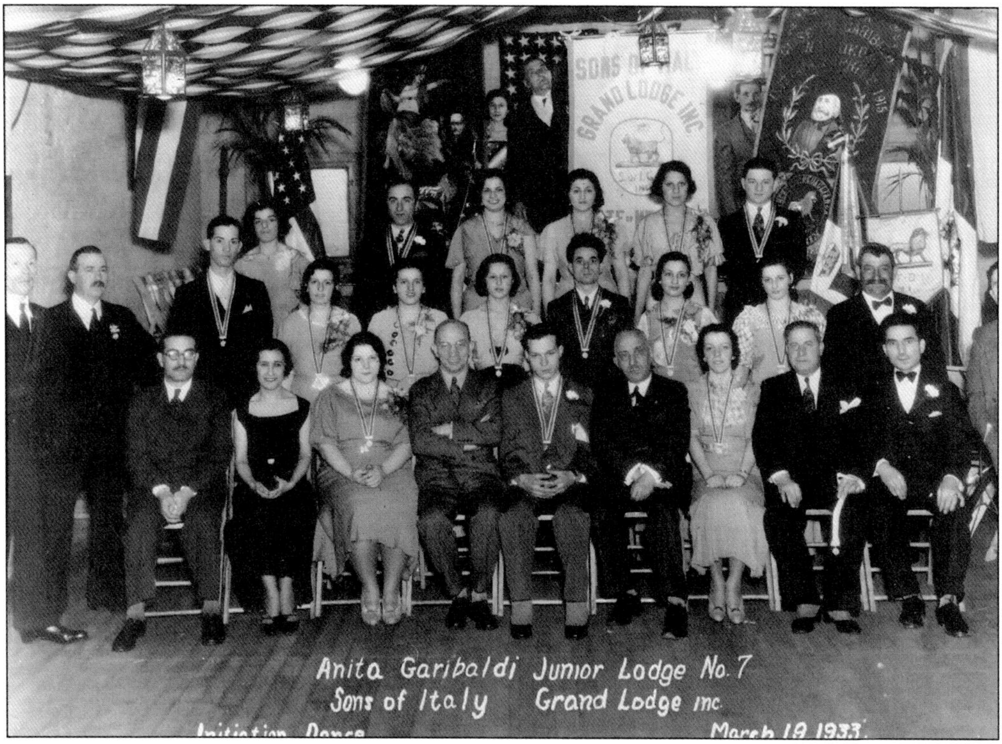

On March 10, 1933, the Anita Garibaldi Junior Lodge No. 7 Sons of Italy held its initiation dance. (Collection of the Staten Island Historical Society.)

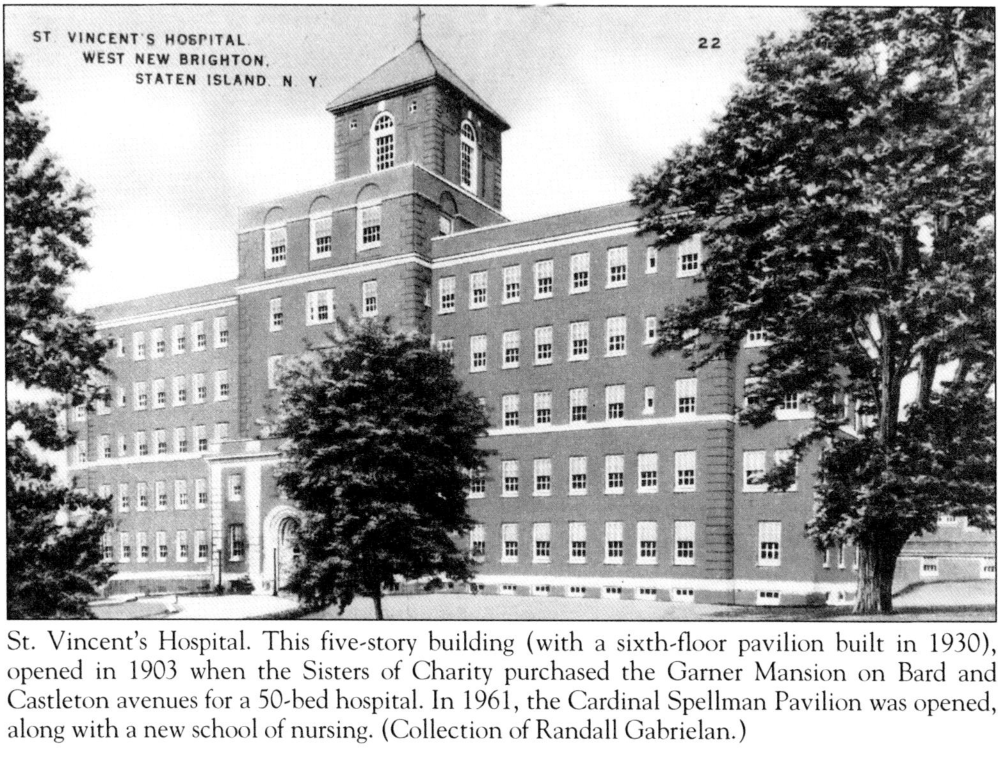

St. Vincent's Hospital. This five-story building (with a sixth-floor pavilion built in 1930), opened in 1903 when the Sisters of Charity purchased the Garner Mansion on Bard and Castleton avenues for a 50-bed hospital. In 1961, the Cardinal Spellman Pavilion was opened, along with a new school of nursing. (Collection of Randall Gabrielan.)

Five

1940–1949

The Gathering Storm

*The Lascaux caves, known for *c*. 20,000 B.C. wall paintings , discovered in France, 1940.

*FDR reelected to third term as president, 1940.

*Author F. Scott Fitzgerald, artist Paul Klee, and American social worker Lillian D. Wald die, 1940.

*Penicillin developed as an antibiotic of choice by Howard Florey, 1940.

*United States declares war on Germany and Italy, World War II continues; Japan attacks Pearl Harbor (December 7), 1941.

*English novelist Virginia Woolf, Irish author James Joyce, and American baseball player Lou Gehrig die, 1941.

*National Gallery of Art opens in Washington, D.C., 1941.

*Enrico Fermi splits the atom, 1942.

*The first electronic "brain" (computer) developed in New York, 1942.

*U.S. Supreme court rules Nevada divorces valid in America, 1942.

*C.S. Lewis writes *The Screwtape Letters*, and Irving Berlin writes "White Christmas," 1942.

*Russian composer and pianist Sergey Rachmaninoff dies, 1943.

*Betty Smith writes *A Tree Grows in Brooklyn*, 1943.

*"Zoot suits with reet pleat" became popular men's fashion, 1943.

*Poliomyelitis, a virus that attacks the central nervous system through the blood, kills nearly 1,200 and leaves thousands more, mostly children, crippled in the U.S., 1943.

*FDR wins fourth term as president, with Harry S. Truman as vice president, 1944.

*"Battle of the Bulge" at Ardennes begins, and D-Day (June 6) landings made in Normandy as World War II continues, 1944.

*Jean-Paul Sartre writes *No Exit*, 1944.

*Dutch artist Piet Mondriaan and Norwegian artist Edvard Munch (best known for *The Scream*) die, 1944.

*Budapest falls, Mussolini killed, Hitler commits suicide (April 30), U.S. drops atomic bombs on Hiroshima (August 6) and Nagasaki (August 9), and FDR dies in office, 1945.

*"V.E. Day" (May 7) marks end of war in Europe, 1945.

*World War II ends after Japanese surrender, August 14, 1945.

*General George S. Patton killed in auto accident, 1945.

*Juan Peron elected president of Argentina, 1946.

*British Prime Minister Winston Churchill gives the "Iron Curtain" speech, 1946.

*Chilean poet Gabriela Mistral wins the Nobel Prize for Literature, 1946.

*Dr. Benjamin Spock writes *Baby and Child Care*, 1946.

*R.E. Byrd conducts the South Pole expedition, 1946.

*Peace treaties signed in Paris, and India proclaims independence, 1947.

**The Diary of Anne Frank* published, 1947.

*Abraham Levitt and sons Alfred and William help solve the GI's housing problem by creating Levittown, the American prototype suburb in Long Island, New York, 1947.

*The transistor invented by Bell Laboratories scientists, 1947.

*The Dead Sea Scrolls (c. 22 B.C.–100 A.D.) discovered in Wadi Qumran, 1947.

*Jackie Robinson becomes first black in Major League baseball, 1947.

*Tennessee Williams wins Pulitzer Prize for *A Streetcar Named Desire*, 1948.

*Mohandas Gandhi, known as the Mahatma, shot and killed, January 31, 1948.

*Israel declared a state, 1948.

*Harry S. Truman elected president, 1948.

Babe Ruth dies, 1948.

**Sexual Behavior in the Human Male* written by Alfred C. Kinsey, 1948.

*Arthur Miller writes *Death of a Salesman*, Norman Vincent Peale writes *A Guide to Confident Living*, and Eleanor Roosevelt writes *This I Remember*, 1949.

*Apartheid established in South Africa, 1949.

*United Nations warned of imminent civil war in Korea, 1949.

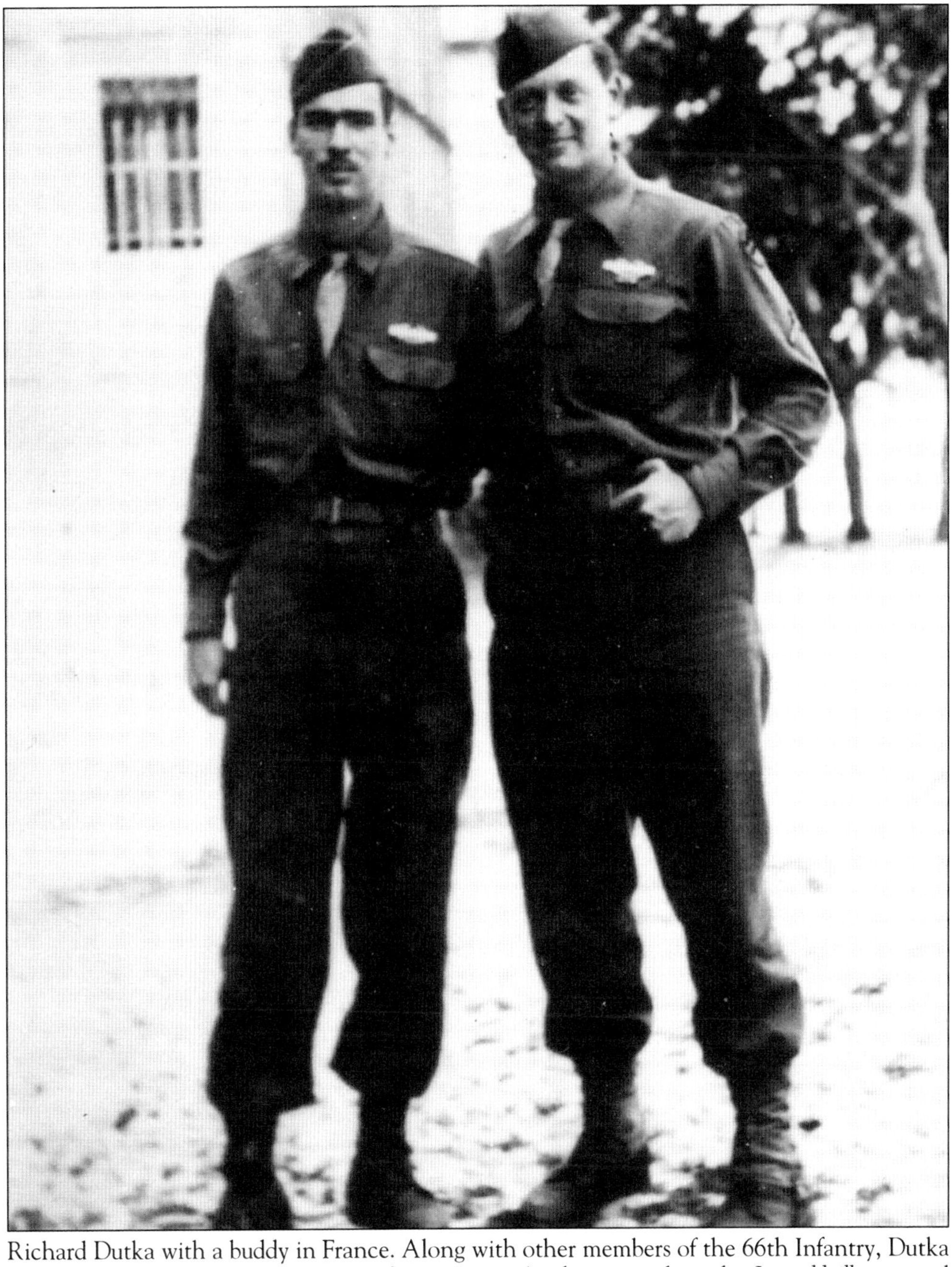

Richard Dutka with a buddy in France. Along with other members of the 66th Infantry, Dutka was part of a sea disaster kept secret for 40 years. As the troop ship, the *Leopoldville*, crossed the English Channel on Christmas Eve of 1944, it was struck by an enemy torpedo. The ship was carrying 2,500 men of the division known as the Black Panthers. Dutka told *Daily News* reporter Bill Farrell in an August 5, 1984 interview, "Suddenly, without warning, a torpedo hit us mid-ship. It was an almost instantaneous knockout." Eight hundred men died in the surprise attack. The survivors went on to serve in France. Dutka and four other members of the 66th Division representing the division were honored by the government of France. (Collection of Marion and Richard Dutka.)

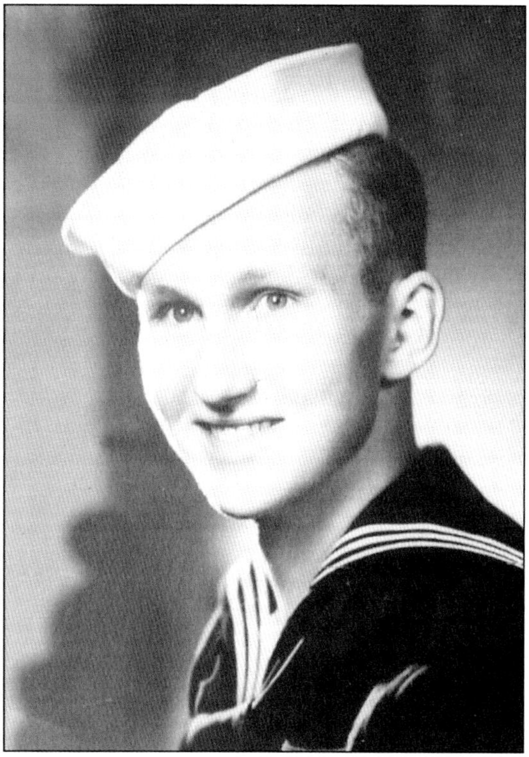

Al Holtermann in uniform in 1943. Holtermann served with the 3rd Fleet in the Pacific during the war. (Collection of Edith and Al Holtermann.)

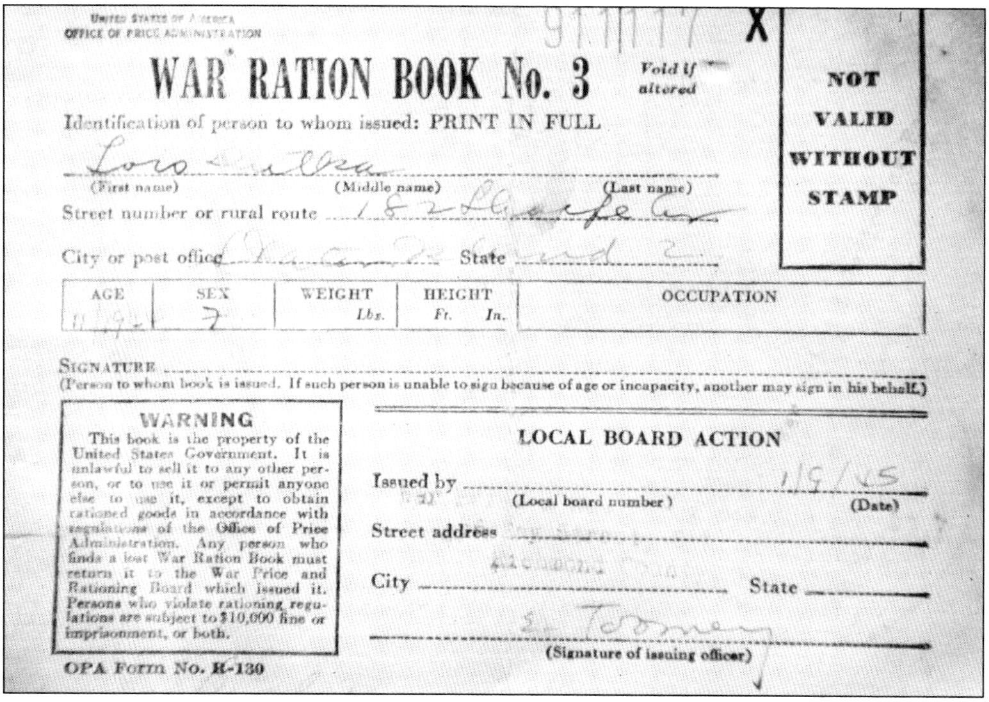

UNITED STATES OF AMERICA
OFFICE OF PRICE ADMINISTRATION

WAR RATION BOOK No. 3

Void if altered

NOT VALID WITHOUT STAMP

Identification of person to whom issued: PRINT IN FULL

(First name) (Middle name) (Last name)

Street number or rural route

City or post office State

AGE	SEX	WEIGHT	HEIGHT	OCCUPATION
		Lbs.	Ft. In.	

SIGNATURE
(Person to whom book is issued. If such person is unable to sign because of age or incapacity, another may sign in his behalf.)

WARNING
This book is the property of the United States Government. It is unlawful to sell it to any other person, or to use it or permit anyone else to use it, except to obtain rationed goods in accordance with regulations of the Office of Price Administration. Any person who finds a lost War Ration Book must return it to the War Price and Rationing Board which issued it. Persons who violate rationing regulations are subject to $10,000 fine or imprisonment, or both.

OPA Form No. R-130

LOCAL BOARD ACTION

Issued by (Local board number) (Date)

Street address

City State

(Signature of issuing officer)

Book of ration stamps for Lois Dutka. During the war, rationing was used to conserve needed goods such as food, clothing, and gasoline. Families received books of ration coupons that could be redeemed for those items. (Collection of Marion and Richard Dutka.)

A series of telegraphs sent and received by Richard Dutka during the war. They lent a particularly personal note to the lives of soldiers. One telegraph informs him of the birth of twin daughters born while he was overseas. (Collection of Marion and Richard Dutka.)

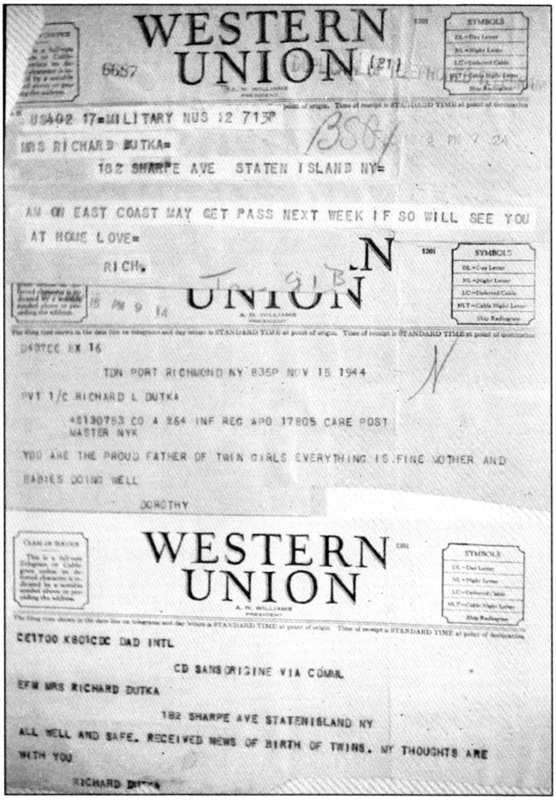
WESTERN UNION

US402 17=MILITARY NUS 12 713P

MRS RICHARD DUTKA=

182 SHARPE AVE STATEN ISLAND NY=

AM ON EAST COAST MAY GET PASS NEXT WEEK IF SO WILL SEE YOU AT HOME LOVE=

RICH.

UNION

D401CC BX 16

TDN PORT RICHMOND NY 835P NOV 15 1944

PVT 1/C RICHARD L DUTKA

42130783 CO A 264 INF REG APO 17805 CARE POST MASTER NYK

YOU ARE THE PROUD FATHER OF TWIN GIRLS EVERYTHING IS FINE MOTHER AND BABIES DOING WELL

DOROTHY

WESTERN UNION

CE1T00 K801CDC DAD INTL

CD SANSORIGINE VIA COMML

EFM MRS RICHARD DUTKA

182 SHARPE AVE STATENISLAND NY

ALL WELL AND SAFE. RECEIVED NEWS OF BIRTH OF TWINS. MY THOUGHTS ARE WITH YOU

RICHARD DUTKA

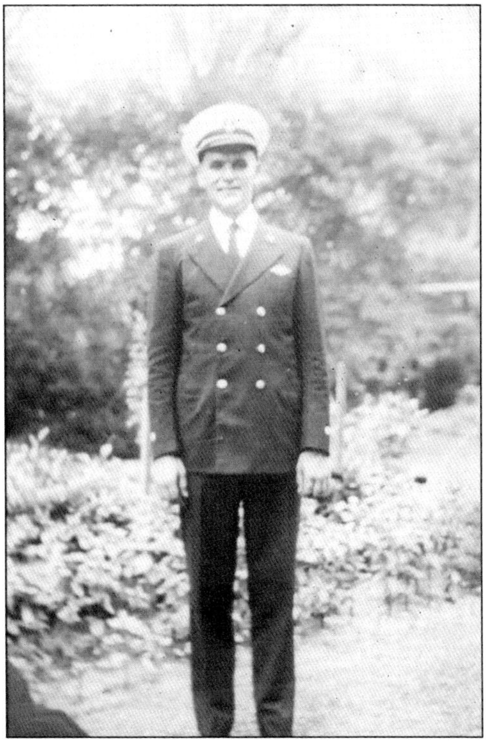

In 1944, Charles Holtermann served in the Merchant Marines. (Collection of Edith and Al Holtermann.)

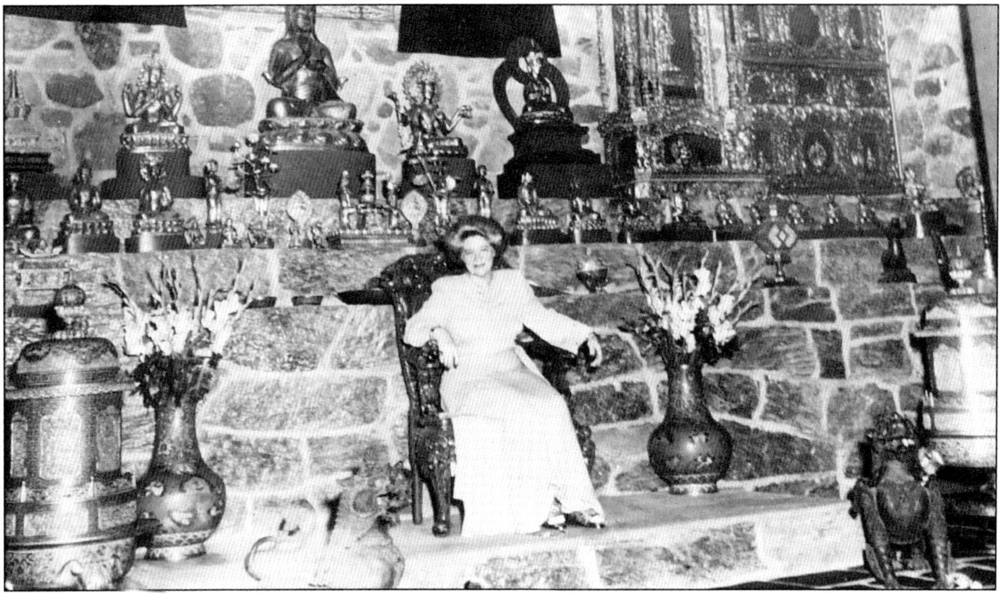

Jacqueline Klauber, an art dealer, whose professional name was Jacques Marchais. Here she presides at the October 5, 1947 opening of the Jacques Marchais Tibetan Museum. Jacques Marchais had a life-long passion for Tibetan art that evolved into the desire to share and preserve her impressive collection in a museum. The opening was covered by *Life Magazine* in its December 8, 1947 issue. Following her death shortly thereafter, friends and supporters raised funds to keep the museum open. The museum houses one of the finest collections of Tibetan art in the western world. (Collection of the Jacques Marchais Museum.)

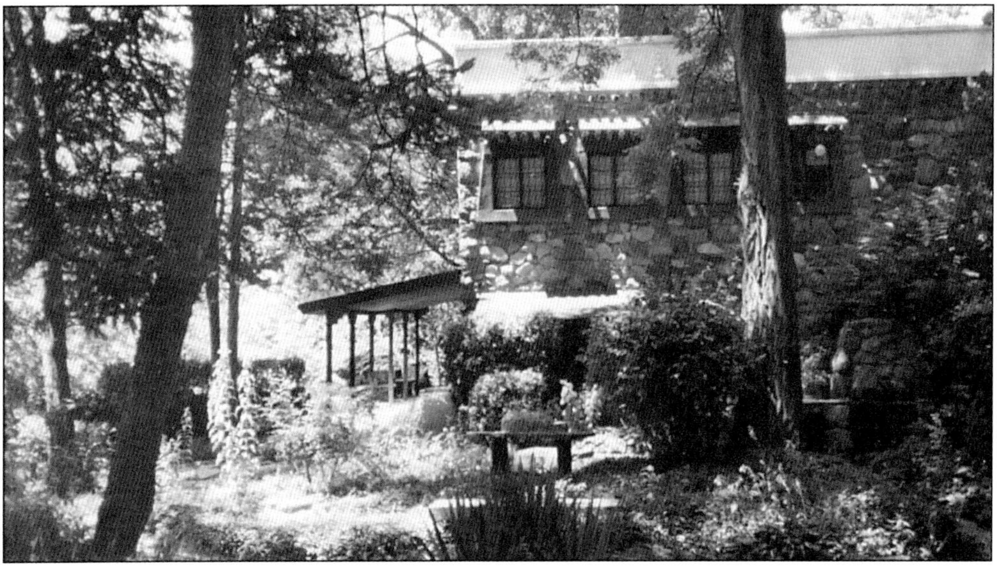

Jacques Marchais Tibetan Museum. The museum, located on Lighthouse Hill, is composed of two buildings designed to resemble a Tibetan monastery. In 1991, museum curator Barbara Lipton and Sen. John Marchi welcomed his Holiness the 14th Dalai Lama to the museum. His Holiness said, "There is a real danger of the disappearance of the unique Tibetan culture." He added that while at the museum he felt as if he were in Tibet. (Collection of the Jacques Marchais Museum.)

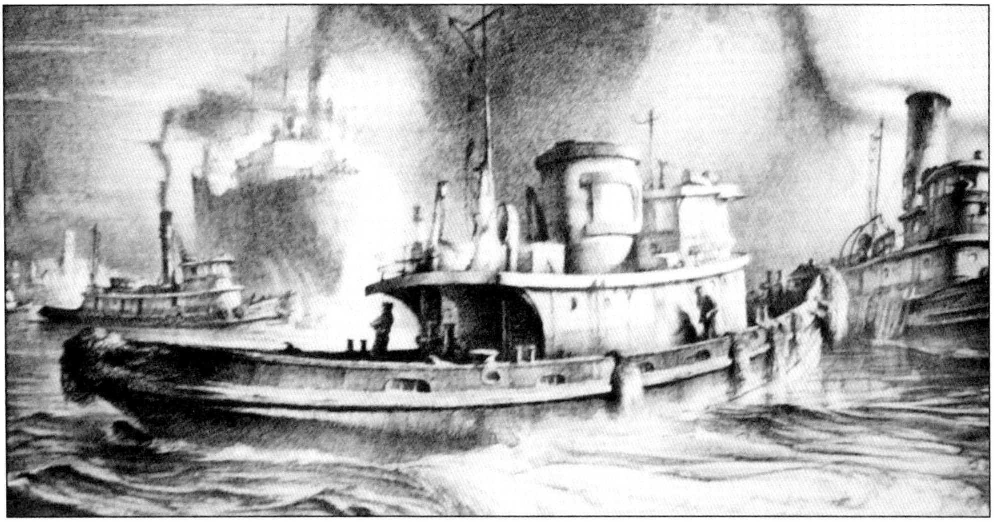

Painting by artist John A. Noble, "*The Procession of Tugs*." Noble wrote of the painting: "In the foreground, beginning to go astern, is the *Dazellaird*, and to her right is a wooden-shipping board tug of 1919, World War I design, which type furnished one of the mainstays of New York tug companies for a generation. Tugs #1 and #2 are each products of different wars. The *Dazellaird* is an Army tug of WWII. In the background is the *J.J. Timmons*, a tug characteristic of 1900 or before. These three tugs, which often worked together, have dropped a light tanker off the Bayonne shore. As an afterthought, I put in a Civil War side wheel tug making this picture a century of tugs. The last is the only vessel I have drawn that I have never seen—however, the temptation was great." (Courtesy of the John A. Noble Collection.)

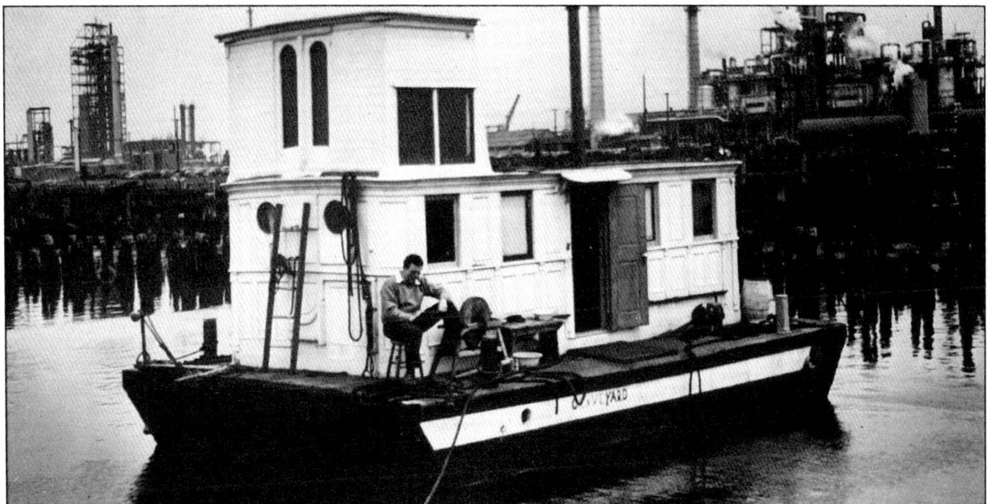

John A. Noble on his studio houseboat at Port Johnson. A maritime artist, he was born in 1913 in the American Hospital in Paris. Noble's father was John Noble, a famous landscape artist who later the founded the Provincetown Art Association. Noble grew up surrounded by artists and art; and throughout his life he was drawn to sea and the wonderful sailing vessels that inhabited it. "Nobody loved sailing vessels more and watched them more than I," he wrote. "My life's work is to make a rounded picture of the American maritime endeavor of modern times." The Noble works in this volume are described by the artist, quotes taken from Erin Urban's *Hulls and Hulls in the Tide of Time*. (Courtesy of the John A. Noble Collection.)

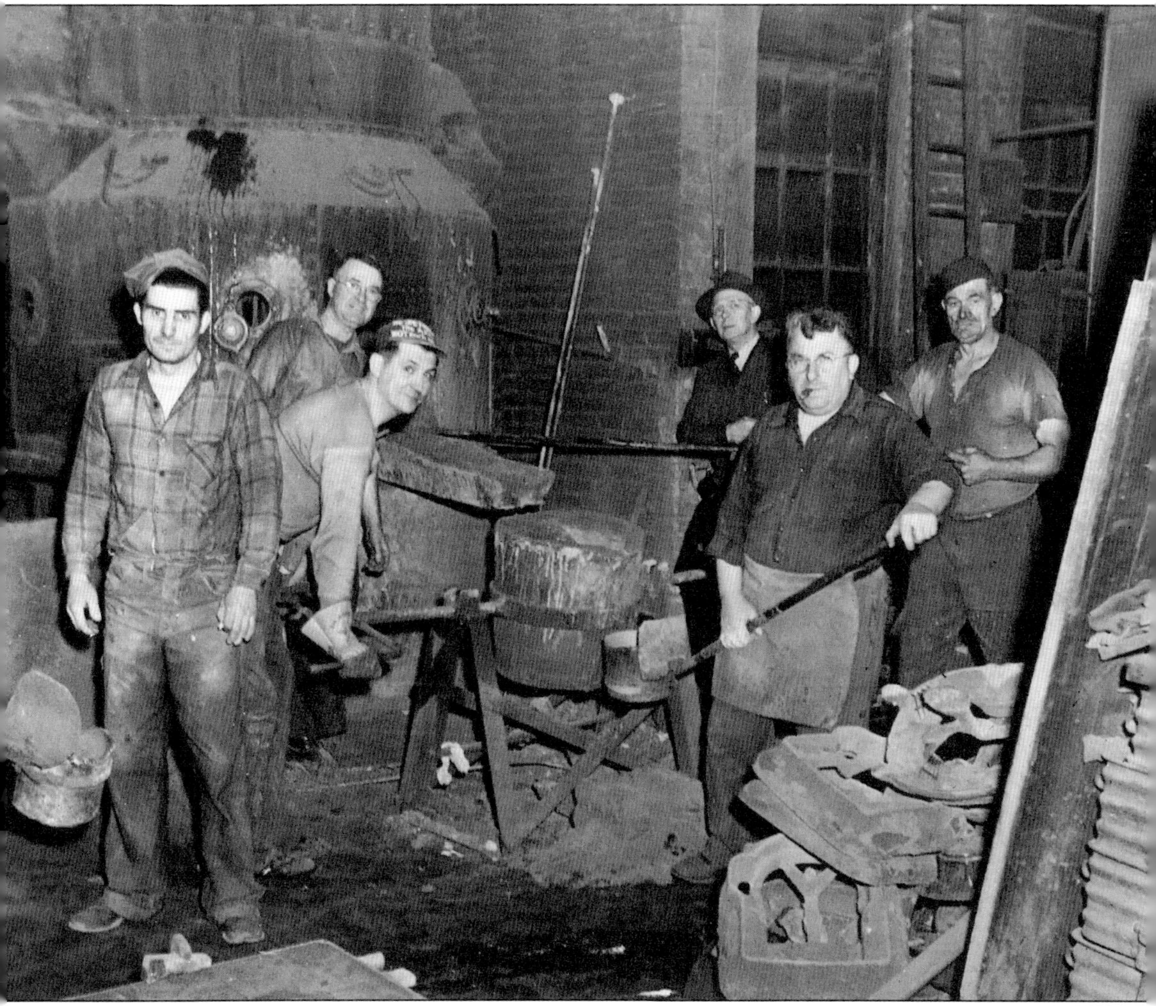

The S.S. White Foundry in 1947. (Collection of the Staten Island Historical Society.)

The Rest Club, Fresh Kills, Travis, 1947. (Collection of Arleen Brahn.)

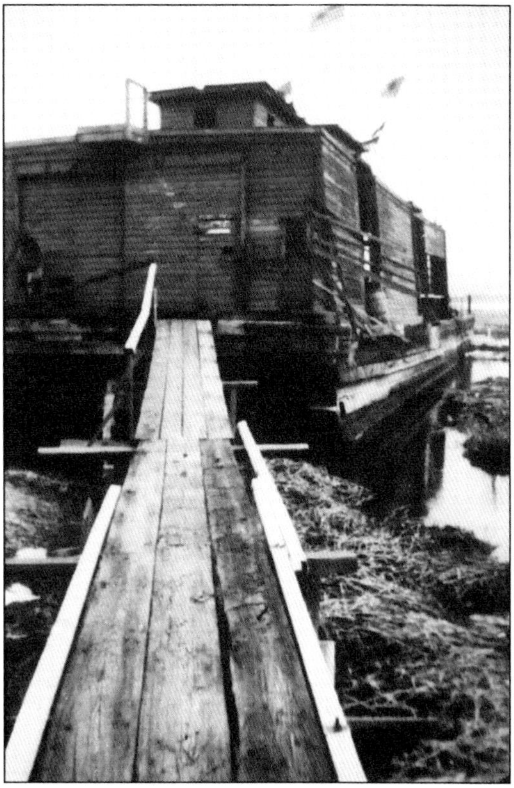

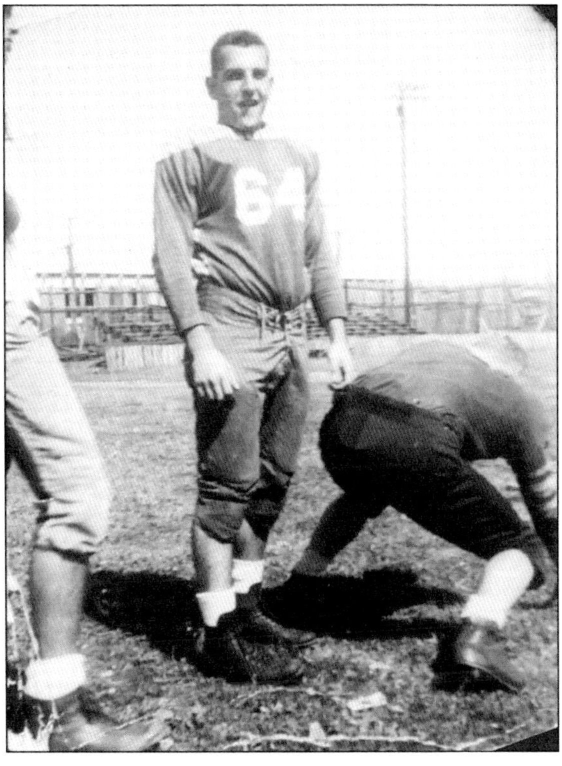

Joe Cugini at Weissglass Stadium in 1948 as part of the Crabb Post League Champs. (Collection of the Cugini Family.)

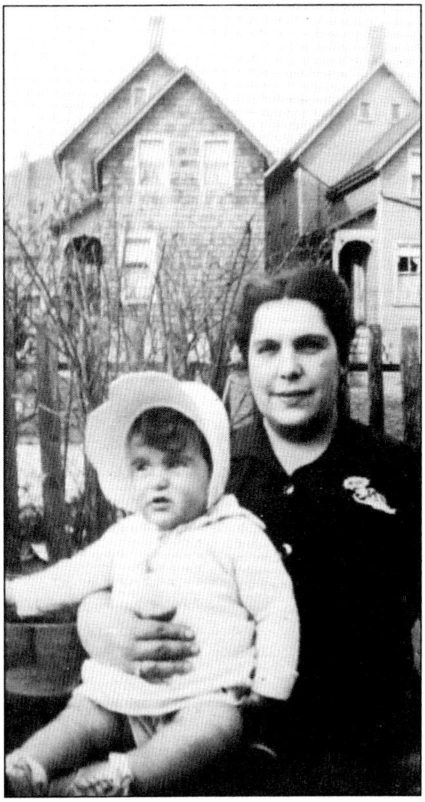

Donata Cugini with baby Dorothy at Post Avenue, Port Richmond, in 1943. (Collection of Dorothy Cugini Nolan.)

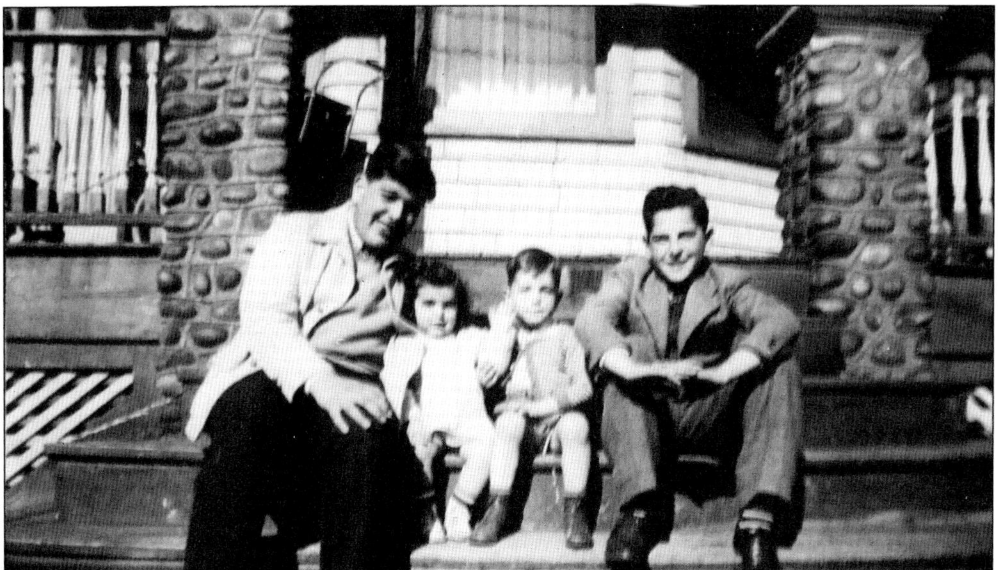

Christy, Dorothy, Robert, and Joe Cugini on the steps of their Post Avenue home in 1944. (Collection of the Cugini Family.)

Jimmy, Joan, and infant Ted, with their father, Buddy Harris, on Easter Sunday, 1941. (Collection of Noreen and Ted Harris.)

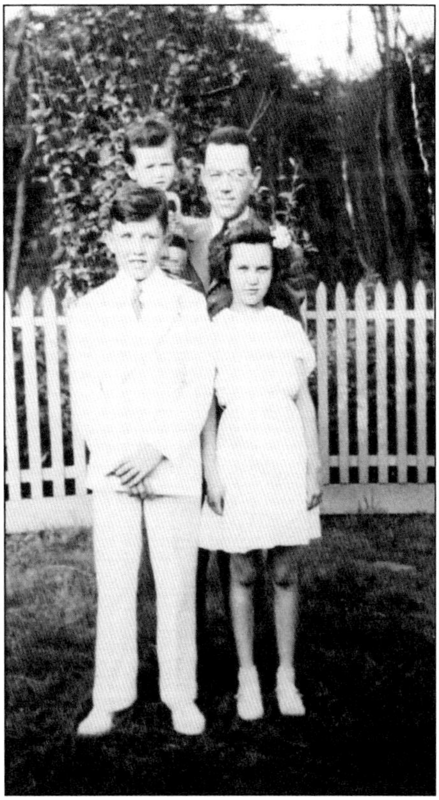

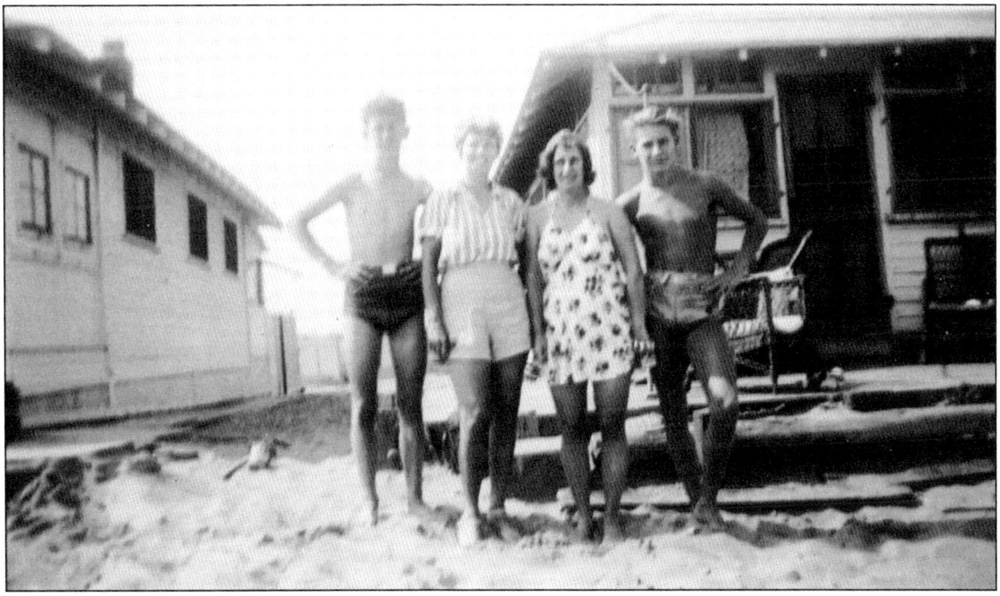

Muriel and Nelson Still, and Ruth and David Decker Jr. at Cedar Grove Beach in 1948. (Collection of Marjorie Johnson.)

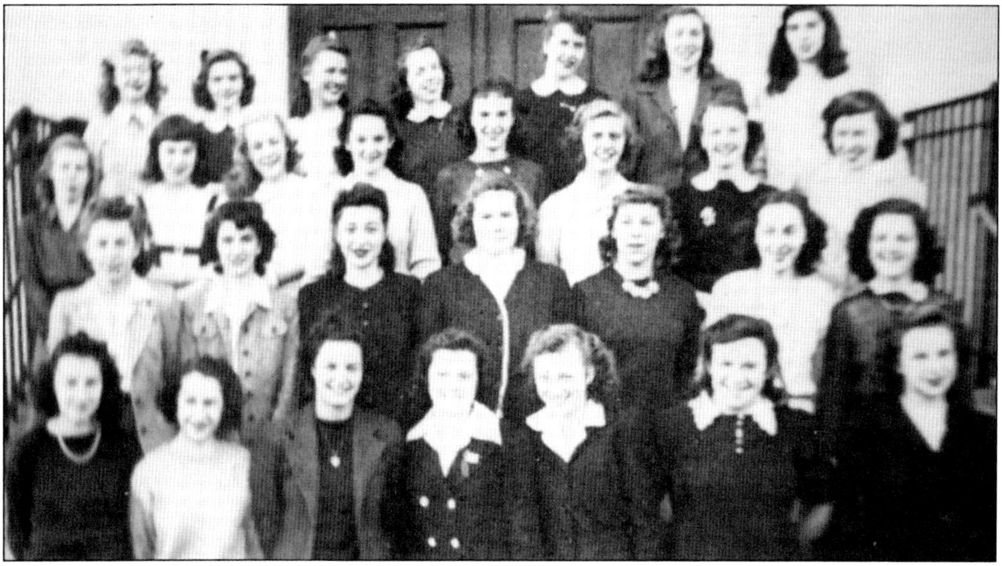

The Girls' Hockey Team at New Dorp High School in 1945. Listed from left to right are as follows: (front row) Jean Hollowell, Lois Johnson, Mary Silva, Barbara Gaines, Marianne Moerlins, Marilyn Martin, and Doris Wills; (second row) Louise Moerman, Eleanor Levanti, Virginia Moschella, Ann Higbee, Edith Armend, Naomi Robinson, and Margaret Vazzana; (third row) Jean Terkildsen, Barbara Wilson, Christine Thing, Helen Dwyer, Marily Rawling, Jacqueline Levis, Joan Hollowell, and Katherine Young; (back row) Joan Feist, Lois Couillard, Natalie Burditt, Ruth Ann Couillard, Pat Ruch, Myra Waida, and Catherine Ewing. Miss Heywang was the faculty adviser. (Collection of Edith and Al Holtermann.)

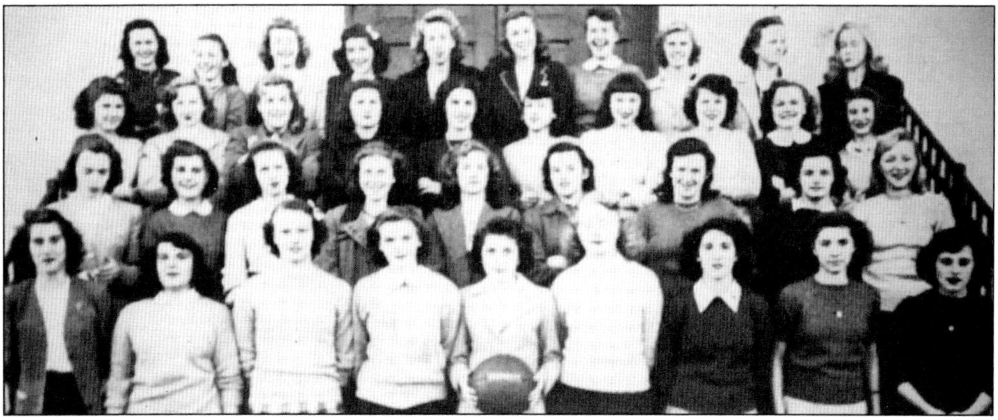

The Touchdown Club at New Dorp High School in 1945. The yearbook notes that girls are becoming more and more active in sports, and Lois Couillard is expected to be the outstanding female athlete when Edith Armend graduates. Listed, from left to right, are as follows: (front row) Vivian Serra, Alyce Crocco, Joan Hollowell, Lois Couillard, Marianthe Politis, Joan Feist, Angelina Gambino, Kathlyn Bordas, and Charlotte O'Donnell; (second row) Ruth Ann Couillard, Sonja Urheim, Doris Wills, Charlotte Cregan, Dorothy Sorenson, Louise Ayuso, Marilyn Martin, Mary Silva, and Pat Woerner; (third row) Elizabeth Privacky, Doris Skinner, Barbara Metcalfe, Peggy Sullivan, Mildred Serra, Carolyn Molla, Barbara Wilson, Marilyn Willshaw, Jean Salmonsen, and Grayce Bartolomeo; (back row) Eva Cannon, Natalie Burdett, Olivia Scheibelein, Doris Ackerman, Marilyn Jenkins, Myra Waida, Pat Ruch, Jacqueline Levis, Lorraine Asmann, and Christine M. Thing. (Collection of Edith and Al Holtermann.)

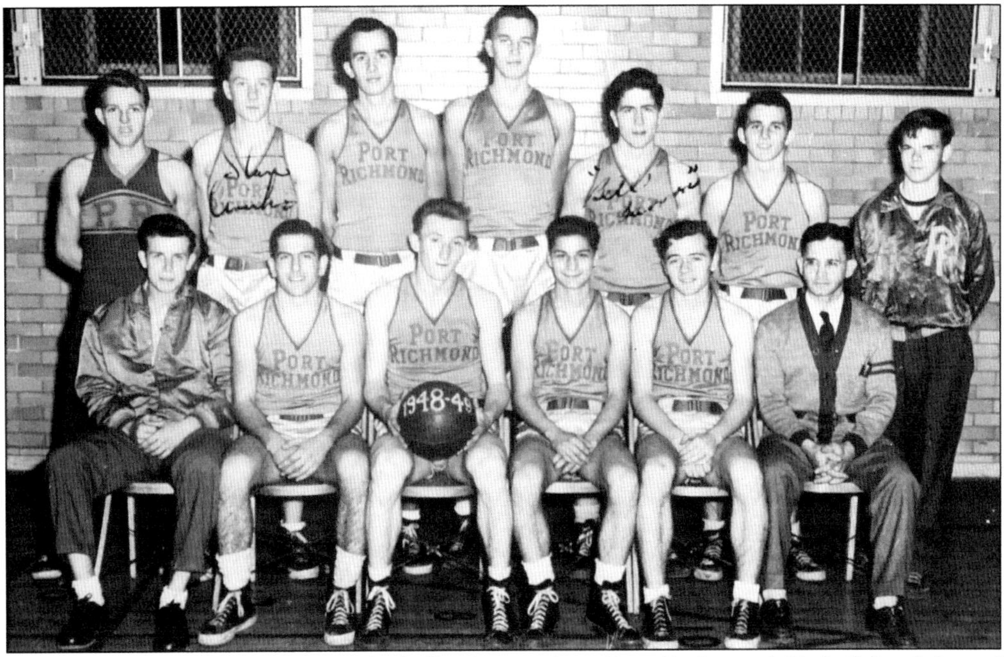

The 1948-49 New York City Basketball Champs from Port Richmond High School. Listed from left to right are as follows: (front row) manager John Leanza, Joe Cugini, captain Dan O'Rourke, Phil Lombardo, Ernie Farris and coach Trella; (back row) Bill Brunda, Stan Cwirko, George Blomquist, Larry Lovington, Bill Barron, and Paul Takash. (Collection of the Cugini Family.)

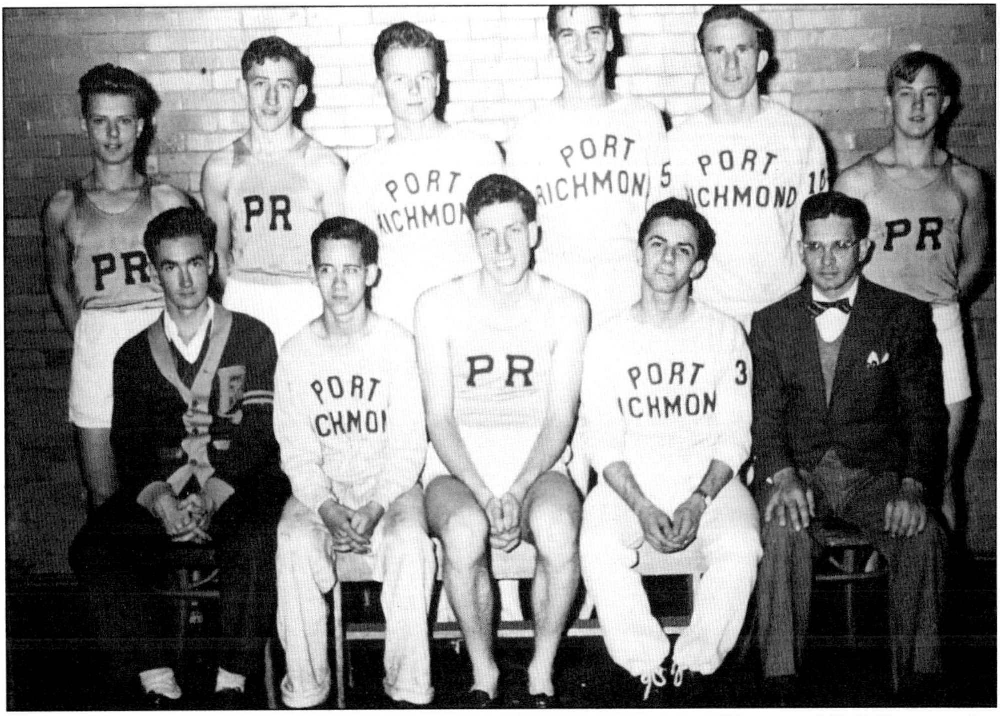

The Port Richmond Track Team with coach Trella. (Collection of Claire and Bill Drinnan.)

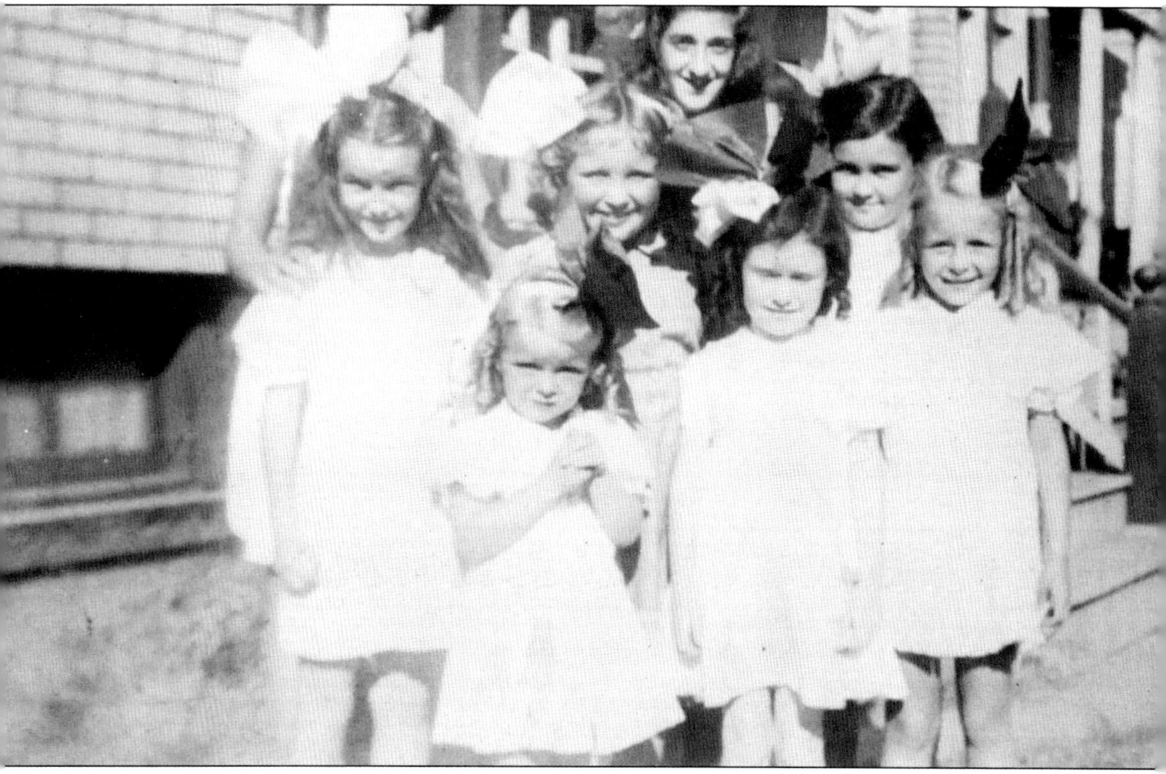

Claire Drinnan's eighth birthday party on September 31, 1944. Included among the guests are Betty Yost (Claire is next to her), Jessie Lynn Forest, Dorothy Edwards, and Carol Forrest. The older girl is of the Deppe family. (Collection of Claire and Bill Drinnan.)

Six

1950–1959

The Fast-Changing Fifties; From the Baby Boom to the Beatniks

*Senator Joseph McCarthy accuses members of State Department of being Communists and Communist sympathizers, 1950.

*U.S. State Department official Alger Hiss convicted of perjury, 1950.

*Korean Conflict begins, 1950.

*Singer Al Jolson, poet Edna St. Vincent Millay, and author George Bernard Shaw die, 1950.

*Clifford Odets writes *The Country Girl*, 1950.

*Antihistamines emerge as treatment of colds and allergies, 1950.

*Australian tennis team beats U.S. for the Davis Cup, 1950.

*"Bebop" yields to "Cool Jazz," 1950.

*King Abdullah of Jordan assassinated in Jerusalem, 1951.

*Julius and Ethel Rosenberg convicted of espionage and sentenced to death, 1951.

*Rachel Carson writes *The Sea Around Us*, and J.D. Salinger writes *The Catcher in the Rye*, 1951.

*Color television introduced in America, 1951.

*Dwight D. Eisenhower elected U.S. President, 1952.

*Albert Schweitzer wins Nobel Peace Prize, 1952.

*Samuel Beckett writes *Waiting for Godot*, 1952.

*Eva Peron of Argentina, the subject of the Broadway hit *Evita*, dies at age 33, 1952.

*Fashion designer Christian Dior gains favor in Paris haute couture, 1952.

*Sen. Joseph McCarthy "witch-hunt" hearings conducted from 1952 to 1954.

*Josef Stalin, Welsh poet Dylan Thomas, and playwright Eugene O'Neill die, 1953.

*Simone de Beauvoir writes *The Second Sex*, 1953.

*U.S.S.R. explodes the hydrogen bomb, 1953.

*Lung cancer first attributed to cigarette smoking, 1953.

*Dr. Jonas E. Salk develops the polio vaccine, begins inoculating children in Pittsburgh, Pennsylvania, 1954.

*French artist Henri Matisse dies, 1954.

*William Golding writes *Lord of the Flies*, 1954.

*Supreme Court bans segregation by color in public schools, 1954.

*Scientists Albert Einstein and Alexander Fleming die, 1955.

*Agatha Christie writes *Witness for the Prosecution*, 1955.

*Dorothy Hodgkin discovers vitamin B12 as treatment for pernicious anemia, 1955.

*The Italian liner *Andrea Doria* sinks off Nantucket Island after colliding with the *Stockholm*, 1956.

*American artist Jackson Pollock, H.L. Mencken, and Bertolt Brecht die, 1956.

*American actress Grace Kelly weds Prince Rainier of Monaco, 1956.

*Eisenhower wins second term as U.S. president, 1956.

*Fidel Castro arrives in Cuba to overthrow dictator Fulgencio Batista, 1956.

*John F. Kennedy writes *Profiles in Courage*, 1956; wins Pulitzer Prize, 1957.

**Around the World in 80 Days*, *The Ten Commandments*, and *The Seventh Seal* among the popular films of 1956.

*Soprano Maria Callas makes her New York debut in Bellini's opera *Norma*, 1956.

*Elvis Presley becomes a popular rock 'n roll star, 1956.

*Undefeated Rocky Marciano retires from boxing, 1956.

*Dr. Seuss writes *The Cat in the Hat*, 1957.

*The Common Market formed after "The Six" sign the Rome Treaty, 1957.

*U.S.S.R. launches the first earth satellites, Sputnik I and II, 1957.

*Mexican artist Diego Rivera and American actor Humphrey Bogart die, 1957.

*Thirteen-year-old Bobby Fischer becomes chess champion, 1957.

*Alaska becomes the 49th state of the U.S., 1958.

*Charles De Gaulle elected President of France, and Nelson A. Rockefeller elected governor of New York, 1958.

*Lorraine Hansberry writes *A Raisin in the Sun*, and Boris Pasternak (author of *Dr. Zhivago*) wins the Nobel Prize for Literature, 1958.

*American golfer Arnold Palmer wins his first Masters' tournament, 1958.

*The National Aeronautics and Space Administration (NASA) established, 1958.

*The "Beatnik" movement spreads from California throughout the U.S. and Europe, 1958.

*Belgium granted reforms in the Congo, 1959.

*Hawaii becomes the 50th state of U.S., 1959.

*American architect Frank Lloyd Wright, and film director Cecil B. DeMille die, 1959.

*Pope John XXIII calls first Ecumenical Council since 1870, 1959.

*U.S.S.R. launches a rocket carrying two monkeys, 1959.

**La Dolce Vita* and *Ben Hur* among popular films, 1959.

*"Nutcracker Man" skull, approximately dated 600,000 B.C., found in Tanganyika by Louis S.B. Leakey, 1959.

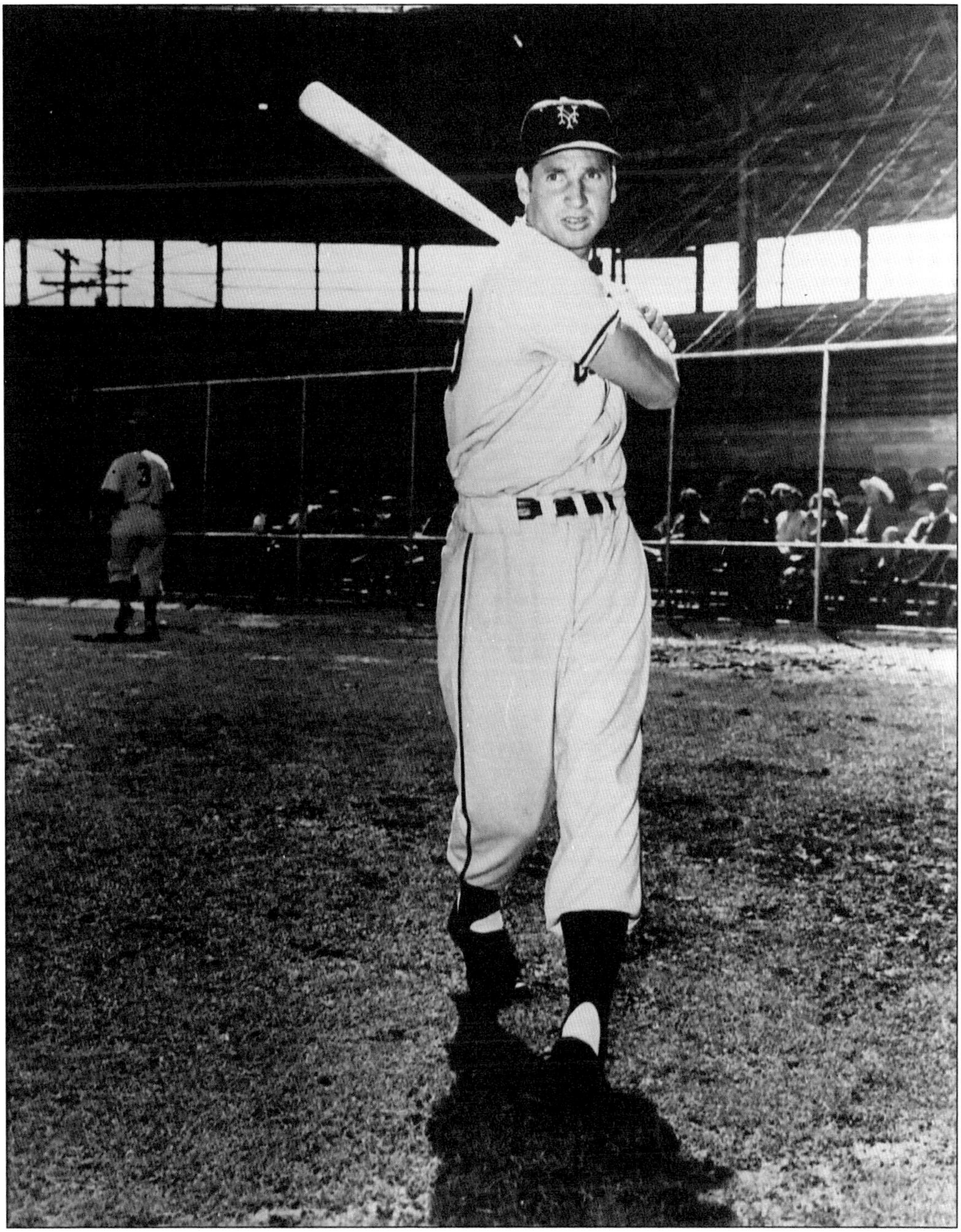

On October 3, 1951 in Brooklyn at the Polo Grounds. Robert Brown ("Bobby") Thomson gained baseball superstardom with his "shot heard 'round the world." The "Staten Island Scot" hit a three-run homer in the ninth inning of the third playoff game against the Brooklyn Dodgers, bringing victory to the Giants. The final score was 5-4 for the National League pennant. Thomson was converged upon by manager Leo Durocher, coach Freddy Fitzsimmons, and center fielder Willie Mays. Born in Glasgow, Scotland, in 1923, the well-liked Thomson graduated from Curtis High School. Today the 76-year-old athlete is the first ambassador of the NJ chapter of the Arthritis Foundation. (Courtesy of the Baseball Hall of Fame Library, Cooperstown, New York)

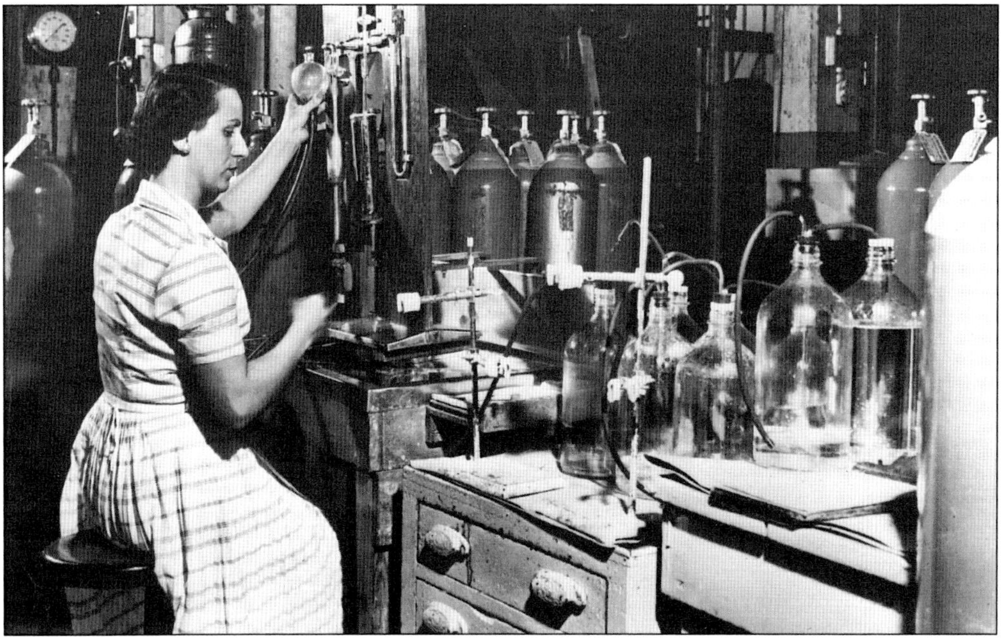

Photograph entitled *Gas Test*. In this image we see a technician at work in 1958 in the S.S. White Dental company, in Princes Bay. The photograph is from the collection of Joseph Helmer. (Collection of Staten Island Historical Society.)

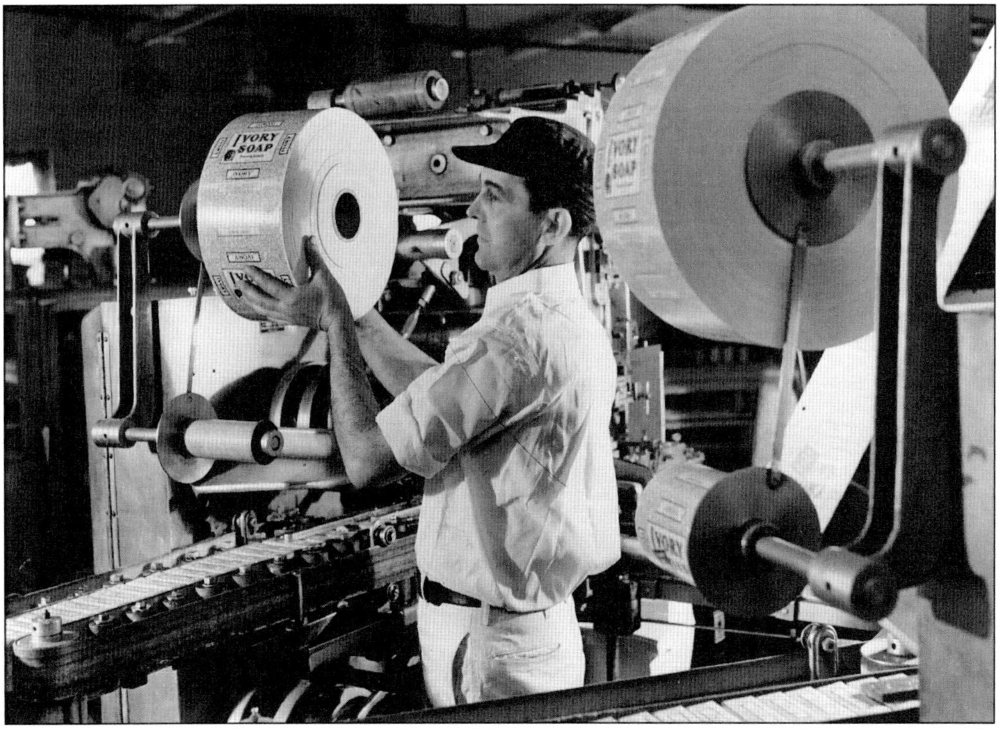

Ivory soap. In the 1950s, a plant worker is lifting a role of wrappers for the company's "old faithful," Ivory soap. The photograph is from Port Ivory. Today, the product is unchanged except for the wrapping. (Used with permission of Procter and Gamble.)

Post Avenue in the 1950s. (Collection of the Cugini Family.)

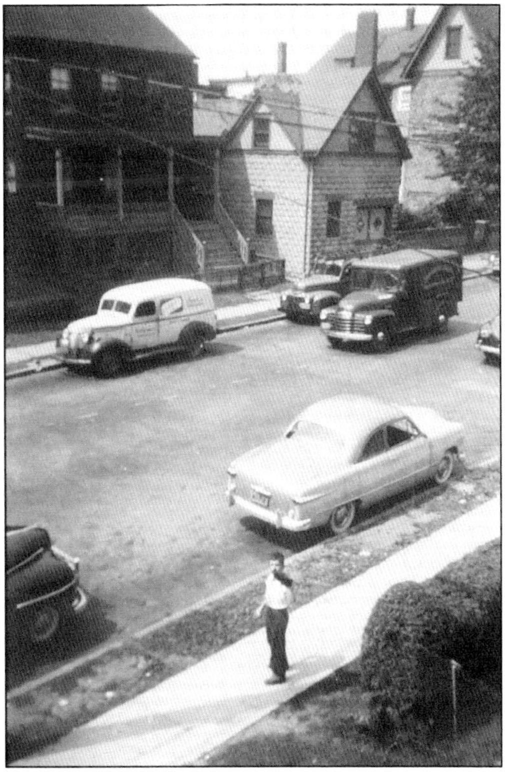

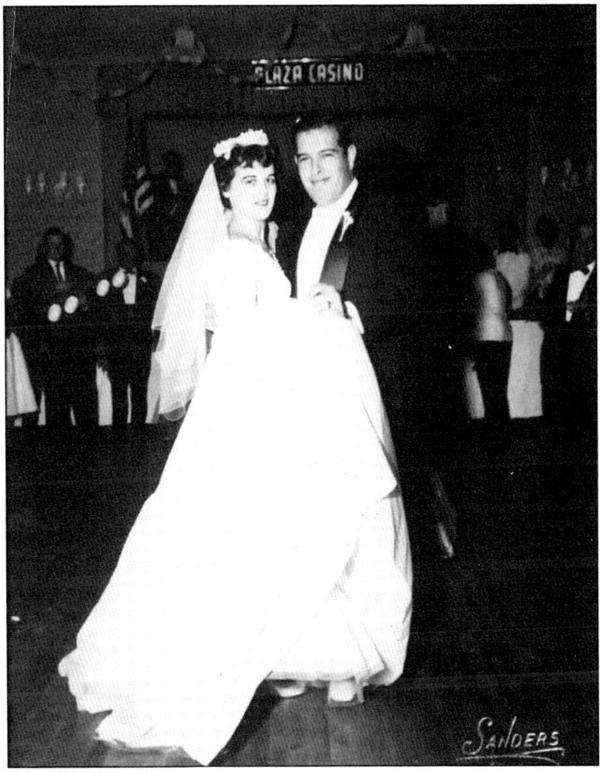

Christy Cugini married Mary Hanley in 1955. They wed at the Plaza Casino, a popular spot for wedding receptions. (Collection of the Cugini Family.)

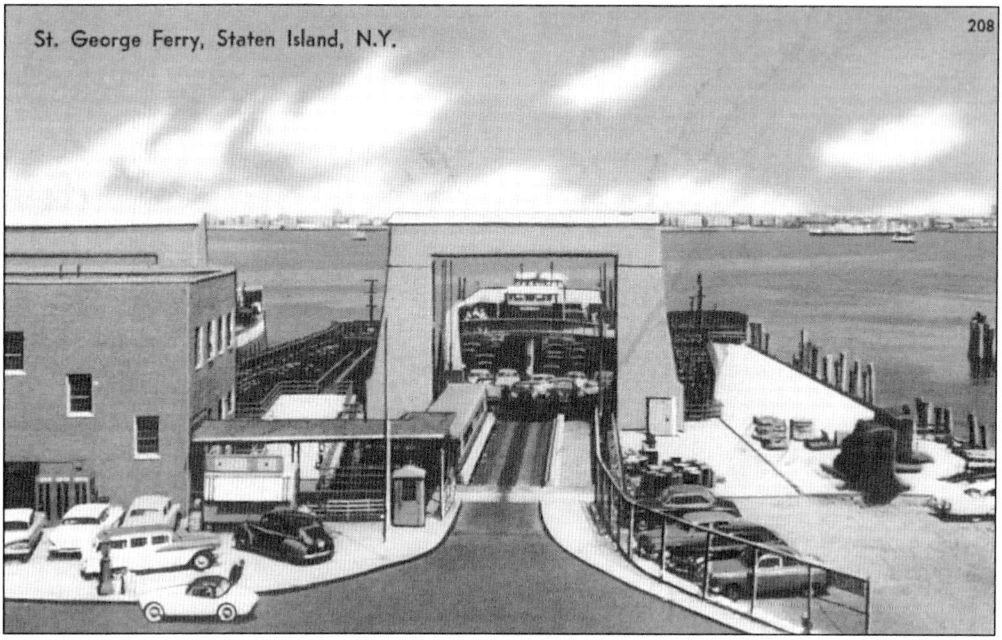

The Brooklyn 69th Street Ferry, part of the St. George Ferry Terminal, built in 1951. The new ferry terminal was fireproof and replaced the 41-year-old terminal destroyed in a catastrophic fire on June 25, 1946. The nine-alarm fire, in which three persons died and 280 were injured, started in the train station. Island fire companies were aided by fireboats and engine companies from Manhattan and Brooklyn. The new terminal, which cost $25 million, was dedicated five years later. (Collection of William P. Blaine.)

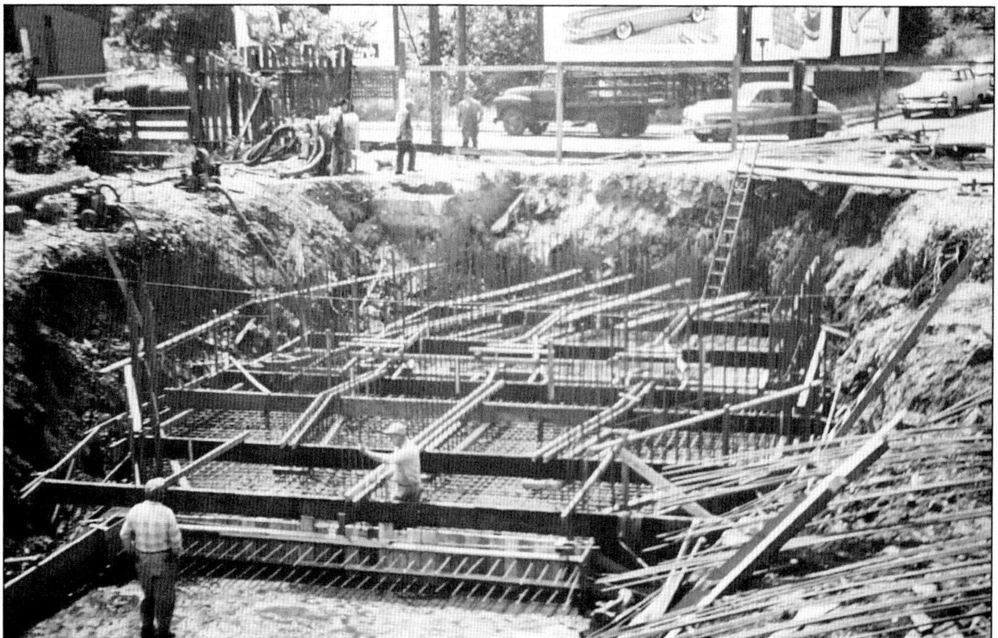

The Nicholas Avenue sewer lines, 1958. The billboard advertising Chevrolets announces "Its Got Git! Chevrolet." (Collection of Claire and Bill Drinnan.)

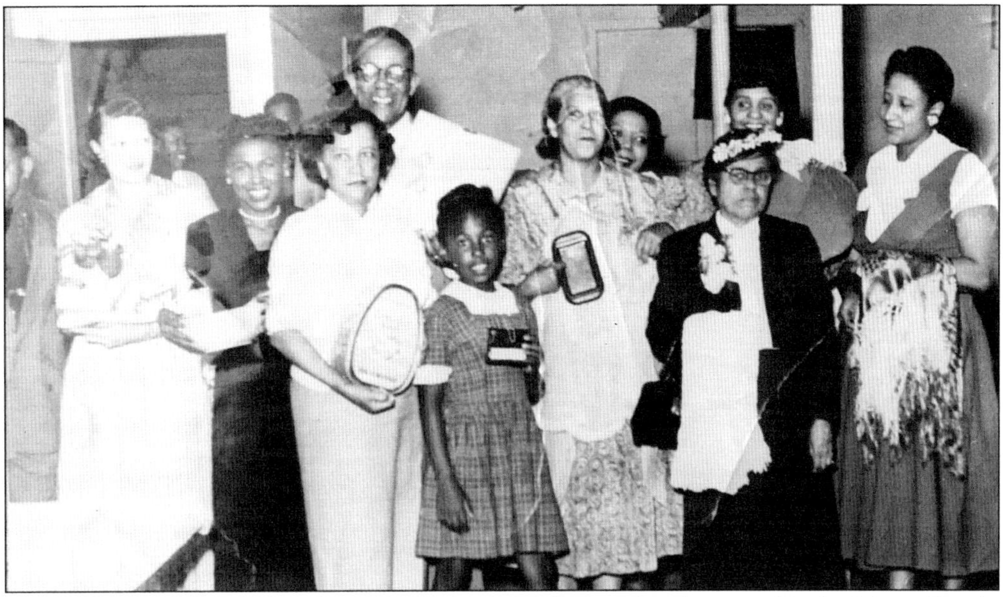

In 1956, the NAACP held a Chinese auction as a fund-raiser. (Collection of Evelyn Morris King.)

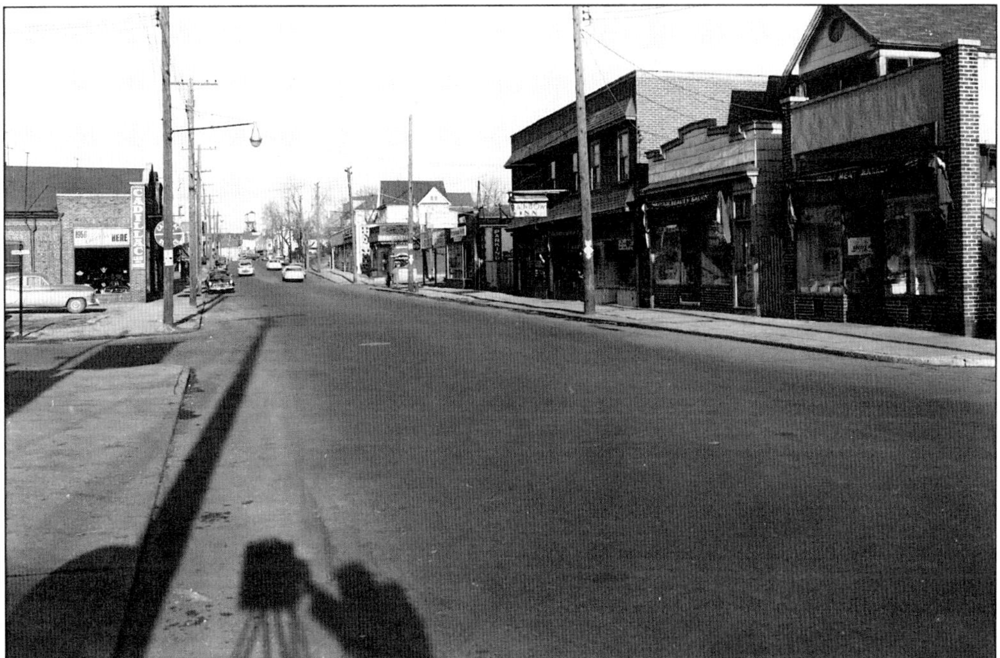

Photograph taken on January 5, 1956. The photographer, Herbert L. Flamm, is caught in silhouette in the lower left corner. Up the street is the Rainbow Inn at 459 Richmond Avenue, next to the Mayfair Beauty Salon and Miceli Meat Market. A Cadillac showroom is at the left. Staten Island has been captured by many fine photographers, both professional and amateur, ranging from the illustrious Alice Austen to W.J. Grimshaw, Percy Sperrs, Mike Falco, Jim Romano, and Bill Higgins, many of whose photographs grace this book. (Collection of the Staten Island Historical Society.)

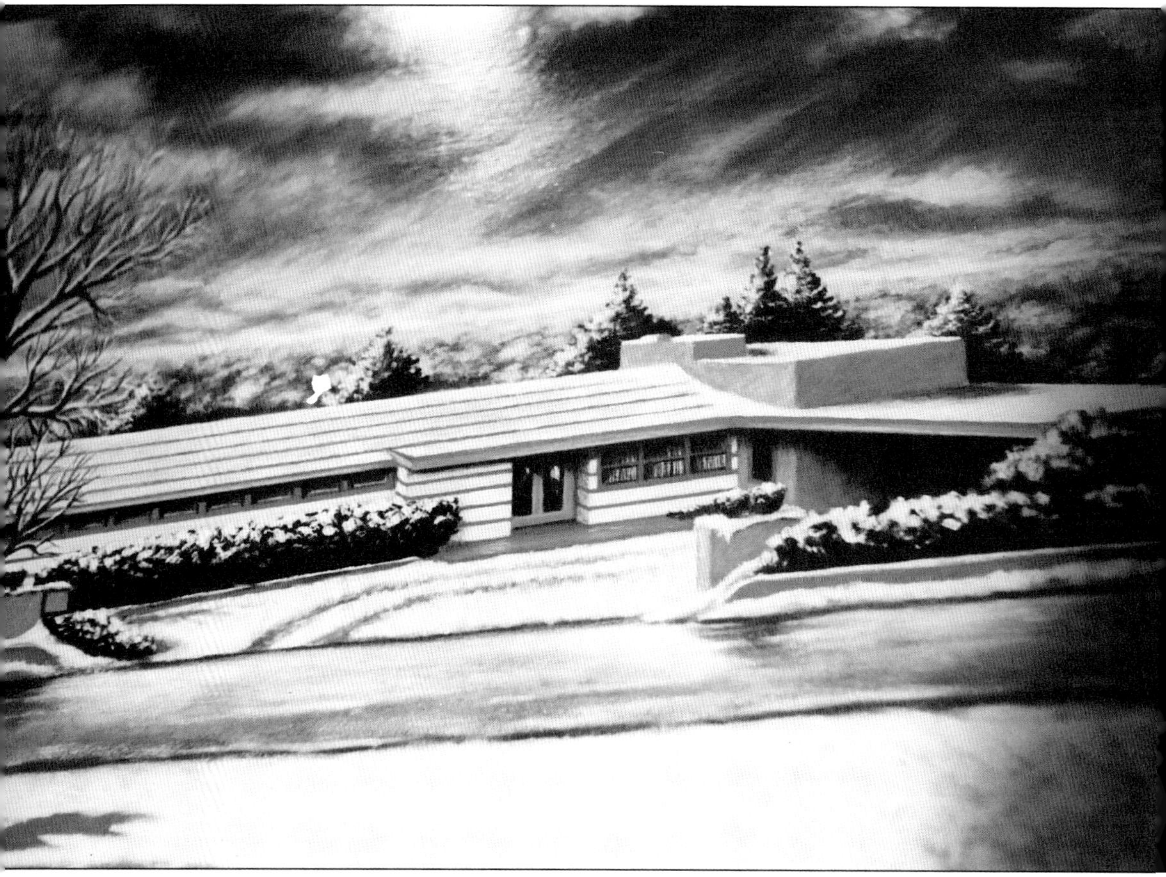

The Frank Lloyd Wright residence called "Crimson Beech," owned by Catherine Cass. Her husband, William, heard Frank Lloyd Wright being interviewed. A personnel agency executive living in Queens, Cass was in the market for a home. His imagination soared, and he asked Catherine about having Frank Lloyd Wright design their home. Mrs. Cass, who was familiar with Wright's work, felt it might be a strenuous undertaking. After acquiring land on Lighthouse Hill, the Casses worked with the Wright organization to have the prefabricated home built. Crimson Beech, so named for a marvelous tree in the front yard, is the only Frank Lloyd Wright-designed residence in New York City. Beautifully maintained, Crimson Beech is a New York City landmark and has received an award from the Frank Lloyd Wright Conservancy. (Collection of Catherine Cass.)

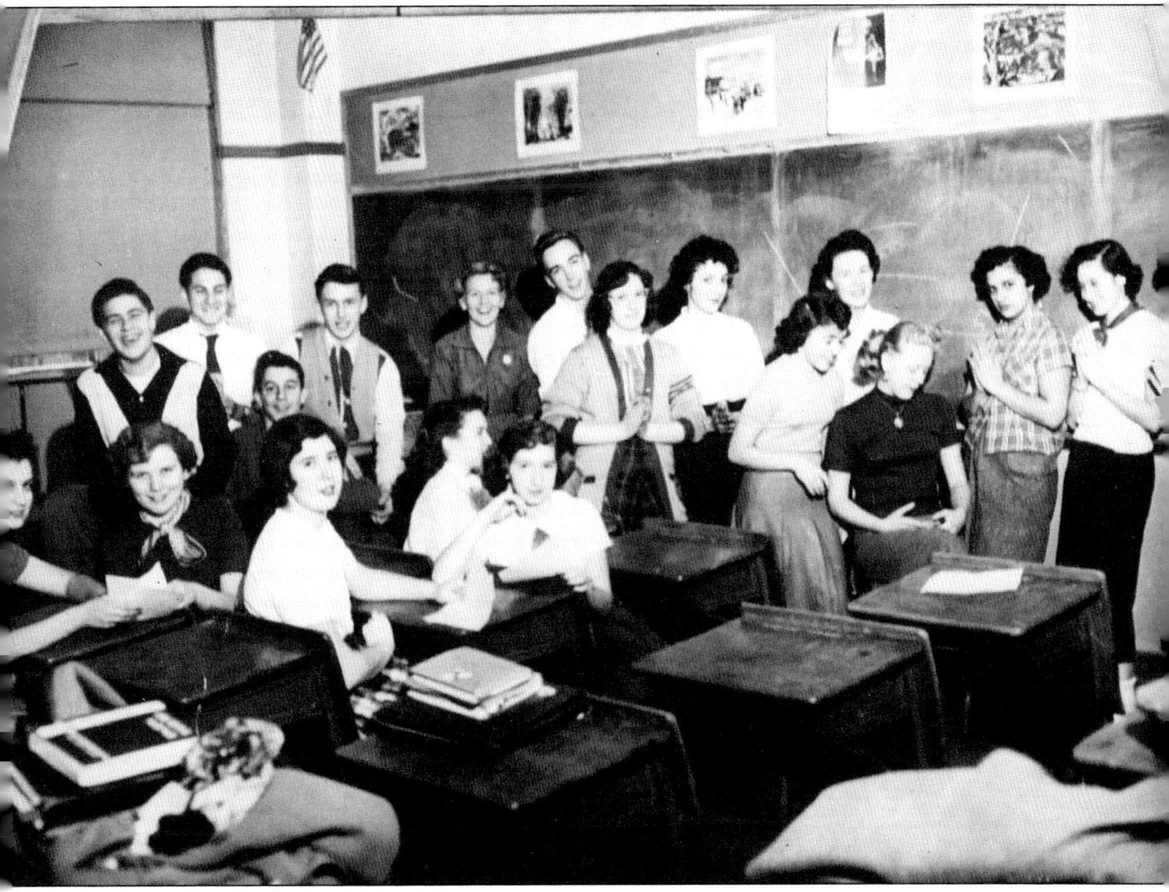

Aspiring thespians of the Footlighters Club of Port Richmond High School. Here they pose with drama coach Bernadette Foley in a December 1952 photograph. (Port Richmond High School Archives.)

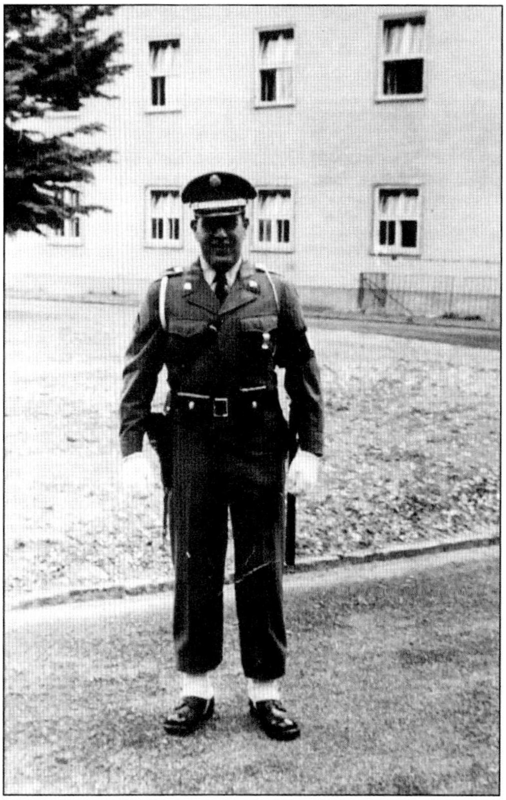

Christy Cugini in 1952 during the Korean War. Part of the military police, Cugini was stationed in Augsberg, Germany. (Collection of the Cugini Family.)

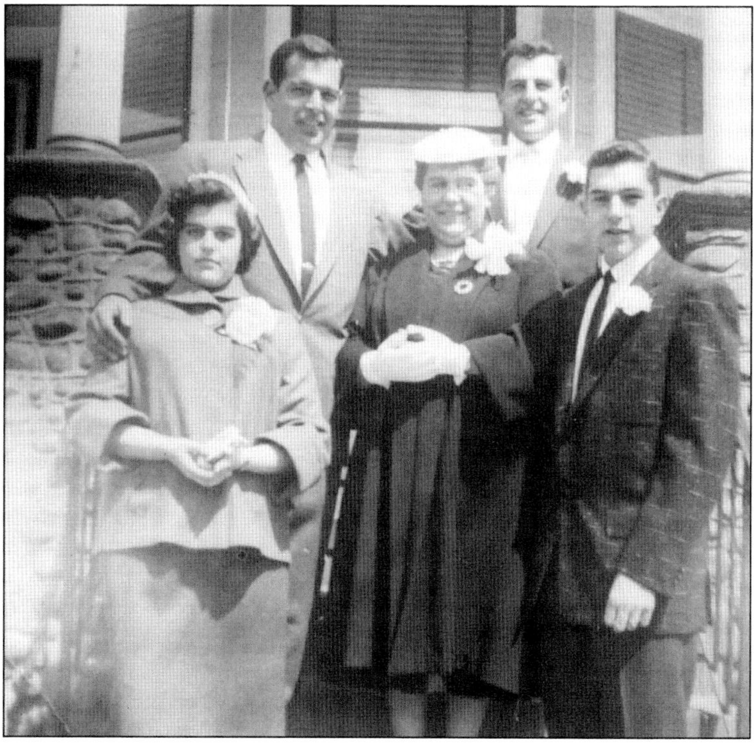

The Cugini family in 1955 on Easter Sunday at 1051 Post Avenue, Port Richmond. They are Dorothy, Christy, (mother) Donata, Joseph, and Robert. (Collection of the Cugini Family.)

In 1955, Penny Holtermann was two years old, the daughter of Edith and Al Holtermann. (Collection of Edith and Al Holtermann.)

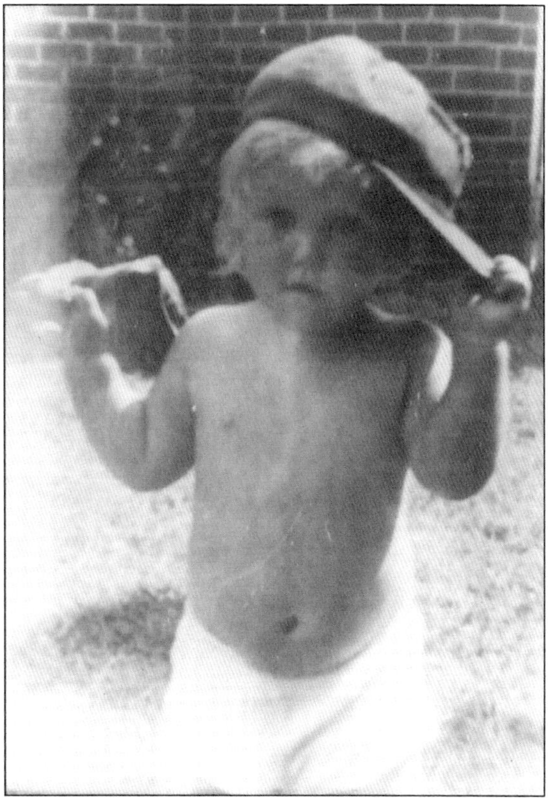

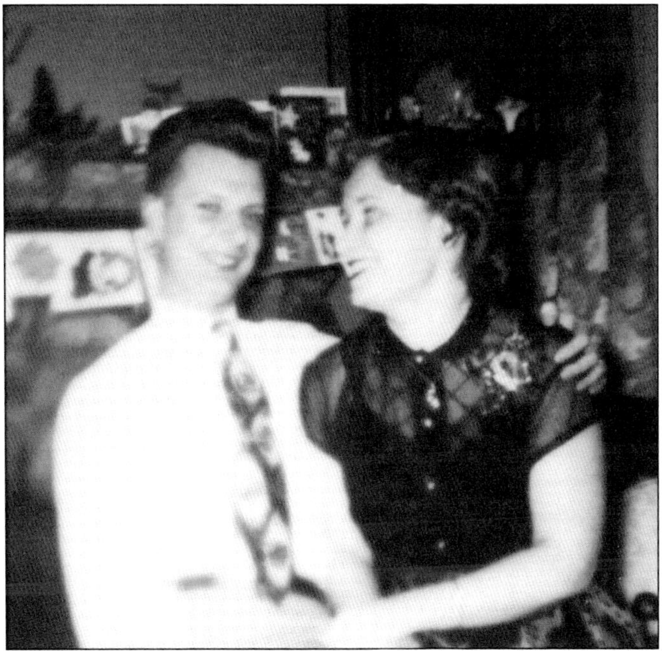

Bill and Claire Drinnan in 1952. Both lifelong Staten Islanders and graduates of Port Richmond High School, Bill went on to pursue an engineering degree at City College, while Claire graduated from Hunter College with a degree in business education and a major in economics. Bill worked in the engineering division of borough hall for 25 years under six borough presidents. The Drinnans are sailing enthusiasts, and Bill has worked on many alumni social events for Port Richmond High School. (Collection of Claire and Bill Drinnan.)

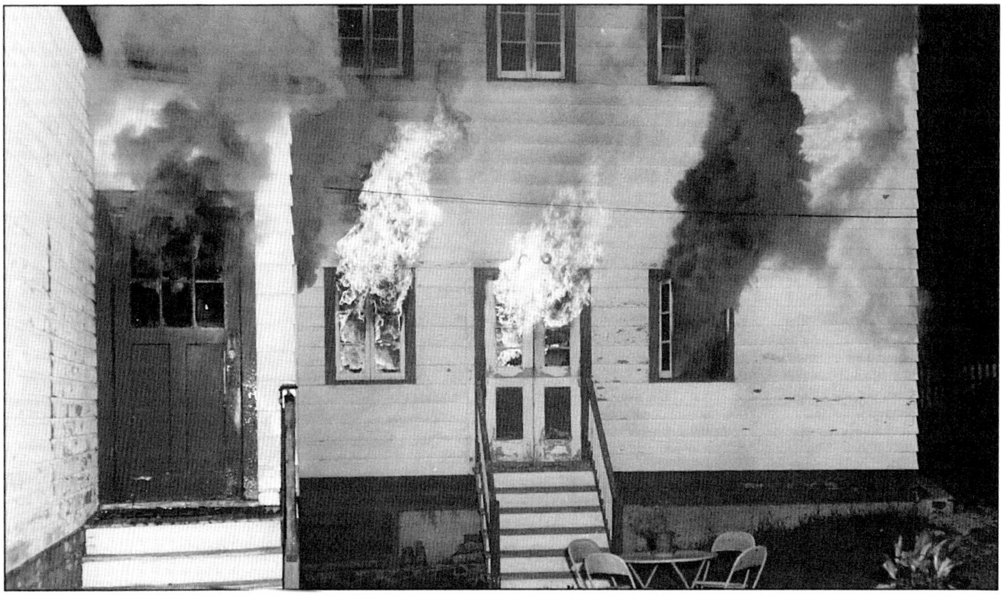

Fire at the Old Mill Restaurant. In the early morning hours of August 22, 1957, a fast-spreading blaze gutted the picturesque Old Mill Restaurant in Grasmere, spreading so quickly through the wooden structure that the interior was completely ablaze before firemen arrived. Eight fire companies responded to the two-alarm call. The photograph was snapped by freelance news photographer John Padula at the rear of the building moments before hoses were brought into play on the structure. Once recognized as one of the leading eating places in the metropolitan area and "recommended by Duncan Hines," the restaurant never reopened. A Chase Manhattan Bank branch now occupies the site, at the corner of Hylan Boulevard and Clove Road. (Collection of A. Richard Boera.)

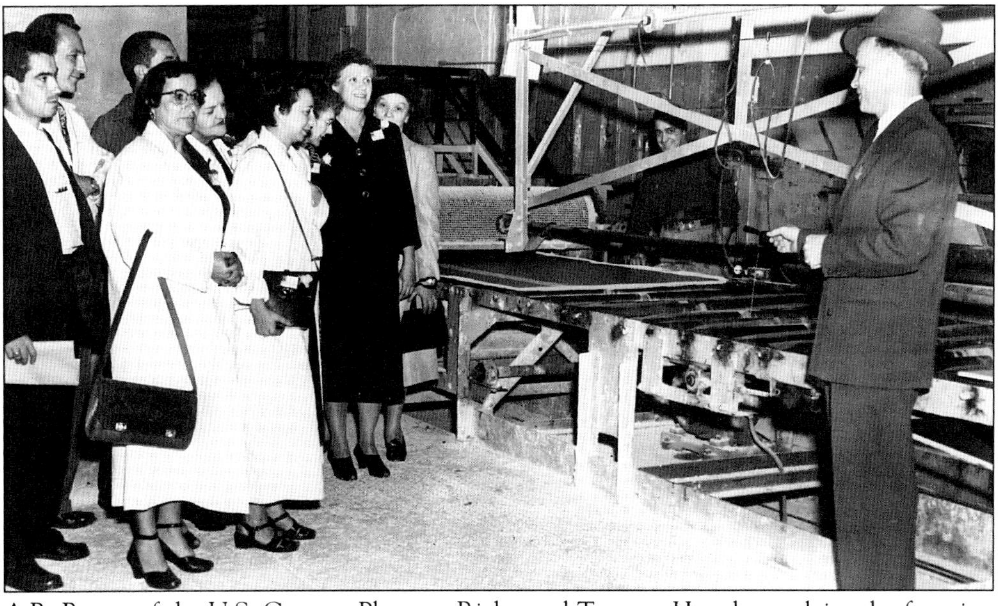

A.R. Rump, of the U.S. Gypsum Plant on Richmond Terrace. Here he explains the function of a rotating knife to a group of teachers on October 16, 1952. (Collection of the Staten Island Historical Society.)

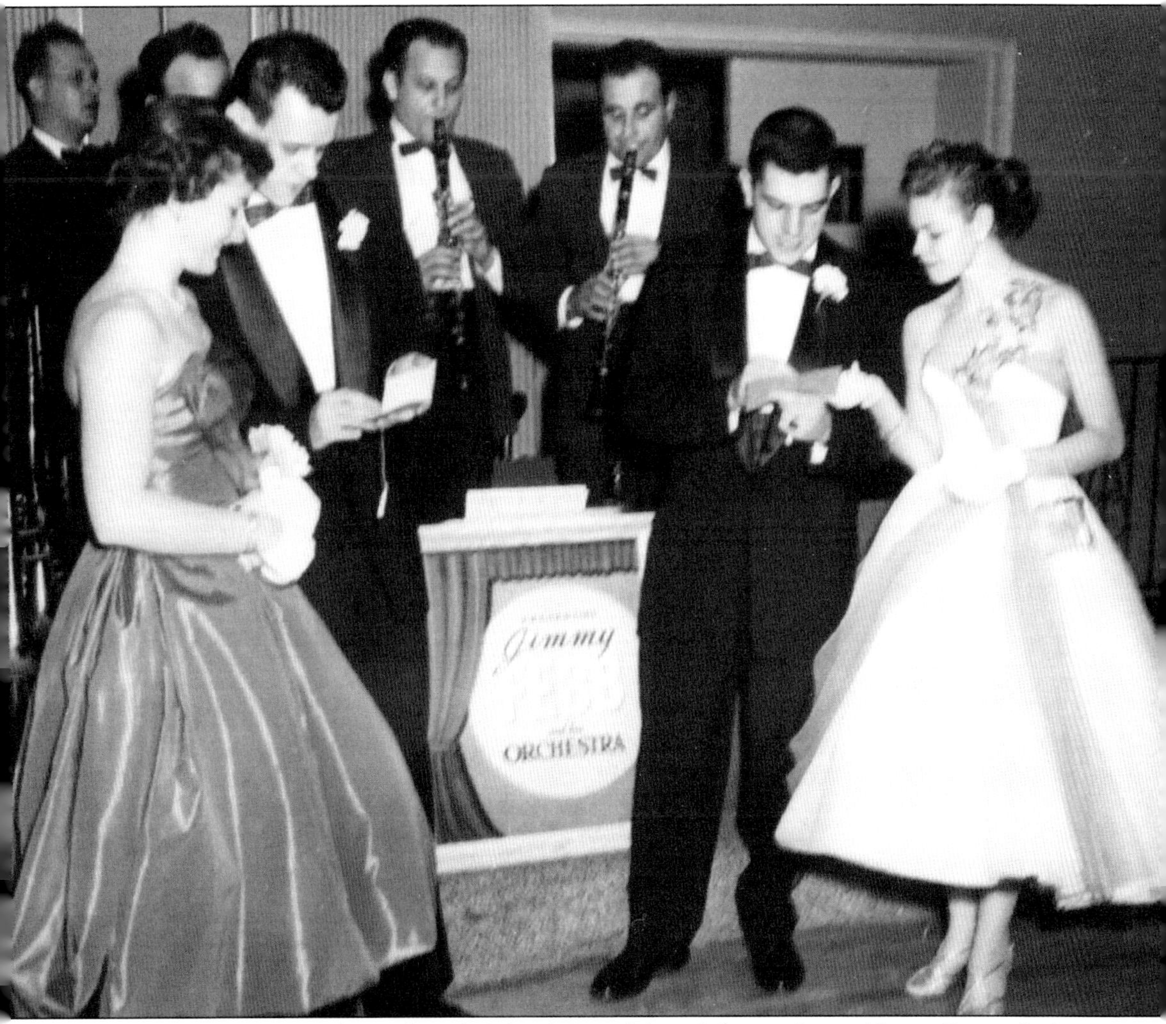

The 1958 prom, Port Richmond High School. Listed from left to right are Nancy Payne, Jack Cooper, class president Bob Cugini, and Diane Robisky, now Cugini. Music was provided by Jimmy Febb. (Collection of the Cugini Family.)

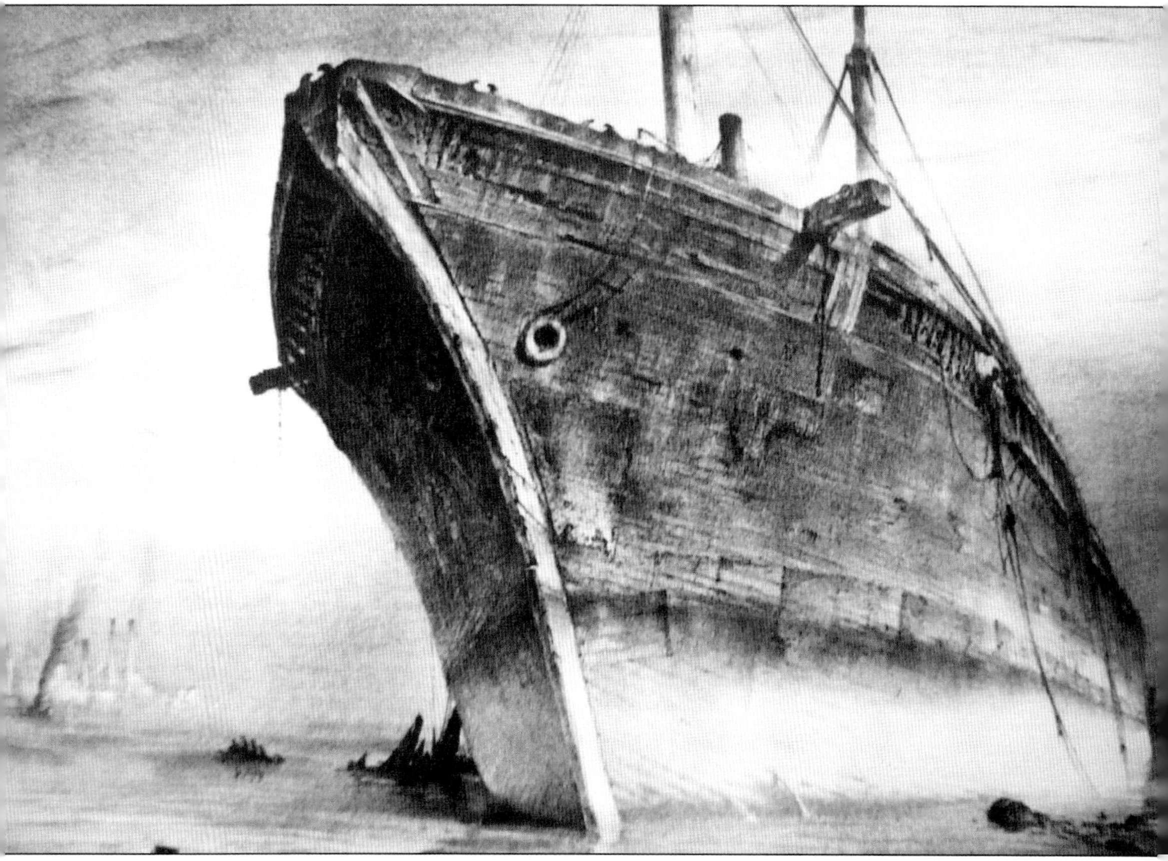

The Cape Horner. "In 1874, Sewall of Bath launched a 1,532-ton ship, the *Occidental*," Noble wrote. "A moratorium should be declared on the destruction of these vessels . . . most glorious of them all, *The Occidental*, beached near the yard in Bath, Maine . . . so that people will be able to behold the near medieval design of the beams, waterways, knees and stanchions to contemplate and muse upon the incredible work of their forebears." (Courtesy of the John A. Noble Collection.)

Seven

1960–1969

The "Give-a-Damn" Years, the Great Society, and Back to the Basics

*John F. Kennedy elected U.S. president, 1960.

*Three women become ministers of the Swedish Lutheran Church, 1960.

*Optical microwave laser built, 1960.

*Harper Lee writes *To Kill a Mockingbird*, 1960; wins Pulitzer Prize, 1961.

*American actor Clark Gable, Oscar Hammerstein II, and Emily Post die, 1960.

*Dag Hammarskjold wins Nobel Peace Prize, 1961.

*U.S. severs diplomatic relations with Cuba, 1961.

*The last journey of the *Orient Express* from Paris to Bucharest, 1961.

*Ernest Hemingway, James Thurber, Grandma Moses, Gary Cooper, Eero Saarinen, and Carl Gustav Jung die, 1961.

*Cuban Missile Crisis; the U.S. blockade of Cuba, 1962.

*Adolf Eichmann hanged, 1962.

*The drug thalidomide causes serious birth defects, 1962.

*Eleanor Roosevelt, American artist Franz Kline, poet e.e. cummings, actor Charles Laughton, and Marilyn Monroe die, 1962.

*Edward Albee writes *Who's Afraid of Virginia Woolf?*, and John Steinbeck wins Nobel Prize for Literature, 1962.

*Pres. John F. Kennedy assassinated by Lee Harvey Oswald, November 22, 1963; Vice President Lyndon B. Johnson sworn in as president.

*Civil Rights march on Washington, D.C.; Dr. Martin Luther King Jr. gives his "I have a dream" speech, 1963.

*Earthquake in Yugoslavia claims about 1,100 victims, 1963.

*French singer Edith Piaf, American poet Robert Frost, Jean Cocteau,

Pope John XXIII, and poet William Carlos Williams die, 1963.

*Incumbent Lyndon Johnson beats Barry Goldwater in U.S. presidential race, 1964.

*Actress Elizabeth Taylor divorces Eddie Fisher and weds Richard Burton, 1964.

*The Verrazano-Narrows Bridge opened, 1964.

*Riots at a soccer match in Lima, Peru, leave three hundred spectators dead, 1964.

**Mary Poppins, Zorba the Greek*, and *Goldfinger* among popular films, 1964.

*Malta becomes independent within Commonwealth, 1964.

*Cole Porter, Gracie Allen, Herbert Hoover, King Paul of Greece,
Pandit Nehru, and Gen. Douglas MacArthur die, 1964.

*The Great Blackout, November 10, 1965,
affects 30 million people (Staten Island was spared).

*Malcolm X shot in New York, 1965.

*Two thousand students at Madrid University demonstrate, fight police, 1966.

*Miniskirts became fashionable, 1966.

*Truman Capote writes *In Cold Blood*,
and Jaqueline Susann writes *Valley of the Dolls*, 1966.

Walt Disney dies, 1966.

*Pope Paul VI issues encyclical on the Vietnamese War, 1966.

*Mitch Leigh's *Man of La Mancha* opens as Broadway musical, 1966.

*Color TV becomes popular, 1966.

*American consumers spend $17, 400 on alcoholic beverages, 1966.

*Expo 67 opens in Montreal, 1967.

*Six-Day War between Israel and Arab nations begins, 1967.

*New York Yankee Mickey Mantle hits his 500th home run, 1967.

*American figure skater Peggy Fleming wins world championship in Vienna, 1967.

*Dr. Christiaan Barnard performs the world's first human heart transplantation, 1967.

*Singer Barbra Streisand gives a concert to 135,000 in Central Park, 1967.

*Bert Lahr ("the Cowardly Lion" in *The Wizard of Oz)*, Vivien Leigh, Spencer Tracy,
Carl Sandburg, Jayne Mansfield, folk singer Woody Guthrie,
Basil Rathbone ("Sherlock Holmes"), and Dorothy Parker die, 1967.

*Violent crime in America increases 57% since 1960, 1968.

*Dr. Martin Luther King Jr. slain, April 5,
and Senator Robert F. Kennedy assassinated, June 6, 1968.

*Jacqueline Kennedy weds Aristotle Onassis, 1968.

*Richard M. Nixon elected president, 1968.

*Astronaut Neil Armstrong "dances" on the moon, July 21, 1969.

*Three hundred thousand hippies and others
attend the Woodstock Music and Art Fair in New York, 1969.

*Judy Garland, American labor leader John L. Lewis,
and North Vietnamese President Ho Chi Minh die, 1969.

*Mario Puzo writes *The Godfather*, and Norman Mailer writes *Armies of the Night*, 1969.

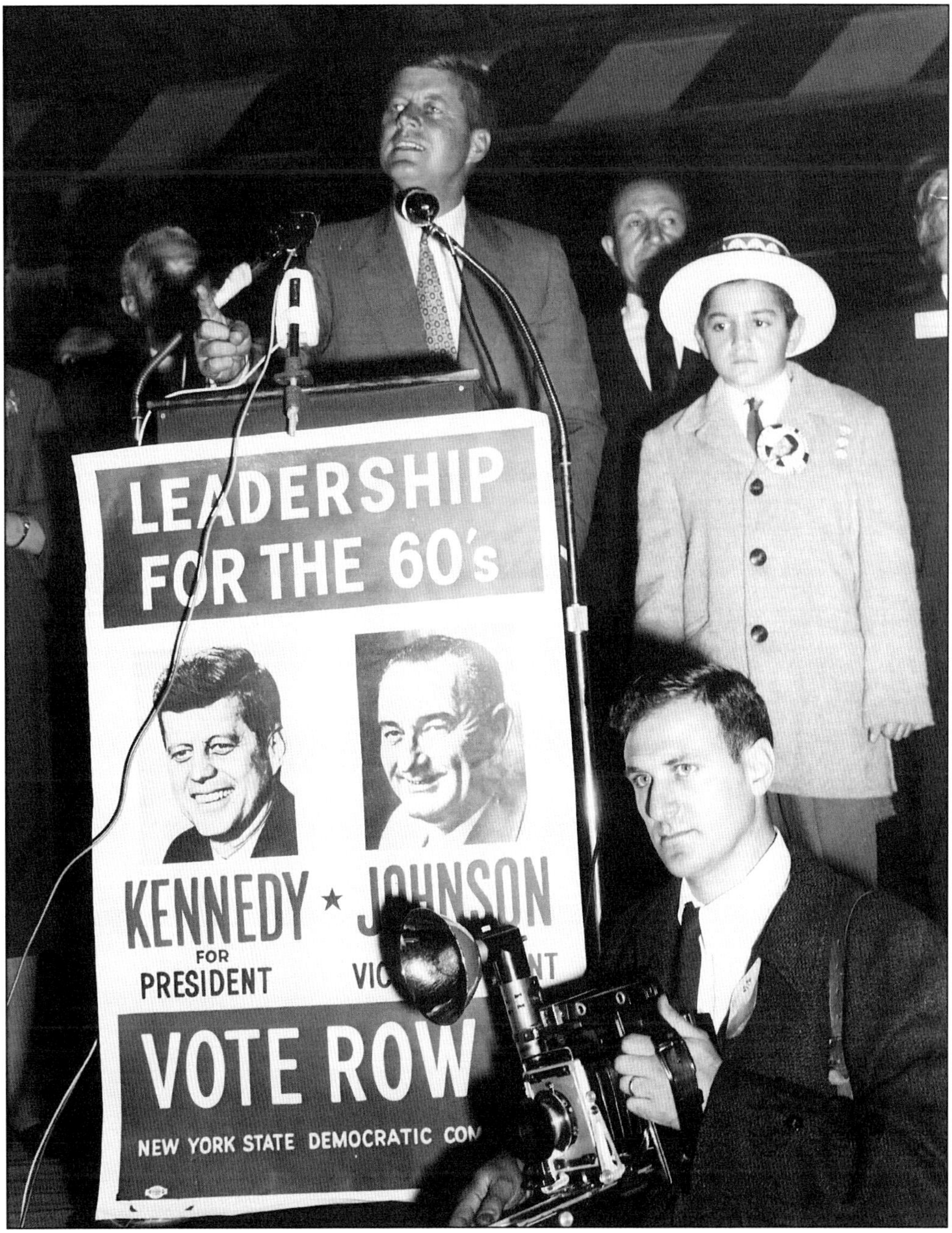

Presidential candidate John F. Kennedy at Labetti Post. Standing next to Senator Kennedy is Philip Massa, assembly candidate, and the handsome young man is a Massa relative. In the foreground is photographer Jim Romano. Usually on the other end of the camera, Mr. Romano, a Kennedy supporter, asked someone to take this picture. (Courtesy of Jim Romano.)

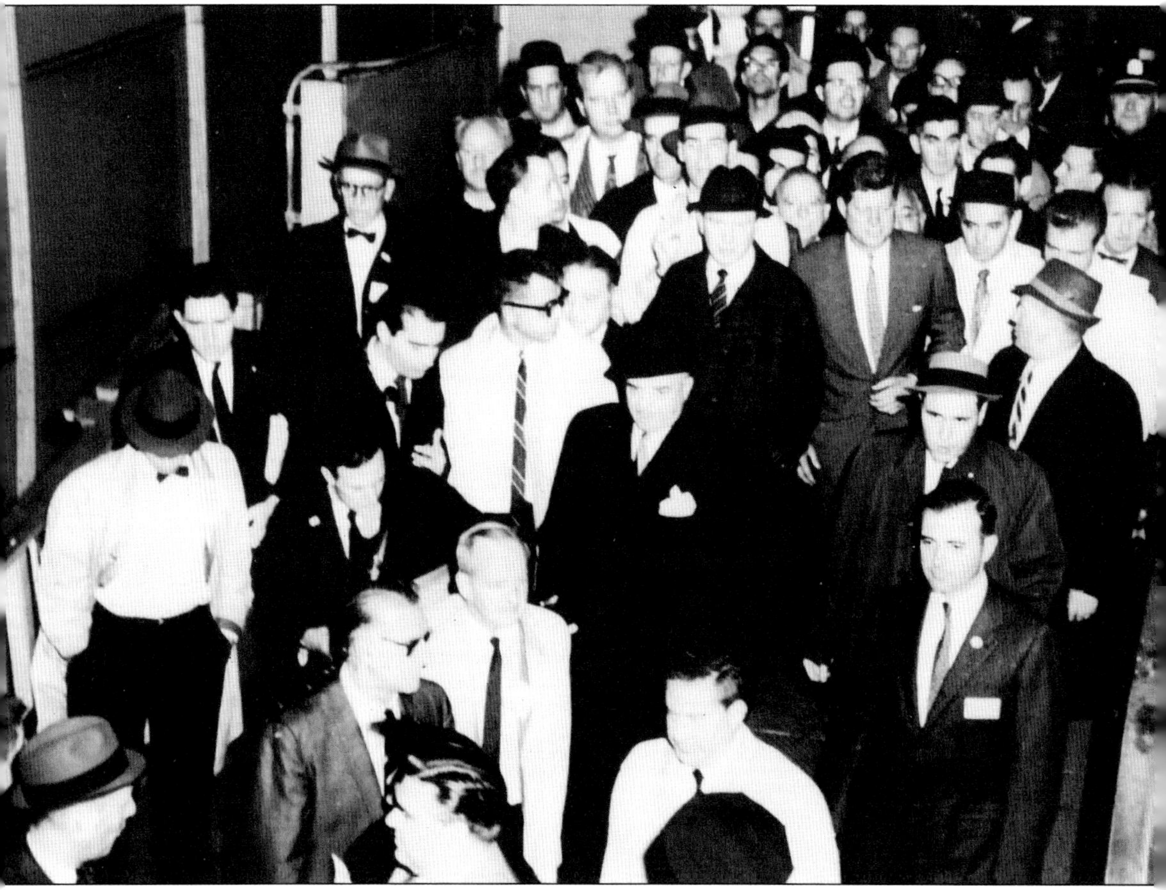

Sen. John F. Kennedy, with the crowd at the St. George Ferry Terminal. In the Friday, October 28, 1960 *Staten Island Advance*, S.S. McSheehy wrote, "Thousands of Islanders screaming and yelling themselves hoarse yesterday gave presidential hopeful John F. Kennedy the greatest ovation ever given to a visitor to this borough." Kennedy, who made the crossing on the ferryboat *Cornelius Kolff*, spoke for 30 minutes to the crowd estimated at 15,000. Kennedy humorously offered his apologies to "any Republican commuters who have been caught unwittingly in this crowd!" Following his introduction by B.P. Albert Maniscalco, Kennedy introduced democratic candidates John M. Murphy for Congress, Ralph Di Iorio for state senate, and assembly candidates Philip Massa and Elaine Kovessy. At the terminal snack bar, Kennedy sat next to Mrs. Rose Feniello of Rosebank and ordered chicken and rice soup, coffee, and a glass of milk. He then boarded the 6:25 *Tides* ferryboat for Brooklyn. (Courtesy of Jim Romano.)

Cable being hung for the Verrazano Narrows Bridge. (Collection of Patricia Pellicru.)

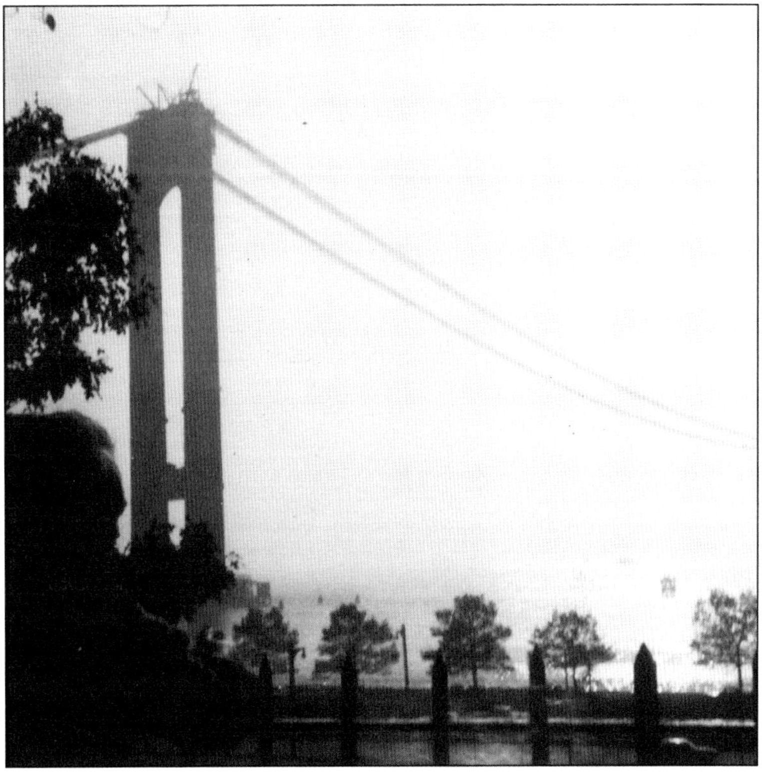

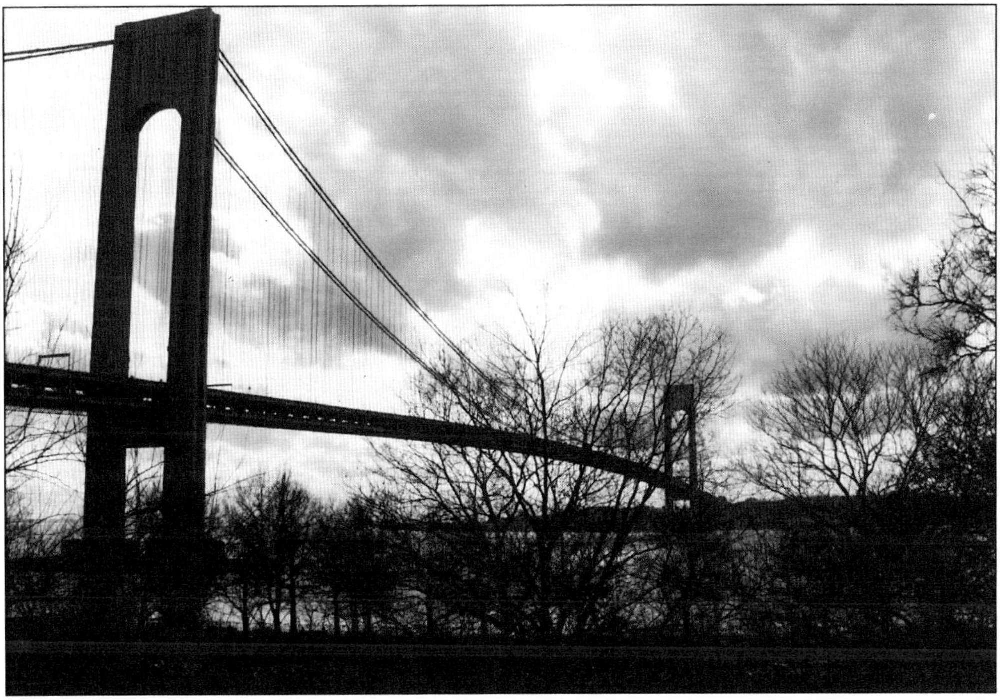

The completed bridge opened on November 22, 1964. The Verrazano is the starting point for the New York City Marathon. (Photograph by John Doherty.)

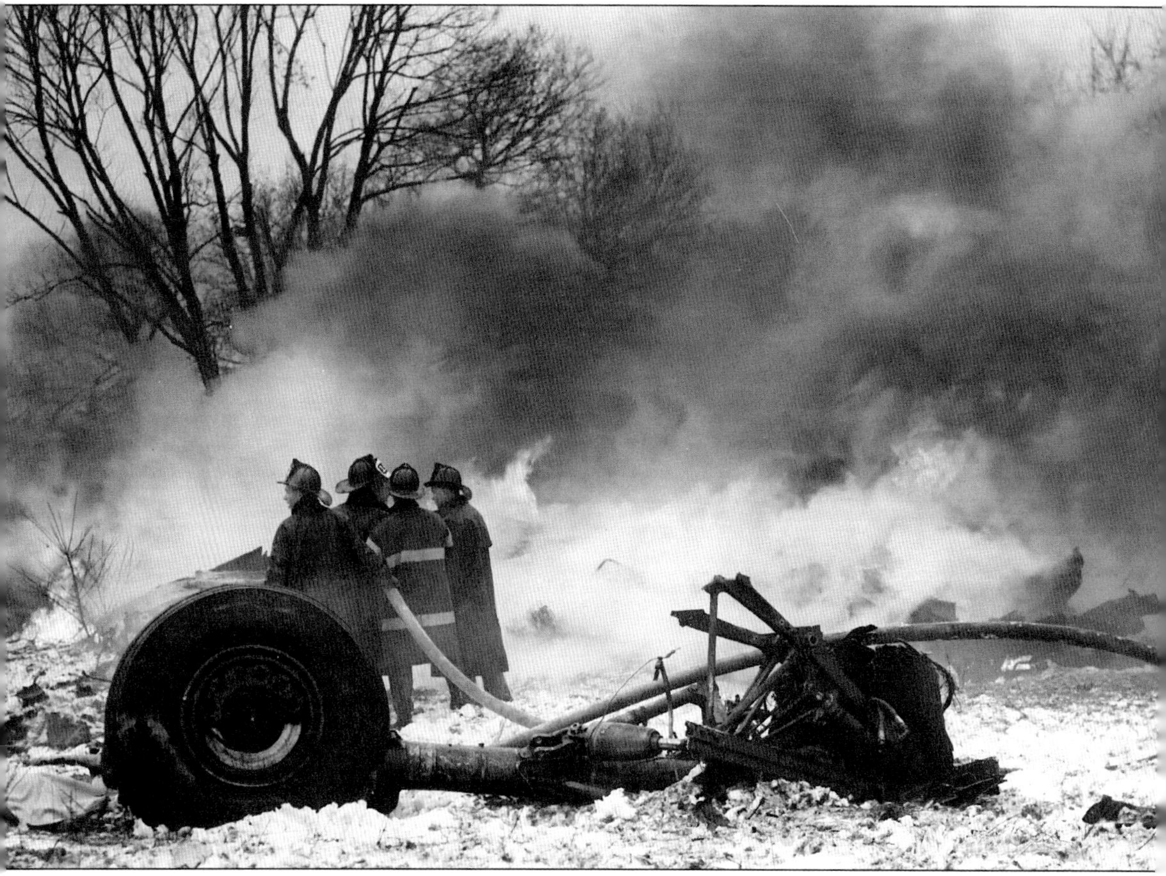

Disaster strikes. One hundred thirty-four persons died in the crash of the United Airlines DC-8 and a TWA Constellation over Staten Island on December 16, 1960. Rescue workers and residents came upon a scene of devastation. The impact sent the DC-8 across the Narrows before crashing into a building in Park Slope, Brooklyn, while the Constellation crashed onto Miller Field in New Dorp. The *Staten Island Advance* reported that a bus driver saw people falling out of the plane as it plummeted. First at the scene were A&P employees John Cronin and Henry Knapp, who found a man gasping for air still strapped in his seat. The men could do little to help the dying man but to throw snow on him. The story of brave 11-year-old Stephen Baltz, who survived for a day, tugged at many people's hearts. (Courtesy of Jim Romano.)

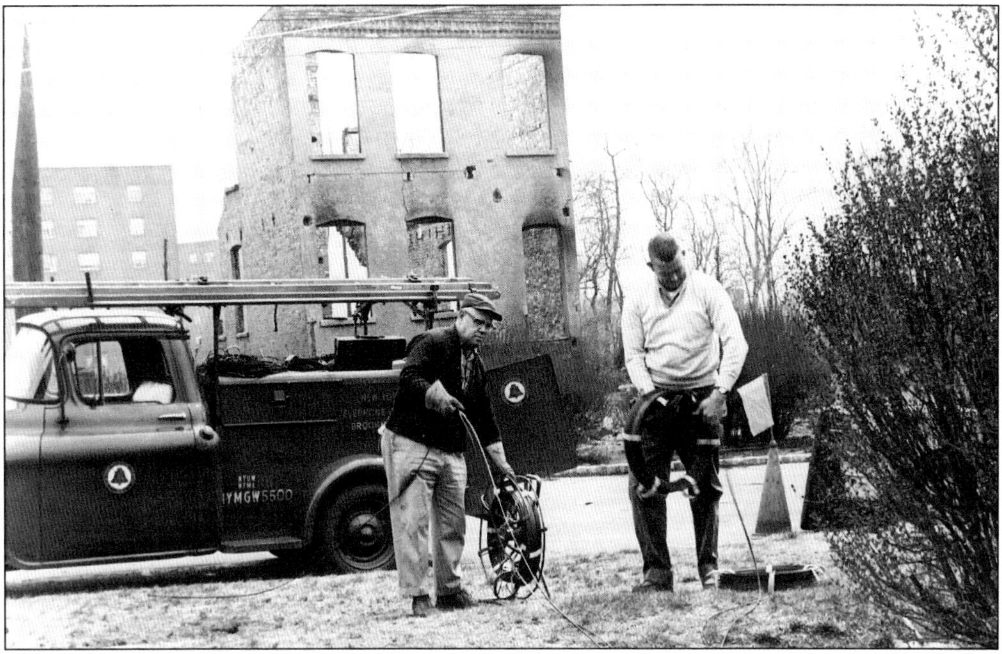

"Black Saturday." Telephone workers do repair work following the brush fires of Black Saturday on the South Shore. The fires of April 23, 1963, destroyed more than 100 homes, left 500 people homeless, and resulted in $2 million in damages. Dry, windy conditions abetted the fires, and firefighters were often rendered helpless when hydrants failed to produce water. A dozen homes in the historic Sandy Ground area were lost to the fire. In 1965, a vast water supply system was built to increase water pressure and prevent another disaster. (Collection of the Staten Island Historical Society.)

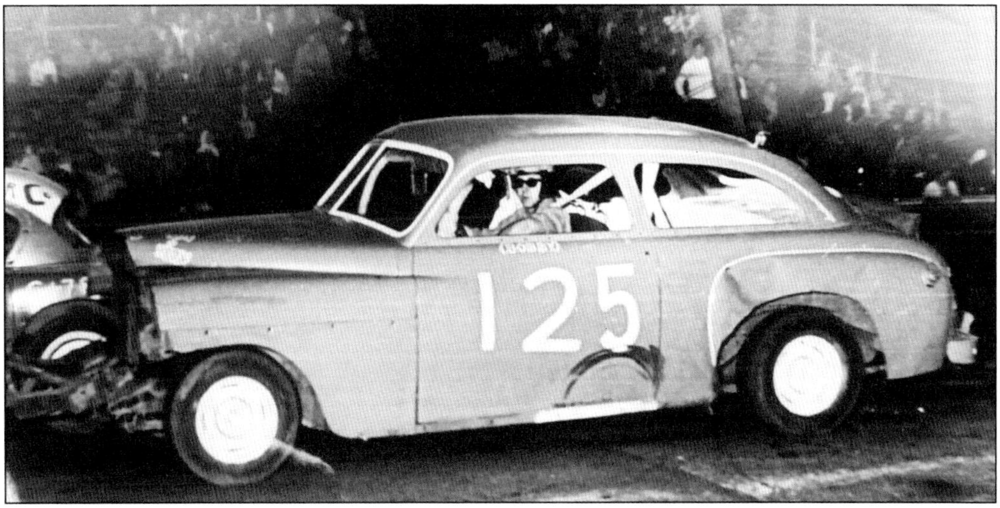

Bob McKeever in Car 125 at the stock-car race at Weissglass Stadium in the summer of 1968. Weissglass Stadium at 1971 Richmond Terrace was named for Julius Weissglass, founder of Weissglass Dairy. A family biography was entitled appropriately *No Spilled Milk*! The stadium hosted many sporting events and stock-car races. Residents can still remember hearing the cheers of the crowds and whir of the cars as they raced around the course. (Collection of Bob McKeever.)

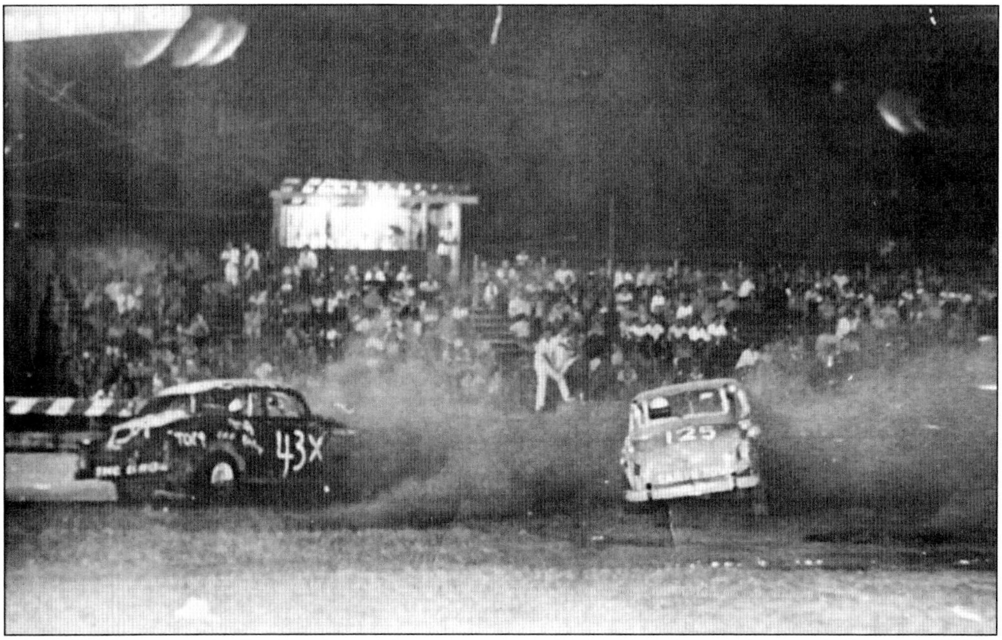

Cars 43X and 125 lend excitement of the stock-car races as they round a turn. (Collection of Bob McKeever.)

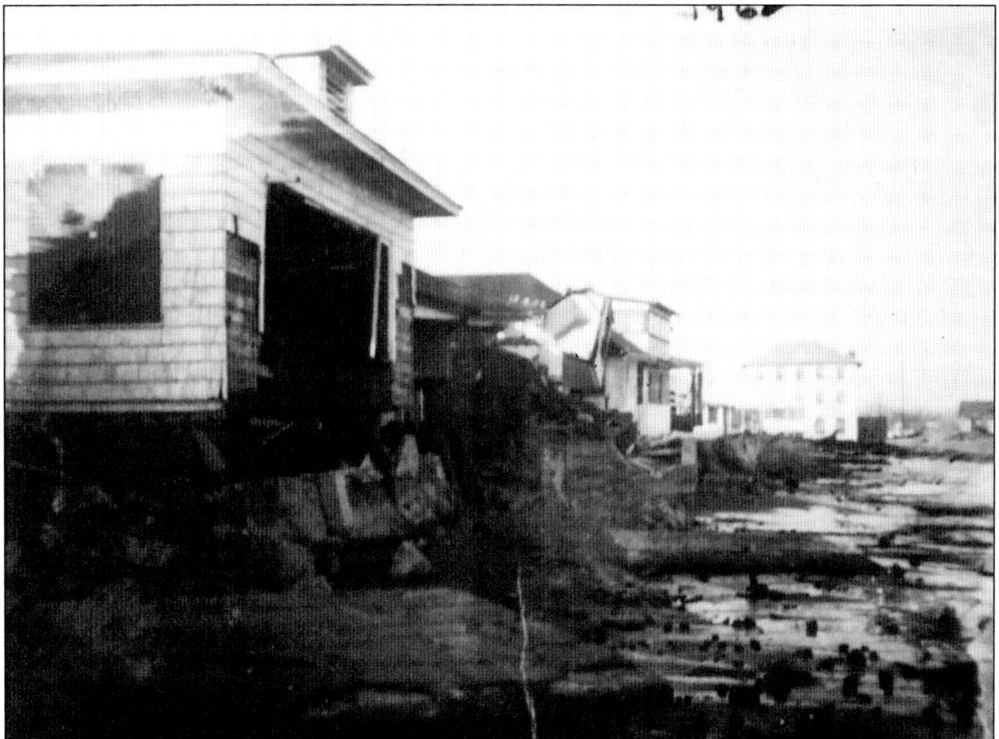

Cedar Grove Beach following the storms of 1962. The stumps of the cedar trees for which the beach was named are visible in the front. St. John's Guild became Staten Island Station during the war. (Collection of Edith and Al Holtermann.)

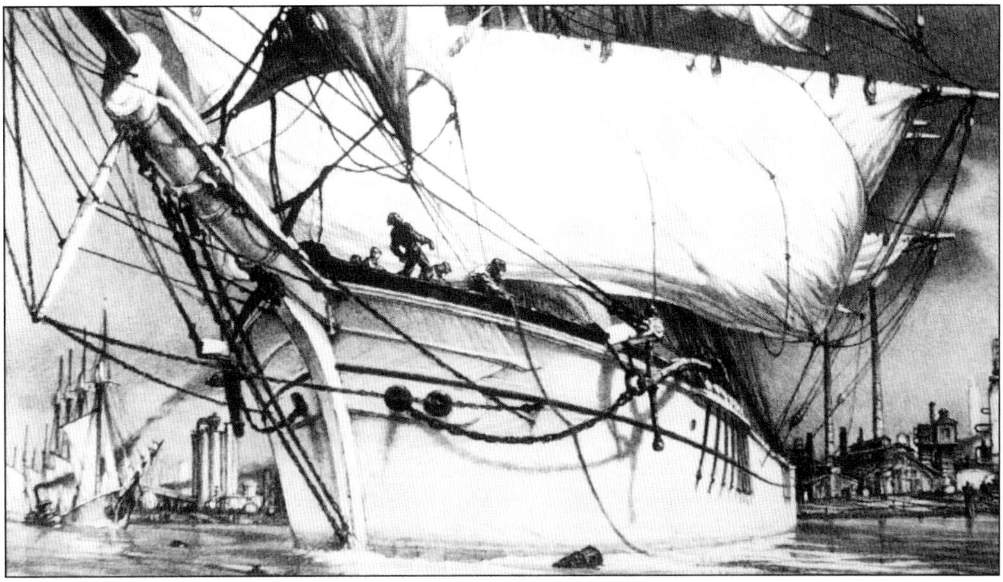

The *Guadalhorce* leaves Bayonne forever, 1969. Bayonne's poet laureate, John A. Noble, chose the sailing ship *Guadalhorce* against the backdrop of Bayonne's oil refineries as his subject for Bayonne's centennial commemorative lithograph. Noble wrote, "She was Bayonne's *Mayflower*, albeit it in reverse. I knew her well. She was one of the most beautiful vessels I have ever seen." (Courtesy of the John A. Noble Collection.)

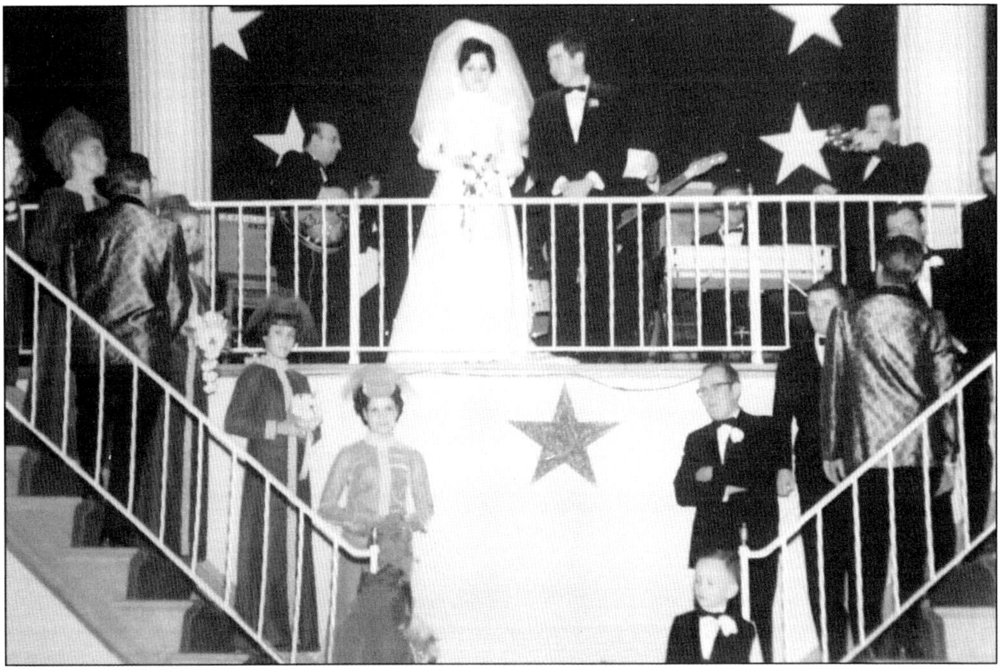

The wedding reception of Ted and Noreen Harris on February 14, 1968, on the impressive staircase of the "Starlight Room" of the Plaza Casino. Listed from left to right, the members of the wedding party shown here are Carol Lundrigan, Sonia Oparski, Valerie Ryschuck, Margaret Lundrigan, ring bearer Joseph Byrne, Joe Byrne, Robert Fleming, Bernard Baldinger, and James Lundrigan. (Collection of Noreen and Ted Harris.)

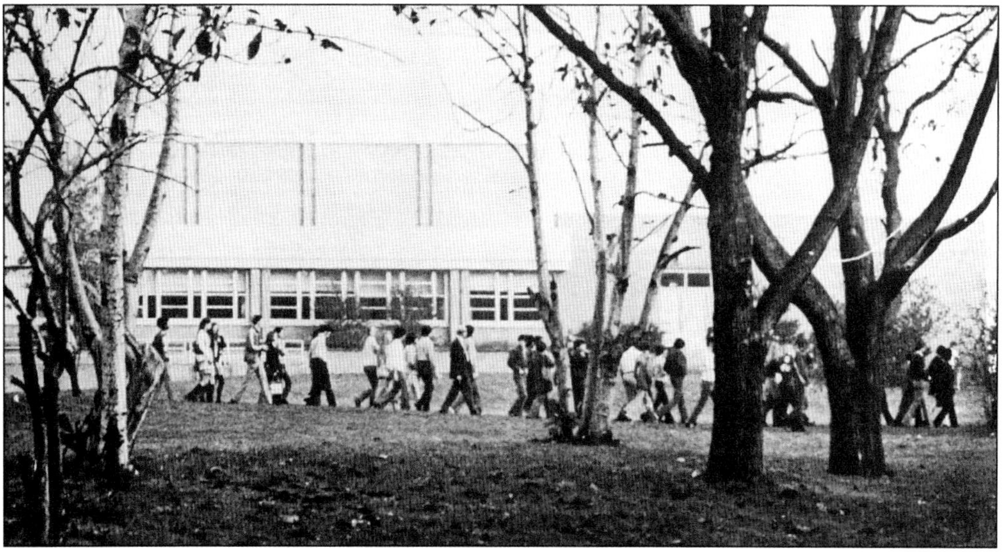

Susan Wagner High School, built in 1968. (Wagner High School Archives.)

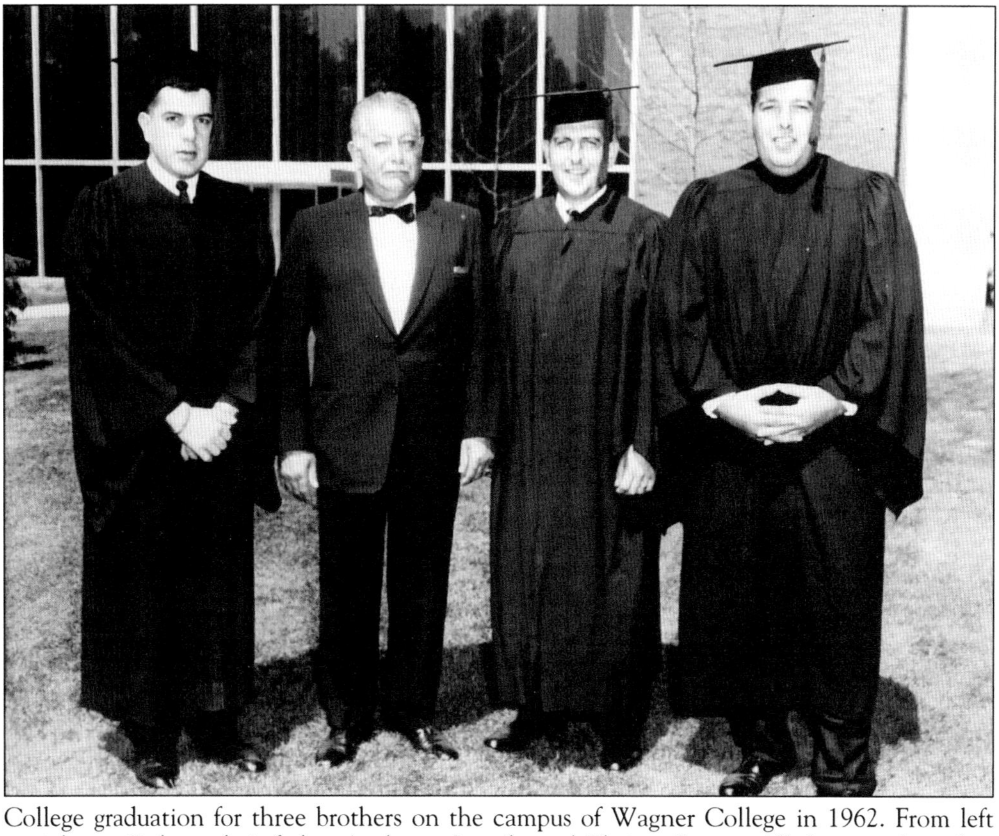

College graduation for three brothers on the campus of Wagner College in 1962. From left to right are Robert, their father Anthony, Joseph, and Christy Cugini. All three graduated in 1962, Robert from Pace University, and Joseph and Christy from Wagner. Today, Robert is a CPA, Joseph is principal of P.S. 46, and Christy is superintendent of schools on Staten Island. (Collection of the Cugini Family.)

Staten Island Community College Groundbreaking program cover, June 2, 1964. The college was the first two-year institution to be sponsored by the Board of Higher Education under the program of the State University of New York. It celebrated its official opening in rented quarters in St. George on September 17, 1956, with the public installation of its first president, Walter L. Willig. Retired NYU professor and Staten Island's devoted representative on the BHE Arleigh B. Williamson and Borough President Albert V. Maniscalco were the local leaders in the movement to establish the college. (Collection of A. Richard Boera.)

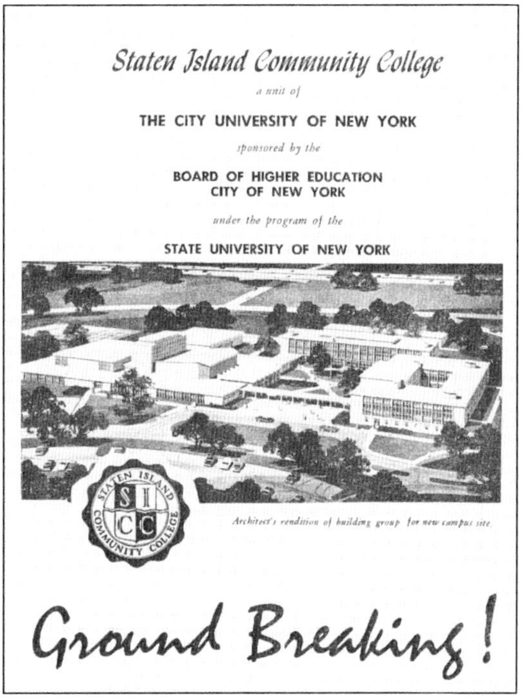

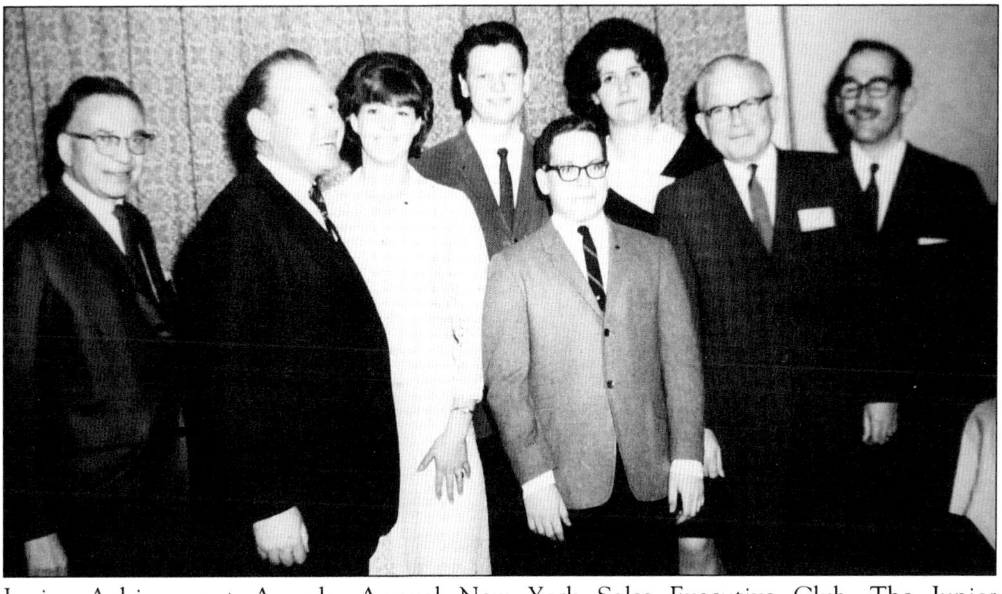

Junior Achievement Awards, Annual New York Sales Executive Club. The Junior Achievement Salesperson of the Year Contest was held on March 15, 1966, at the Hotel Roosevelt. Listed from left to right are Jules B. Singer, chairman of the Youth Activities Committee of the Sales Executives Club of New York; Samuel J. Lefrak, president of the Lefrak Organization and founder of Lefrak City; Sheila Press, 1966 Junior Achievement Salesperson of the Year; finalists Richard Dutka, Mark Greitbart, and Jean Powles; Herbert K. Baskin, vice-president of Bankers Trust Company and President of Junior Achievement of New York; and Warren Rohlfs, chairman, Sales Executives Club Junior Achievement Committee. (Collection of Marion and Richard Dutka.)

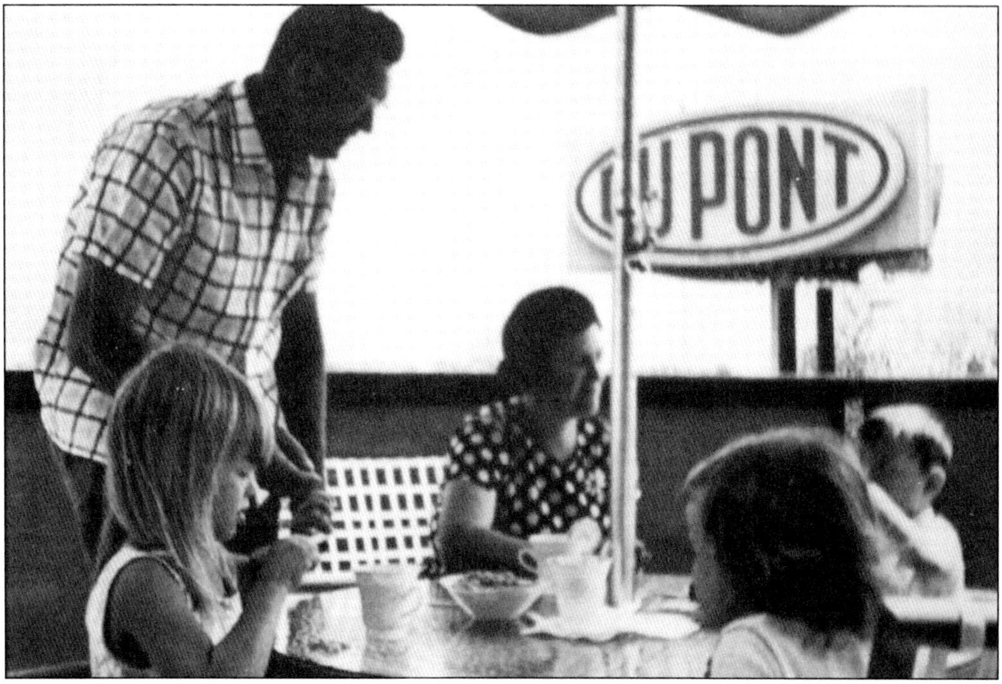

New York World's Fair 1964–65. Richard and Marian Dutka pose with their children Bernadette, Elizabeth, and David. The Dutka family was sent by Procter and Gamble to enjoy the sights at the fair. Because of proximity to the Flushing Meadows, Queens, the 1964–65 World's Fair was the third World's Fair to be held in New York. Called the "Olympics of Progress" by World's Fair President Robert Moses, some of the major attractions included the General Motors "Futurama II," which portrayed life as it may be in the year 2064, the NYC Pavilion scale model "showing every building in the five boroughs,' and General Electric's "Carousel of Progress." The microwave oven and Belgian waffles, as one of this book's authors wistfully recounts, were introduced at the fair. (Collection of Marion and Richard Dutka.)

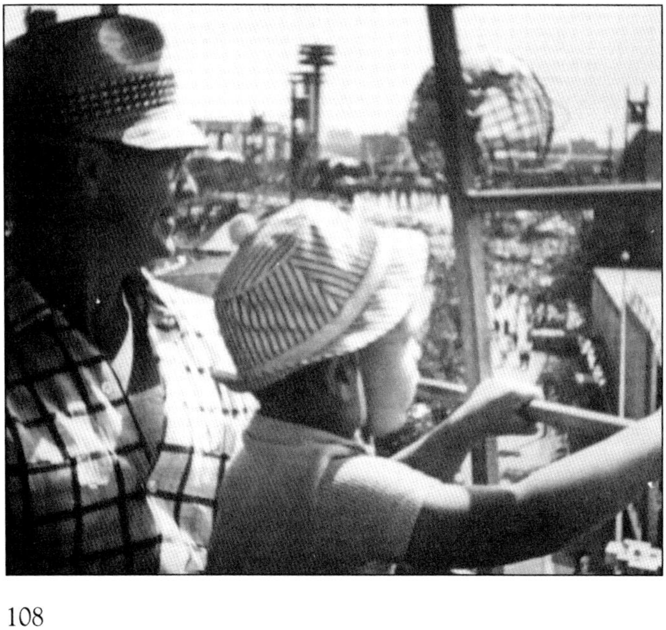

Richard Dutka and his son David in a Skylift at the World's Fair. In the background is the Unisphere. Because of proximity to the Flushing Meadows, Queens, location, many islanders were able to enjoy day trips to the fair, either as a family excursion or educational trip. Today the Unisphere remains, and the New York City Pavilion has become the Queens Museum, which stills houses the scale model of New York City. (Collection of Marian and Richard Dutka.)

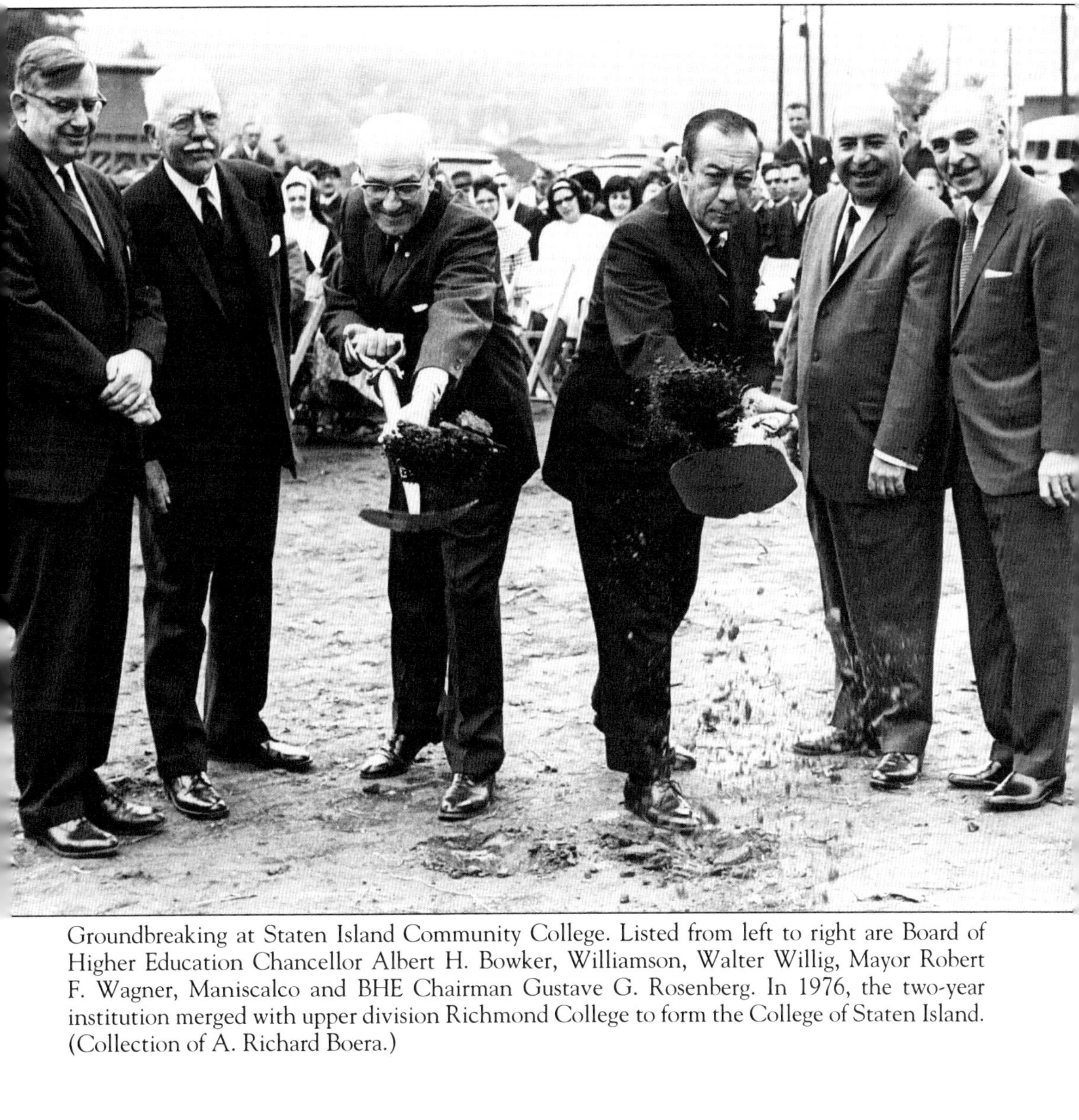

Groundbreaking at Staten Island Community College. Listed from left to right are Board of Higher Education Chancellor Albert H. Bowker, Williamson, Walter Willig, Mayor Robert F. Wagner, Maniscalco and BHE Chairman Gustave G. Rosenberg. In 1976, the two-year institution merged with upper division Richmond College to form the College of Staten Island. (Collection of A. Richard Boera.)

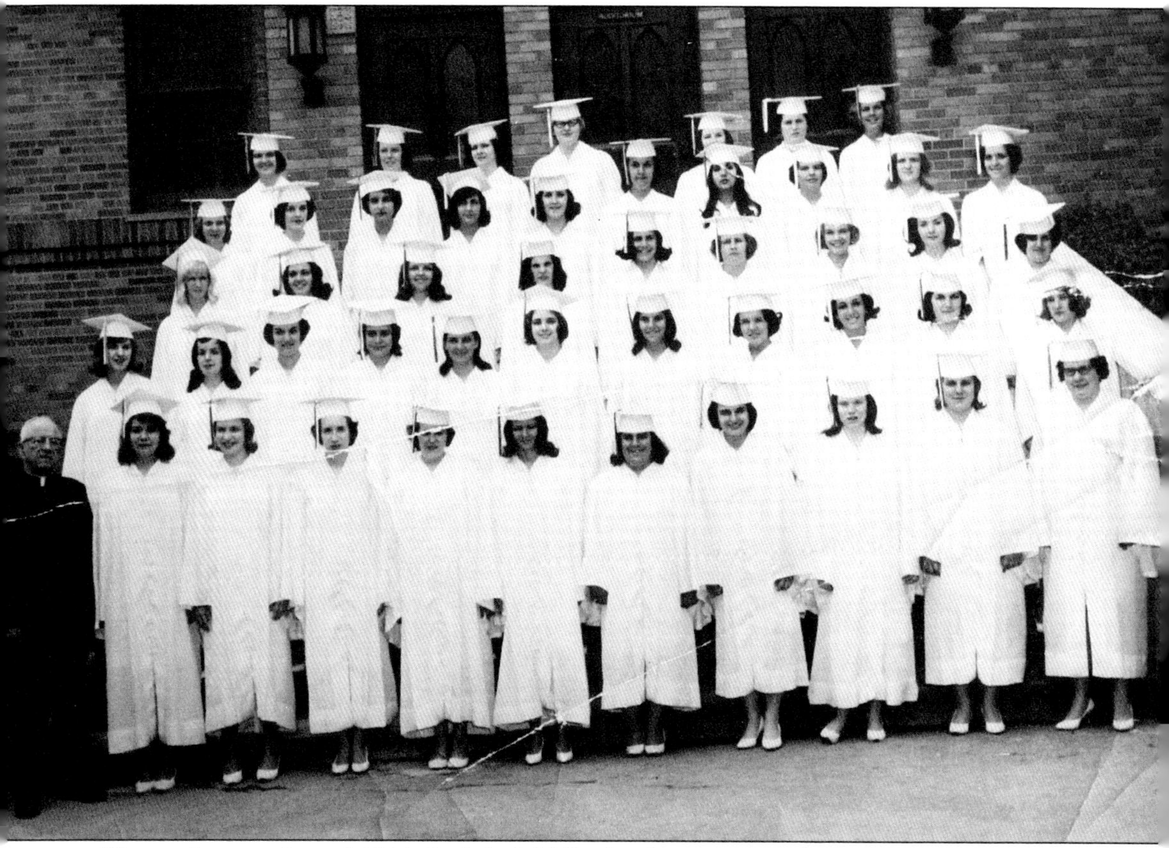

The graduating class of 1964, St. John's Villa Academy in Arrochar. The school located on Cleveland Avenue is operated by the Sisters of St. John the Baptist. (Collection of Ted and Noreen Harris.)

Eight

1970–1979

The "Me" Generation; From Hippies to Yuppies

*The National Guard kills four Kent State University students protesting Vietnam War, 1970.

*Gypse Rose Lee, Charles de Gaulle, Gamal Abdel Nasser, Bertrand Russell, and cartoonist "Rube" Goldberg die, 1970.

*Alexander Solzhenitsyn wins Nobel Prize for Literature, 1970.

*Israel's fourth Prime Minister Golda Meir visits London, 1970.

*Eudora Welty writes *Losing Battles*, Neil Simon writes *Last of the Red Hot Lovers*, and William Saroyan writes *Days of Life and Death and Escape to the Moon*, 1970.

*Jazz musician Louis Armstrong, composer Igor Stravinsky, Coco Chanel, and painter Rockwell Kent die, 1971.

*U.S. bombs North Vietnam and Vietcong supply routes in Cambodia; fighting in Indochina spreads to Laos and Cambodia, 1971.

*TV advertisements for cigarettes banned in America, 1971.

*American 18-year-olds get the right to vote as 26th Amendment to the Constitution ratified, 1971.

*The five-day uprising at Attica prison leaves 10 guards and 32 prisoners dead, 1971.

*Five men arrested by Washington, D.C. police in Watergate affair, 1972.

*Richard Nixon defeats George McGovern in presidential race, 1972.

*Michelangelo's sculpture *Pieta* vandalized by fanatic with a hammer, 1972.

**All in the Family* America's most popular TV show, 1972.

*Poets Marianne Moore and Ezra Pound, gospel singer Mahalia Jackson, J. Edgar Hoover, Harry S. Truman, actors Maurice Chevalier and George Sanders die, 1972.

*Notre Dame wins national collegiate football championship, 1973.

*Spanish artist Pablo Picasso, actors Betty Grable, Edward G. Robinson, Lon Chaney Jr., writer W.H. Auden, British author J.R.R. Tolkien, and Lyndon B. Johnson die, 1973.

*Billie Jean King defeats Bobby Riggs in tennis match, 1973.

*U.S. Supreme Court rules against individual states prohibiting abortion during the first six months of pregnancy, 1973.

*Duke Ellington, pop singer Cass Elliott, Samuel Goldwyn, poet Anne Sexton, Agnes Moorehead, Dizzy Dean, Jack Benny, and Amy Vanderbilt die, 1974.

*President Richard Nixon resigns, August 9, 1974.

*Nine Israeli athletes killed in Olympic Village, September 6, 1972.

*Smallpox epidemic in India kills 10,000 to 20,000, 1974.

*Elizabeth Ann Bayley Seton canonized as first American saint, 1975.

*International Brotherhood of Teamsters President James R. Hoffa disappears, 1975.

*First-class postage increased from 10 to 13 cents, 1975.

*Mauna Loa volcano erupts for first time since 1950 in Hawaii, 1976.

*Ethiopian Emperor Haile Selassie, Aristotle Onassis, baseball manager Casey Stengel, playwright Thornton Wilder, artist Thomas Hart Benton, TV writer Rod Serling, King Faisal of Saudi Arabia, and actress Susan Hayward die, 1975.

*The Bicentennial of the United States celebrated, July 4, 1976.

*Reclusive billionaire Howard Hughes, actors Paul Robeson, Rosalind Russell, composers Benjamin Britten and Walter Piston, bandleader Guy Lombardo, J. Paul Getty, and German philosopher Martin Heidegger die, 1976.

*Rev. Sun Myung Moon's Unification Church rejected by NYC Council of Churches, and parents protested against "brainwashing" of Moon's followers called "Moonies," 1976.

*Aerosol spray cans reported damaging to the atmosphere's ozone layer, 1976.

*U.S. President Jimmy Carter pardons nearly all American draft dodgers of the Vietnam War era, 1977.

*"King of Rock 'n' Roll" Elvis Presley, singers Bing Crosby and Maria Callas, and actors Alfred Lunt, Groucho Marx, Charlie Chaplin, and Joan Crawford die, 1977.

*Popular films of 1977 include *Annie Hall* (Woody Allen), *Star Wars* (George Lucas), and *Saturday Night Fever* (John Travolta).

*November 20, 1978, four hundred people die in the Jonestown mass suicide.

*A Gutenberg Bible sells for $2 million at a New York auction, the highest price ever paid for a book, 1978.

*In England, Lesley Brown gives birth to a daughter, the "Test-tube baby," the first child conceived outside a woman's body, 1978.

*Egyptian President Anwar Sadat and Israel Premier Menahem Begin receive the Nobel Peace Prize, 1978.

*Artist Norman Rockwell, anthropologist Margaret Mead, Pope Paul VI, Golda Meir, ventriloquist Edgar Bergen, and author Faith Baldwin die, 1978.

*Margaret Thatcher becomes the Conservative Prime Minister of Britain, 1979.

*William Styron writes *Sophie's Choice*, 1979.

*Egypt and Israel sign peace treaty, March 27, 1979.

*Three Mile Island, Pennsylvania, nuclear catastrophe averted, March 30, 1979.

*American clown Emmett Kelly, hotel owner Conrad Hilton, and actors John Wayne, Merle Oberon, Mary Pickford, and Jack Haley die, 1979.

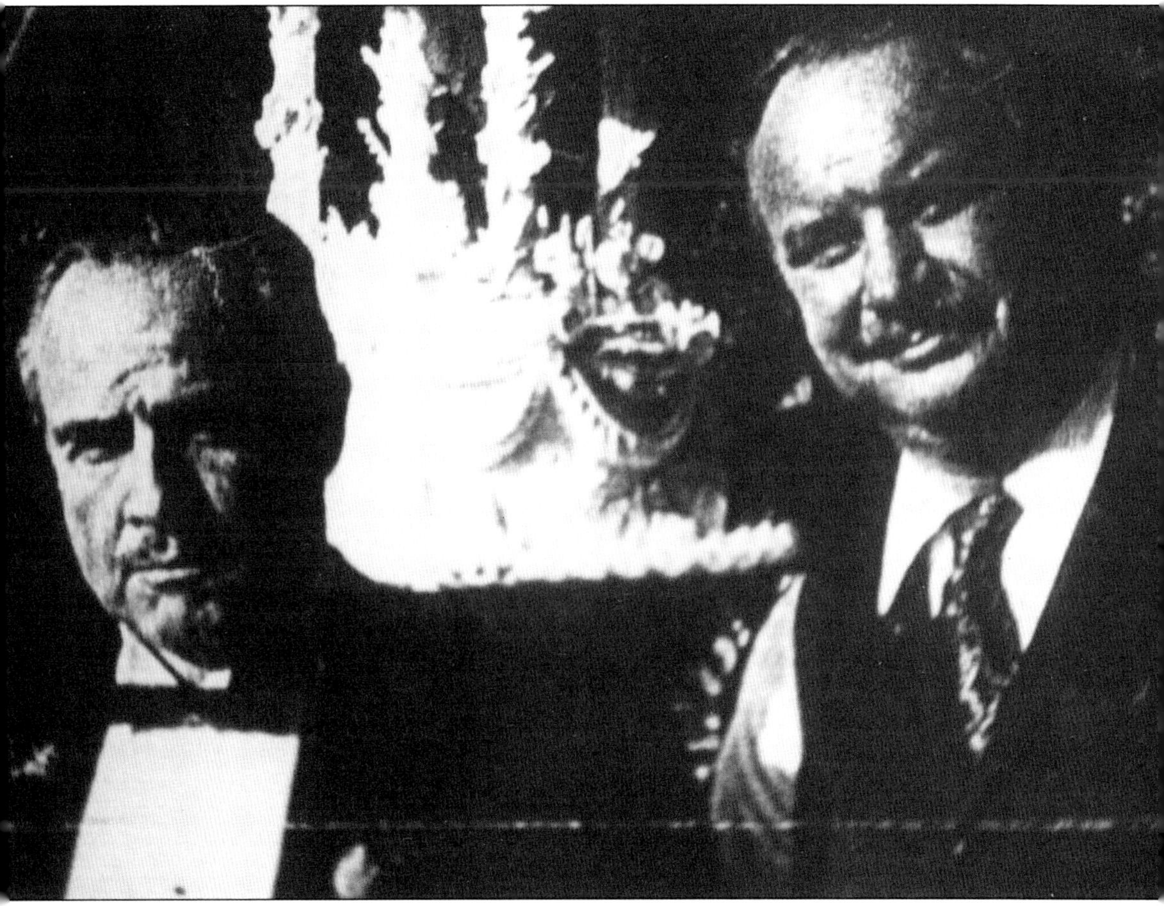

Marlon Brando with Staten Island restaurateur Jack Demyan on the set of *The Godfather*. The movie based on Mario Puzo's best-selling novel garnered Academy Awards for both Best Actor (Brando as Don Vito Corleone) and Best Picture. Much of the film was shot on Emerson Hill, and Demyan's Hofbrau catered food for the crew and cast. Jack Demyan recalled that Brando ordered a steak every other day and that the end of filming was celebrated with a champagne and shrimp party. Because of his artistic abilities, Demyan was asked to make up the "blood" for the gory scene in which the horse head was placed in the producer's bed. Yes, folks, it was paint. (Collection of Jack Demyan.)

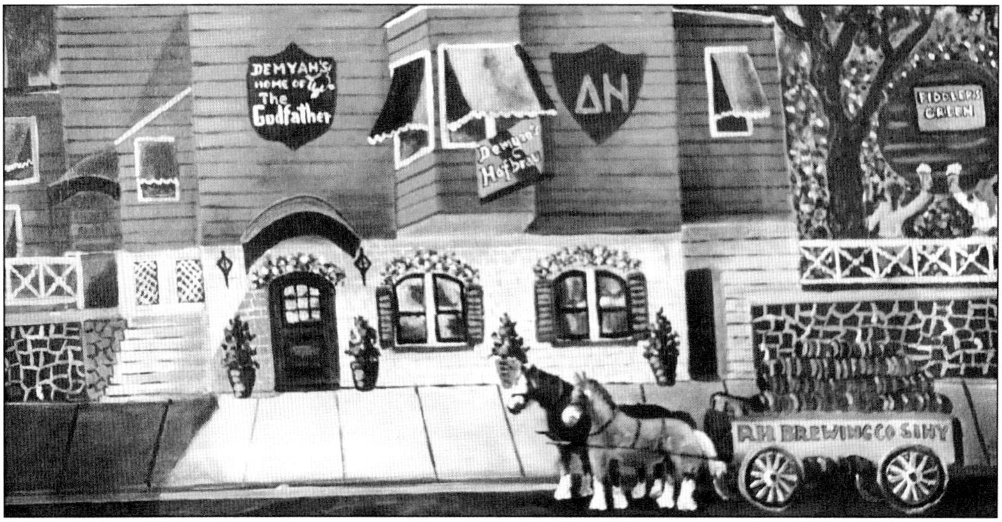

Demyan's Hofbrau is a colorful rendition by owner Jack Demyan. Demyan's was part of the restaurant and offices of the old Bechtel's Brewery. The restaurant, cheerfully decorated with floral paintings by Jack, had rooms named for Demyan's longtime friend, artist John A. Noble, silent-film star Mabel Normand, and the character Miss Wilberforce from Norman Douglas' *South Wind.* Noble, who affectionately called Demyan "Grandpa Moses," wrote when Demyan had legal difficulties, "Jack Demyan is a phenomenon of Staten Island . . . He gave parties with cake aboard a dying ferryboat on its last run and . . . at the opening of a new bridge . . . He is an artist in a most unusual and mysterious way and makes New York a richer and more intriguing place." Demyan's was destroyed in a fire in 1981. (Collection of Jack Demyan.)

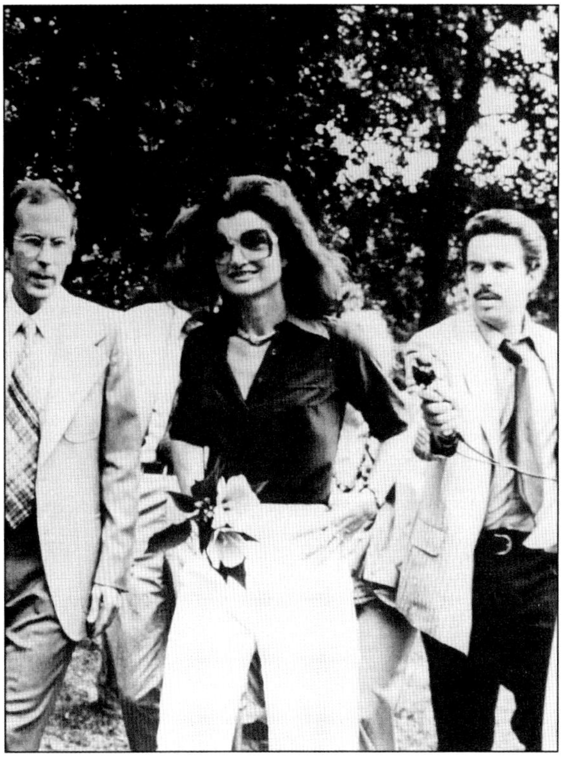

Jacqueline Kennedy Onassis at the Snug Habor Cultural Center. To Mrs. Onassis' side is Barnett Shepherd (left), present head of the Staten Island Historical Society and author of *Sailors' Snug Harbor.* In 1972, the City of New York purchased Snug Harbor for $9.2 million for use as a cultural center. The visit of Mrs. Onassis, then director of the Municipal Arts Society and long known for her interest in the arts and preservation of historic sites, was an auspicious beginning to Snug Harbor's new life. When asked if she would prefer to see Snug Harbor remain a home for old sailors or become a cultural center, she replied, "Well, I like to see it as it is, as an example of how they used to care for our old people . . . But if it were going to fall to a wrecker's ball, it is better to see it become an arts center." (Collection of Barnett Shepherd.)

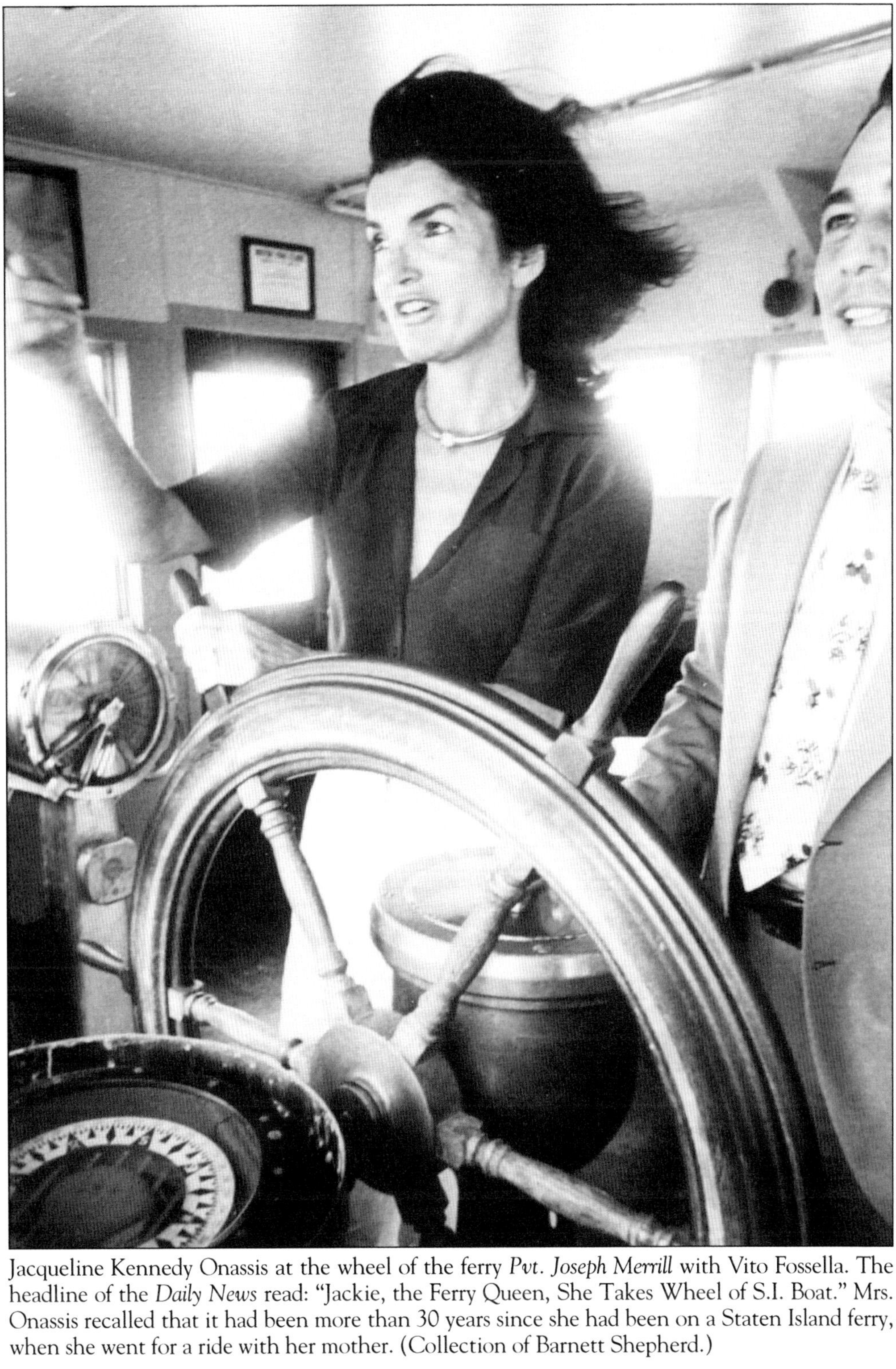

Jacqueline Kennedy Onassis at the wheel of the ferry *Pvt. Joseph Merrill* with Vito Fossella. The headline of the *Daily News* read: "Jackie, the Ferry Queen, She Takes Wheel of S.I. Boat." Mrs. Onassis recalled that it had been more than 30 years since she had been on a Staten Island ferry, when she went for a ride with her mother. (Collection of Barnett Shepherd.)

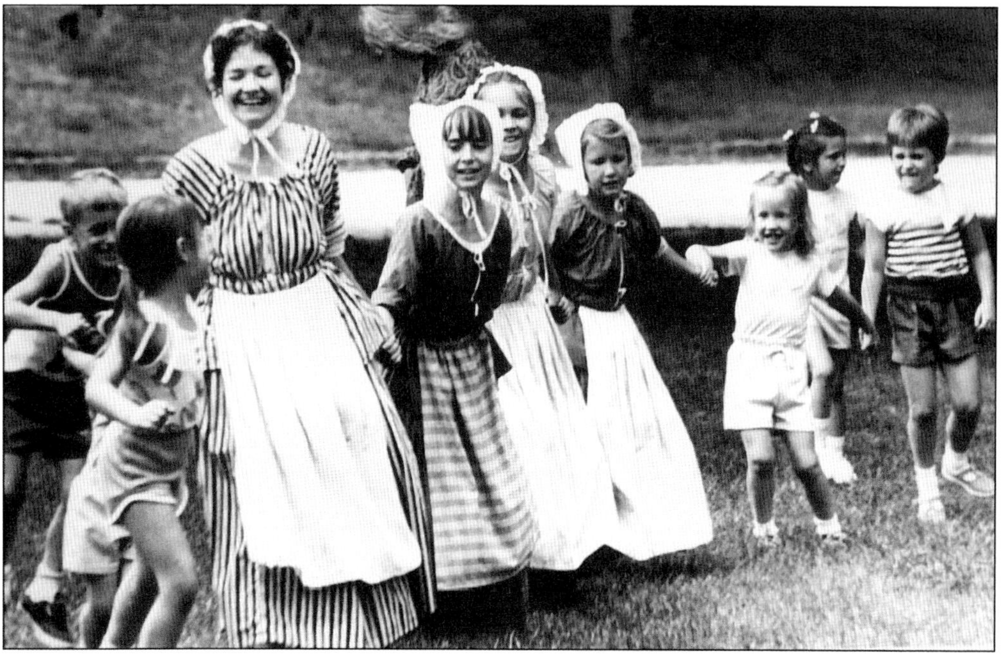

Felicity Beil with students in a summer program at Historic Richmondtown. As a living village, Richmondtown offers many educational programs for children and adults that allow us to "time-travel," i.e., experience life in other eras of history. (Collection of the Staten Island Historical Society.)

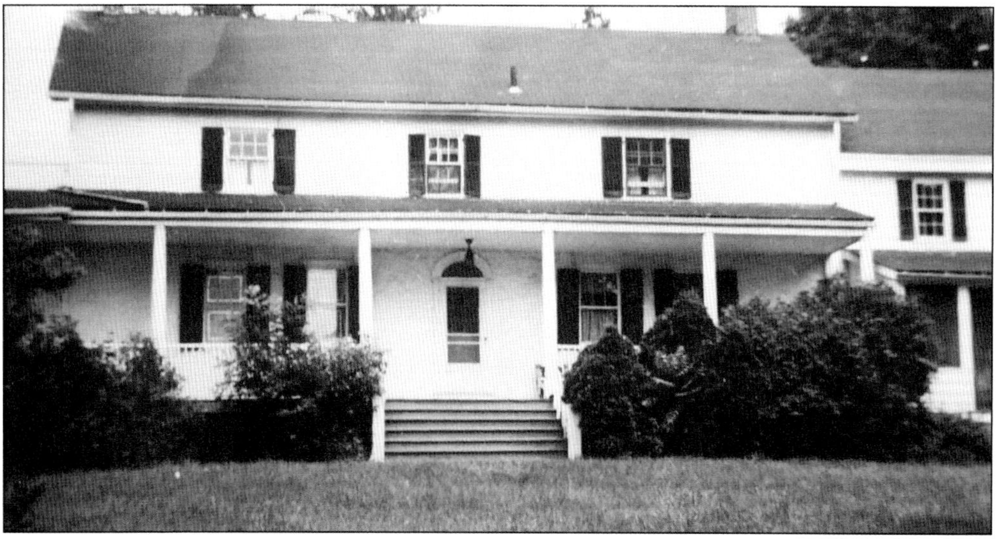

The Poillon-Seguine-Britton House. Built as a simple fieldstone cottage in 1695 by Jacques Poillon, this structure served as the center of the home which was enlarged by the Seguine family to include a second story. A sun porch was added by the Brittons. The home was owned for 25 years by David Decker. Declared a New York City landmark in 1981, the lovely home that overlooked Great Kills Bays was destroyed by fire in 1989. (Photograph by Tony Lanza, collection of Marjorie Johnson.)

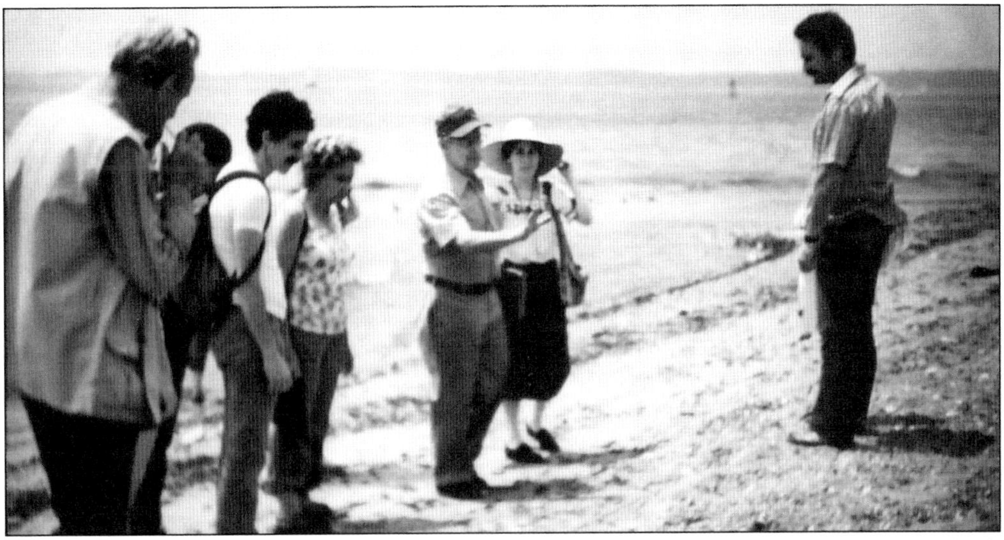

Carlton Beil, in a 1970s photograph. Beil is one of Staten Island's foremost naturalists. He leads a group on a nature walk at the shore in Tottenville. For many years, Beil worked as curator of special exhibits for the Museum of Natural History in New York City. He recalls as a young boy having a nosebleed and being taken by William Davis into the Staten Island Institute of Arts and Sciences. This meeting sparked an interest in the natural sciences that would become a career and avocation. Noted for the meticulous nature of his research, Beil once began a paper on the serpentine rock formations of Staten Island with the "Big Bang." On the right is Beil's daughter Eloise, who was a curator at The Staten Island Institute of Arts and Sciences. (Photograph by Marjorie Johnson.)

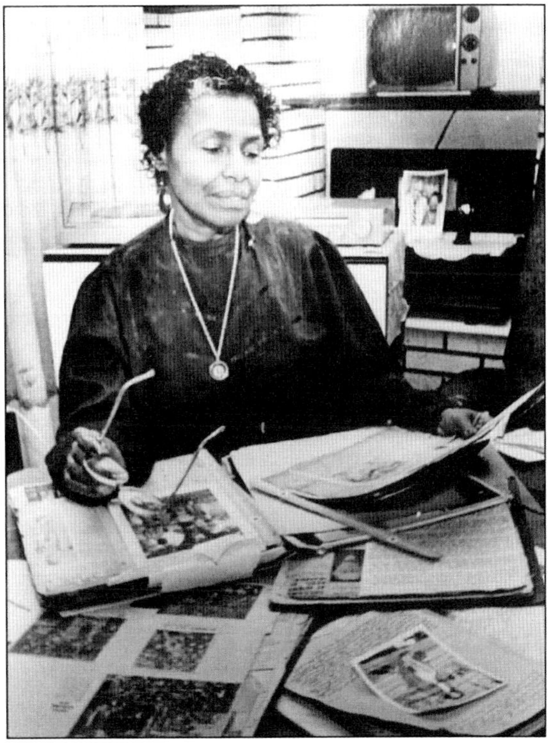

Staten Island historian Evelyn Morris King. Here Mrs. King pores over memorabilia and historical sources. Mrs. King was named as a Woman of Achievement by the *Staten Island Advance* for her contribution to community service and the preservation of history. She recalls that her community service began with taking other children to Sunday school. Mrs. King is the daughter of William Morris, who owned Morris Moving and founded the Staten Island chapter of the NAACP. On her mother's side, she traces her ancestry back to slavery on Staten Island. With Joseph N. Marone, she co-authored *The Black Man in American History*. She founded the Gospel Extravaganza. She also received the John V. Lindsey Prize for Race and Ethnic Relations. A retired schoolteacher, Mrs. King continues to teach African-American history. (Collection of Evelyn Morris King.)

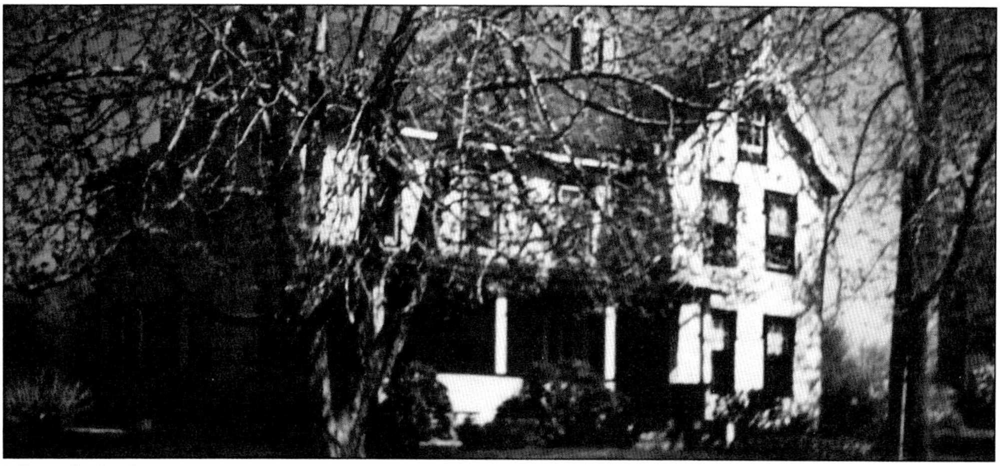

The Ichabod Crane House. In an interesting piece of Staten Island history, author Washington Irving was sufficiently taken with Ichabod Crane's name to use it for the gangling schoolmaster in his time-honored classic *The Legend of Sleepy Hollow*. The December 1987 *Preservation League News* reported that Irving met Colonel Crane during the War of 1812, when Crane was stationed in Sackett Harbor, New York. When Crane retired in 1854, he purchased and moved into the Ozias Ansley farmhouse in Chelsea Heights (today's Travis). Crane expanded and renovated the home in a Gothic Revival style. The home was also owned for many years by the Minto family. Despite efforts to preserve the historic home on 3525 Victory Boulevard, it was demolished in 1989. (Collection of the Minto Family.)

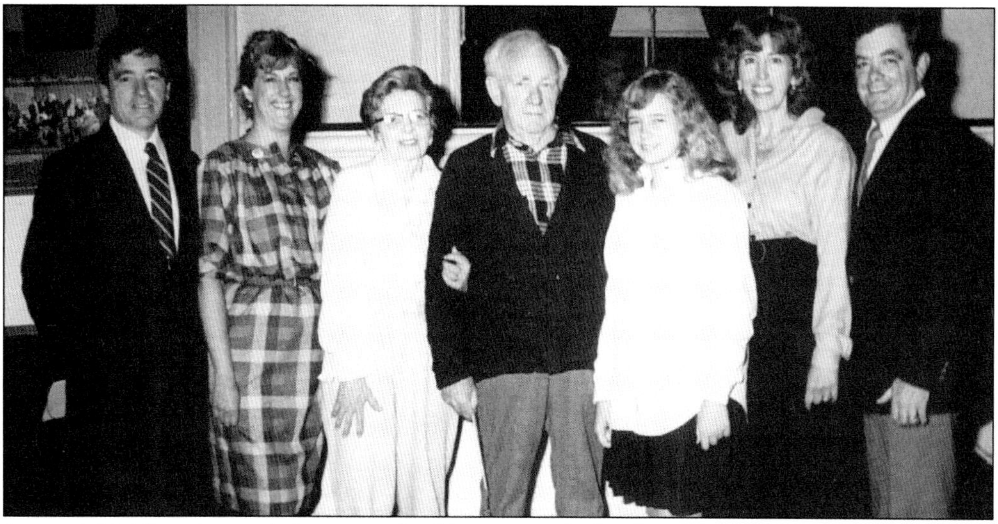

Loring McMillen, borough historian for 54 years, with family. McMillen was instrumental in recognizing and establishing the claim of the Voorlezer House as the oldest standing schoolhouse in the United States. He worked with other preservationists to establish Historic Richmondtown and was in many ways its founding father. He was director of Historic Richmondtown from 1967 to 1978. Barnett Shepherd said of McMillen: "He undoubtedly made a very, very important contribution to preserving Staten Island's history, more than anyone else I can think of." From left to right are William McMillen, director of preservation at Historic Richmondtown; his wife, Judith, director of education; Eleanor McMillen with Loring; granddaughter Lauren; and Loretta and Harlow McMillen, teacher and writer on many historic topics. (Collection of the Staten Island Historical Society.)

Nine

1980–1989

Introducing the Information Age

*English composer and member of "The Beatles" John Lennon shot to death by Mark Chapman in New York, 1980.

*U.S. population reported to be 226,504,825, 1980 Census.

*Mount St. Helens volcano in Washington State erupts, May 20, 1980.

*Ronald Reagan elected 40th U.S. president, 1980.

*Athlete Jesse Owens, comedian Jimmy Durante, film director Sir Alfred Hitchcock, and actors Mae West, Peter Sellers, Steve McQueen, and George Raft die, 1980.

*The *Titanic* wreck found 12,000 feet deep in the North Atlantic Ocean, 1980.

*Polish radio broadcasts a Mass for first time under Polish communist rule, 1980.

*First giant panda cub born in captivity in Mexico, 1980.

*President Reagan shot and wounded by John Hinckley, March 20, 1981.

*Sandra Day O'Connor becomes first woman Justice of the Supreme Court, 1981.

*Anwar Sadat assassinated, October 6, 1981, and Indira Gandhi slain, October 31, 1984.

*Iran releases all 52 hostages, 1981.

*Prince Charles and Lady Diana Spencer wed on July 29, 1981.

*IBM introduces the personal computer (PC), 1981.

*Jamaican reggae musician Bob Marley, actors William Holden and Natalie Wood, IRA hunger striker Bobby Sands, and songwriter Hoagy Carmichael die, 1981.

**USA Today* daily newspaper first published, 1982.

*Gabriel Garcia Marquez of Colombia wins Nobel Prize for Literature, 1982.

*The Boston Celtics win the National Basketball Association championship, 1982.

*Jazz pianist Thelonious Monk, pianist Artur Rubinstein, actors Eleanor Powell, Henry Fonda, Princess Grace Kelly, Ingrid Bergman, John Belushi, and Marty Feldman, the "White Witch" of England Sybil Leek, and psychoanalyst Anna Freud die, 1982.

*Futurist theme park EPCOT opened by Disney World in Florida, 1982.

*The last King of Italy, Umberto, Jack Dempsey, choreographer George Balanchine, R. Buckminster Fuller, Tennessee Williams, Ira Gershwin, David Niven, Gloria Swanson, trumpeter/bandleader Harry James, and Buster Crabbe (*Flash Gordon*) die, 1983.

*Alice Walker wins Pulitzer Prize for *The Color Purple*, 1983.

*AIDS virus discovered independently by American and French research teams, 1984.

*PG-13 film rating established by The Motion Picture Association of America, 1984.

*Pop singer Michael Jackson wins an unprecedented eight Grammy Awards for his album *Thriller*, which sells more than 37 million copies, 1984.

*Standard Oil of California buys and merges with Gulf for $13.2 million, resulting in world's largest corporate merger, 1984.

*Actors Richard Burton and James Mason, William "Count" Basie, McDonald's founder Ray Kroc, publisher Alfred Knopf, Truman Capote, playwright Lillian Hellman, photographer Ansel Adams, and singer Marvin Gaye die, 1984.

*American zoologist Diane Fossey, baseball player Roger Maris, actors Yul Brynner and Rock Hudson, and artists Marc Chagall and Jean Dubuffet die, 1985.

*13-year-old Ruth Lawrence receives degree in mathematics from Oxford University, 1985.

*Terrorists kill 13 people at Leonardo da Vinci Airport in Rome, Italy, December 27, 1985.

*Space shuttle *Challenger* explodes moments after take-off, killing seven crew members including Christa McAuliffe, the first "teacher in space," 1986.

*133,000 evacuated after reactor exploded at Chernobyl (nuclear) Power Station in Kiev, U.S.S.R., 1986.

*Desmond Tutu becomes the first black Archbishop of Cape Town, South Africa, 1986.

*The 100th anniversary of the Statue of Liberty celebrated, July 4, 1986.

*The "Baby M" surrogate mother loses her court battle, 1987.

*World famous dancer Fred Astaire, choreographers Michael Bennett and Bob Fosse, actresses Mary Astor and Rita Hayworth, comedian Jackie Gleason, actor Danny Kaye, pianist Liberace, Andy Warhol, and classical guitarist Andres Segovia die, 1987.

*George Bush defeats Democrat Michael Dukakis in presidential election, 1988.

*Salman Rushdie writes *The Satanic Verses*; is attacked by Muslims for blasphemy, 1988.

*Sculptors Louise Nevelson and Isami Noguchi die, 1988.

*Popular songs of 1988 include "Don't Worry, Be Happy."

*Naguib Mahfouz of Egypt becomes the first African writer to win the Nobel Prize for Literature, 1988.

*Toni Morrison wins Pulitzer Prize for *Beloved*, and physicist Stephen Hawking writes *A Brief History of Time*, 1988.

*Lt. Col. Oliver North convicted of crimes in the Iran-Contra scandal, 1989.

*Czech dissident/playwright Vaclav Havel jailed, then becomes president of Czechoslovakia, 1989.

*The Dalai Lama wins the Nobel Peace Prize, 1989.

*The *Exxon Valde* runs aground in Alaska, spilling 11 million gallons of oil, 1989.

*The Berlin Wall is torn down, November 10, 1989.

*Actors Laurence Olivier, Bette Davis, and Lucille Ball die, 1989.

*Wendy Wasserstein wins Pulitzer Prize for *The Heidi Chronicles*, 1989.

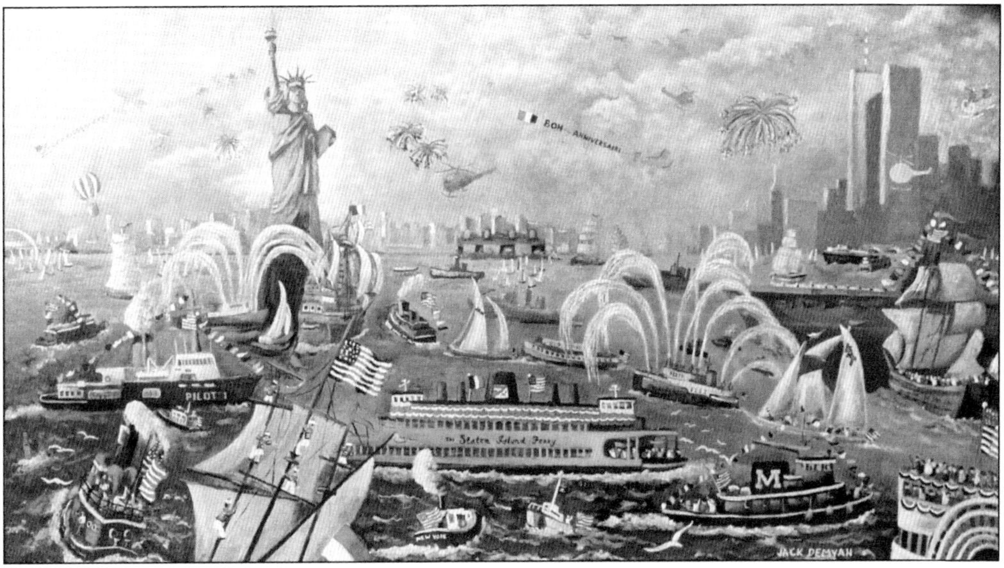

Bon Anniversaire, Miss Liberty, a watercolor by Staten Island artist Jack Demyan. The painting embraces the exuberant celebration commemorating the 100th anniversary of the Statue of Liberty. Prominent in the foreground is a Staten Island ferry. (Collection of Jack Demyan.)

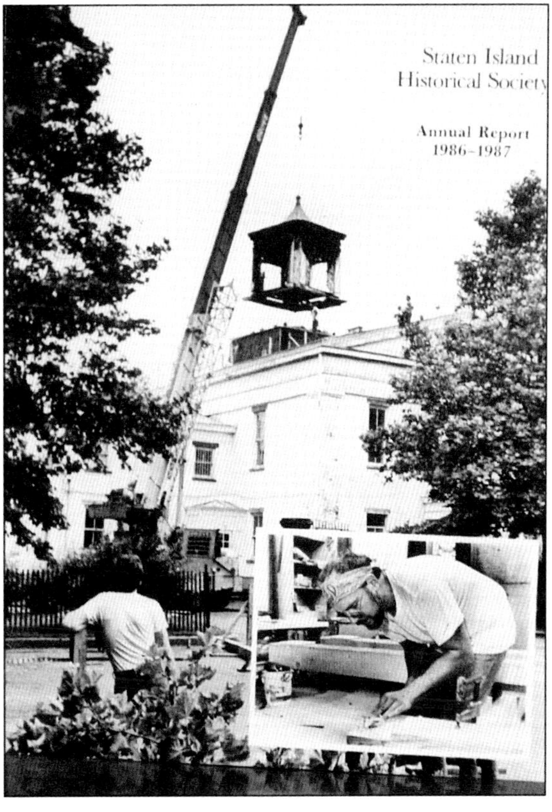

The 1986–87 cover of the Staten Island Historical Society Annual Report. It shows the tower on the courthouse being lifted by a crane. The tower had been struck by lightning in September 1986. When insurance did not cover the entire renovation, $10,000 raised by local donors matched contributions by AT&T, Mobil, and the New York Telephone Company. A lightning rod and weather vane were the gifts of the women's auxiliary of the Staten Island Historical Society. Island Housewrights of Prince's Bay performed the exacting work of reconstructing the tower, including using wooden pegs instead of nails. (Collection of Marjorie Johnson.)

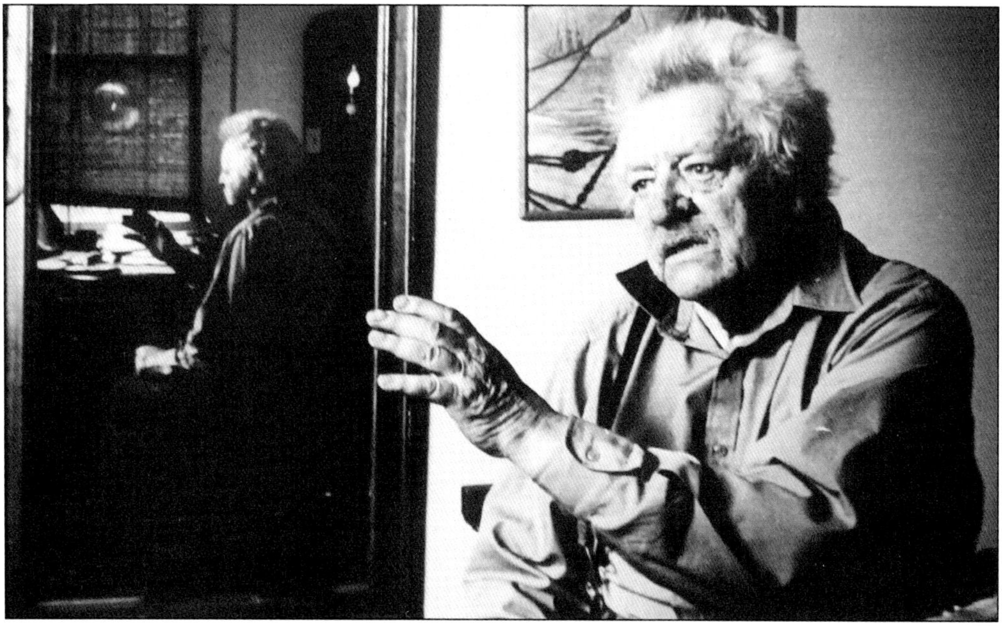

Staten Island artist John A. Noble in 1982, before his death on May 15, 1983, a few months after the death of his beloved wife, Susan Ames Noble. Noble was named an Academician at the National Academy of Design and exhibited at the Brooklyn Museum. At one point he wrote to the *New York Times* and the *Staten Island Advance*, "Before all is over and gone, let us take a wild fling and for once in our City's history name a vessel after a poet—not a politician." Noble's wish was honored in 1986 when two new ferries, *The Alice Austen* and *The John A. Noble*, were launched. While he achieved national recognition, his work is especially loved in Staten Island and Bayonne where he spent so much of his life. His work is housed at the John A. Noble Collection in a former seamen's dormitory at the Snug Harbor Cultural Center. (Courtesy of the John A. Noble Collection.)

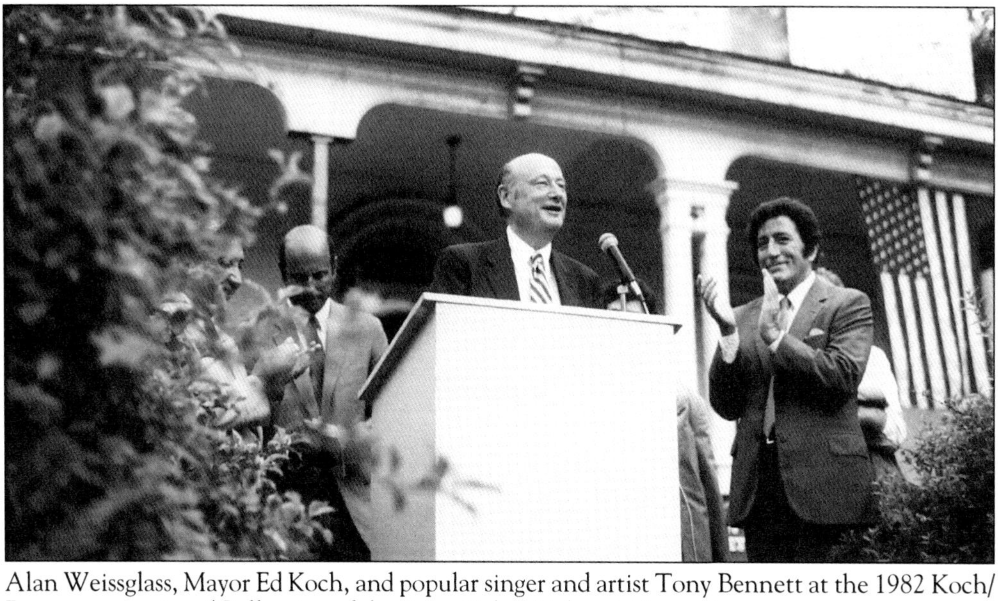

Alan Weissglass, Mayor Ed Koch, and popular singer and artist Tony Bennett at the 1982 Koch/Bennett reception. (Collection of the Snug Habor Cultural Center.)

Ten

1990-Present

Higher Technology, "New Age," and the Future

*Iraq seizes Kuwait, August 3, 1990.

*Lech Walesa elected president of Poland,
and Mary Robinson elected first woman president of Ireland, 1990.

*Nelson Mandela freed after 27 years in prison in South Africa, February 11, 1990.

*Composers Leonard Bernstein and Aaron Copland, singers Sammy Davis Jr., Sarah Vaughan,
and Pearl Bailey, and actors Rex Harrison, Ava Gardner, and Greta Garbo die, 1990.

*West and East Germany reunited, October 3, 1990.

*The Gulf War (Desert Storm) begins in the Middle East, the first war to be televised
by CNN (the 24-hour news channel), then other networks, 1991.

*Anita Hill hearings on sexual harassment by Clarence Thomas, October 1991.

*Russian government threatened by reactionary coup, which fails;
Mikail Gorbachev resigns December 26, and Boris Yeltsin takes over, 1991.

*Los Angeles riots after acquittal of police officers for beating Rodney King, April 30, 1992.

*Bill Clinton becomes president, November 1992.

*World Trade Center bombed by terrorists, February 26, 1993.

*Mass suicide in Waco, Texas, by Davidian cult members, April 19, 1993.

*Rabin and Arafat sign an accord, May 4, 1994.

*Nelson Mandela becomes the first black president of South Africa, May 11, 1994.

*Jacqueline Kennedy Onassis dies of cancer at the age of 64, May 20, 1994.

*O.J. Simpson jailed on double murder charges, 1994; acquitted in 1995 after a lengthy trial.

*Death toll of six hundred following an earthquake in Kobe, Japan, January 17, 1995.

*Federal building in Oklahoma City bombed by American terrorists

Timothy McVeigh and Terry Lynn Nichols; 169 dead, 400 injured, April 19, 1995.

*Diana, Princess of Wales, and her Egyptian boyfriend, Dodi al Fayed, killed in Paris car crash, August 30, 1997.

*Mother Teresa dies in India a week later, 1997.

*Convicted killer (turned born-again Christian) Karla Faye Tucker executed by lethal injection in Texas, 1998.

*Pacific El Niño storms cause tragic mudslides and flooding in Peru, Ecuador, and other locations, 1998.

*Tension mounts between the U.S. and Iraq, talk of attack on Iraqi leader Saddam Hussein; UN Secretary intervenes and averts the attack, at least temporarily, 1998.

*The Olympic games held in Nagano, Japan, where first women's U.S. hockey team and 15-year-old figure skater Tara Lipinski win gold medals, February 1998.

*Alleged scandal—called "The White House Under Fire"—steals headlines for months in 1998, with stories that President Bill Clinton had sexual relations with White House intern Monica Lewinsky and several other women; Clinton denies the charges as independent counsel Kenneth Starr leads the investigation, which has not yet been closed at the printing of this book.

*The most popular movie and biggest box-office hit to date, *Titanic*, reenacts the 1912 tragedy of the ocean liner's collision with an iceberg, killing more than a thousand passengers.

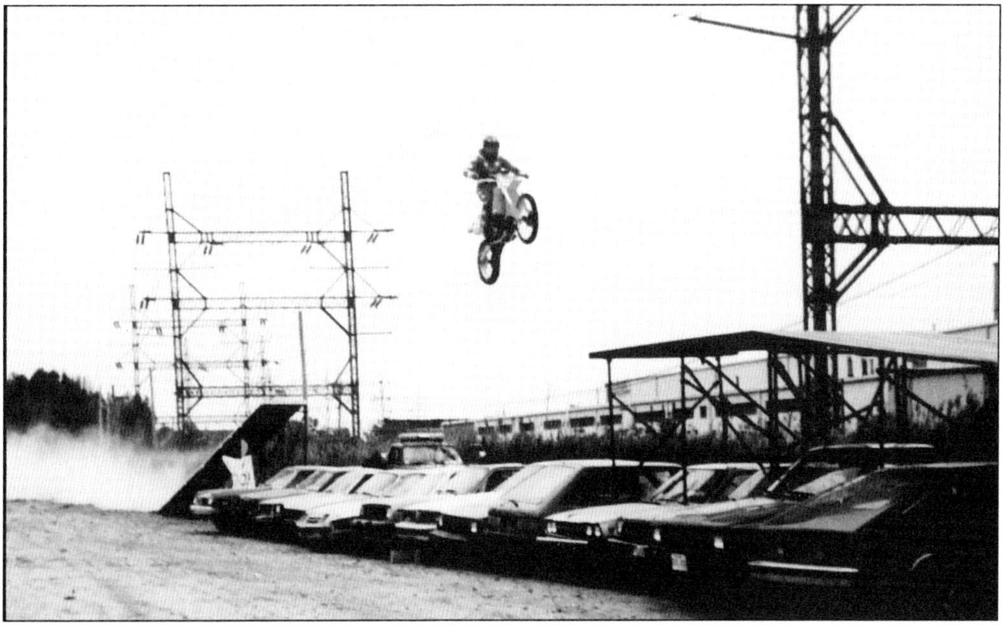

Death-defying leap. Ron Star vaults over 14 cars in a performance to benefit Vietnam veterans. Known as Staten Island's Motorcycle Daredevil, Star has ridden since he was a kid. He was bedridden for a year following a mishap while attempting to jump over 10 cars. Star has a cable television show and works to stress the importance of safety and the dangers of drinking and driving. Ron has also written a script for an action hero, "The Immortal Starfighter," and plans to play the role. He hopes some day to jump over 20 cars, and after that vault the East River to complete a deathbed promise to mother to become more famous than Evel Knievel. (Collection of Ron Star.)

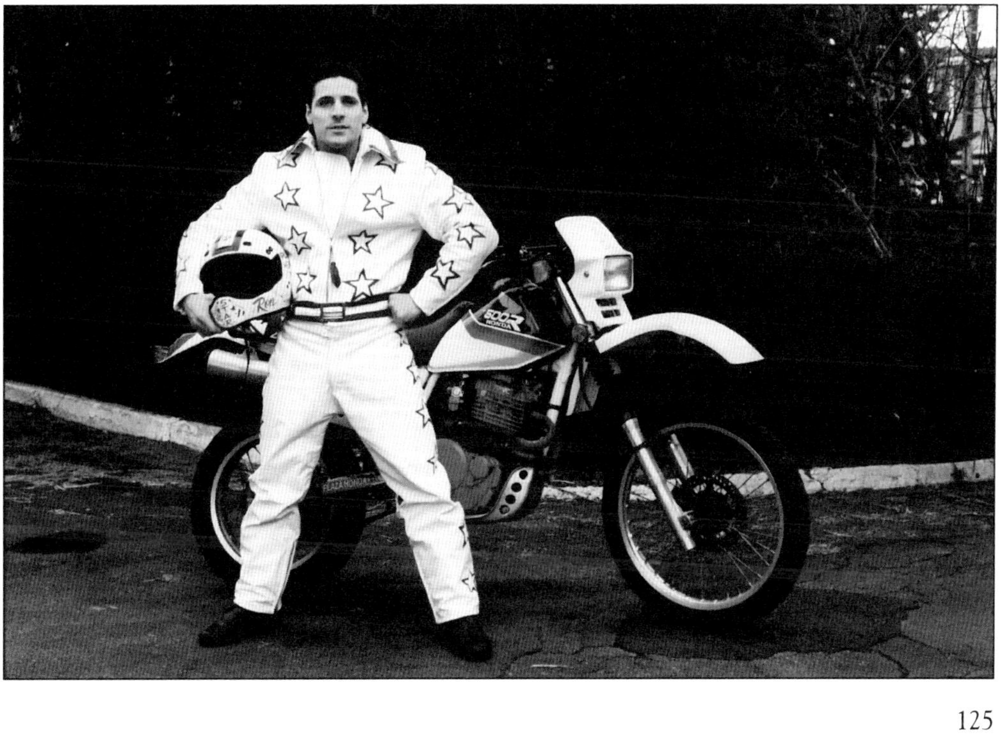

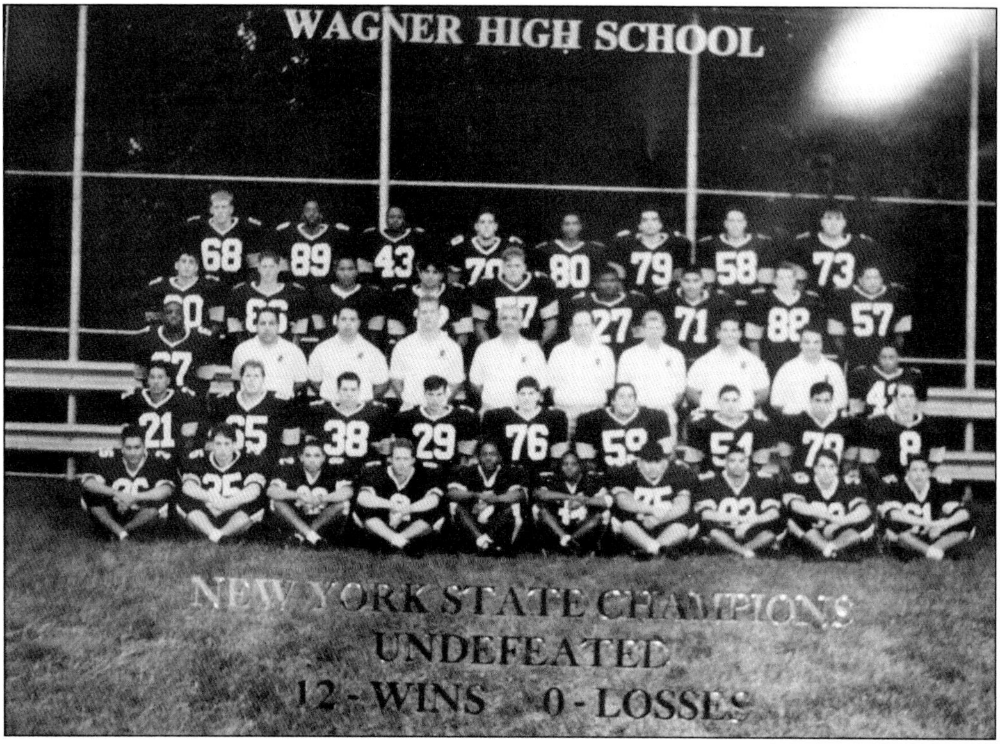

The Wagner High School Football Team, 1992. The team achieved a pinnacle by becoming the New York State Football Champions under coach Allan Peturzo.

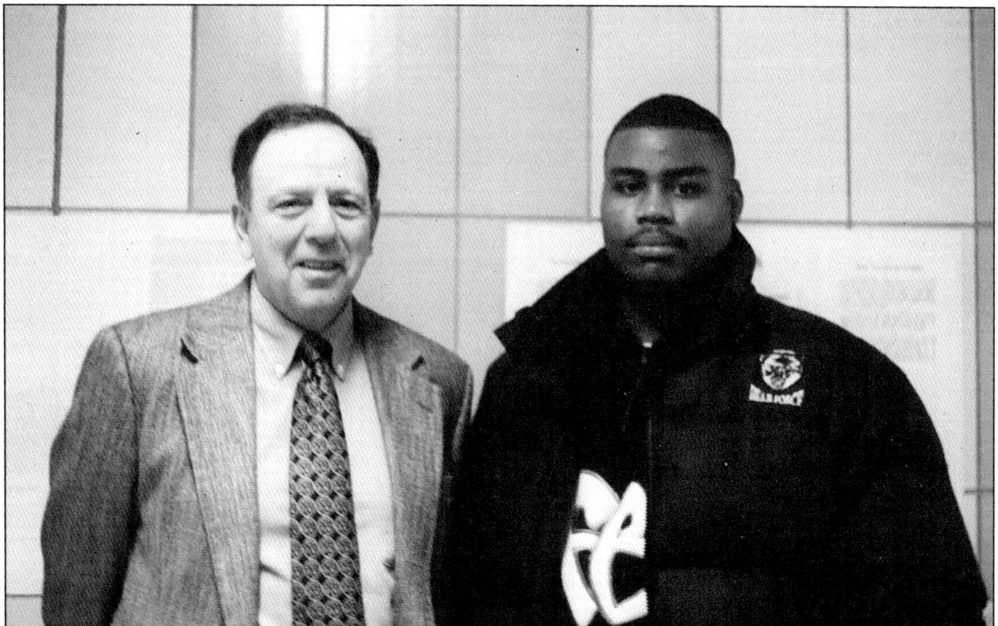

Allan Peturzo with Jarel Carroll. The head coach of Wagner High School's football team, Peturzo started his teaching career at Mt. Loretto and from there went to Tottenville High School. He is a well-loved mentor who has led many teams to championships.

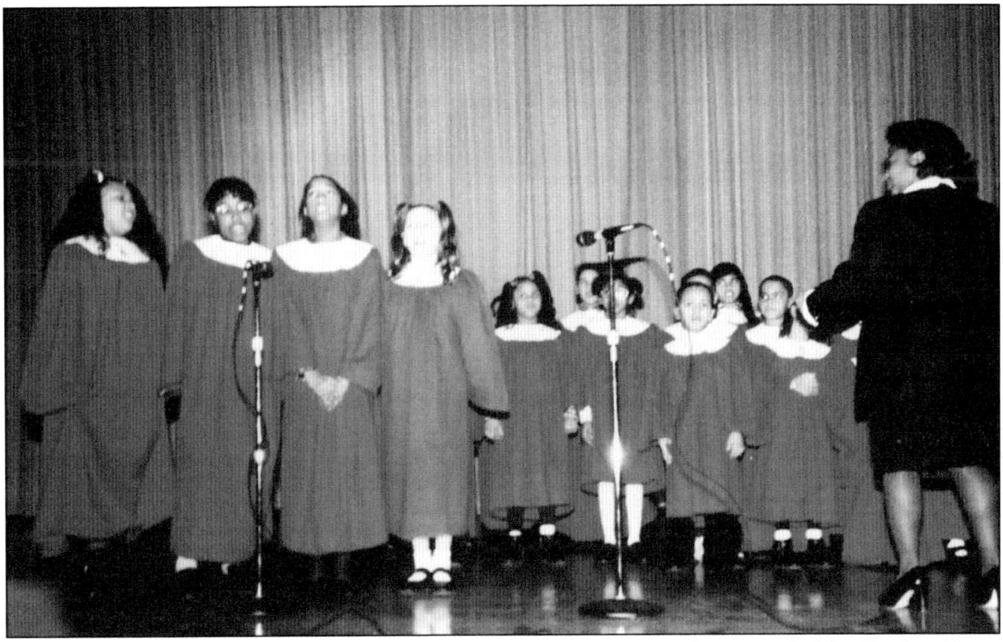

One of the NAACP-sponsored Gospel Extravaganza's groups of singers, led by Evelyn King. (Collection of Evelyn Morris King.)

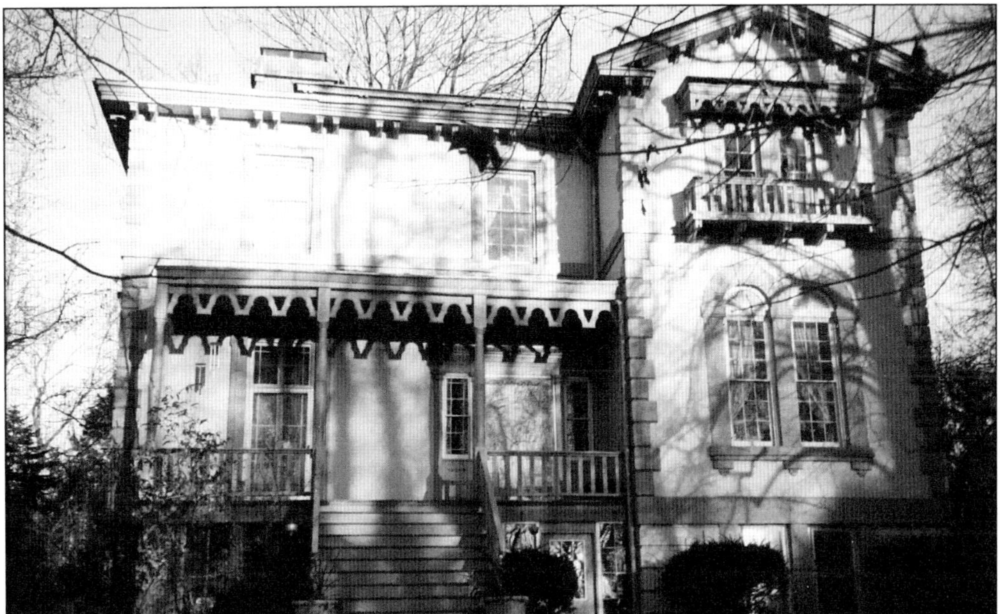

The C.K. Hamilton house at Harvard Avenue in New Brighton. This house was part of the first Staten Island suburban development begun in the mid-19th century by Charles Kennedy Hamilton. The homes in Hamilton Park stand as evidence to the successful efforts of private citizens in preserving historic treasures. The *c.* 1853 Italianate house built on a park-like setting was believed to be the first "cottage." After many years of neglect, it was purchased by the Seeley family, restored, and was an attraction of the Victorian Christmas House Tour, by the Preservation League of Staten Island. (Photograph by Margaret Lundrigan.)

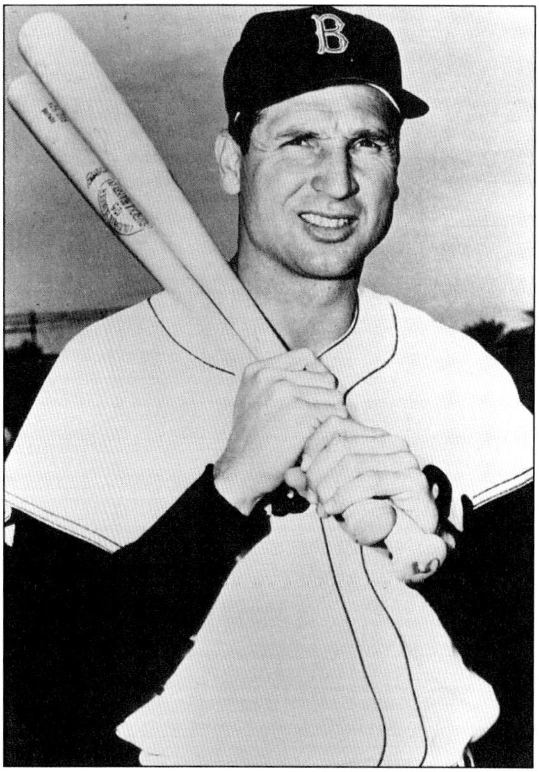

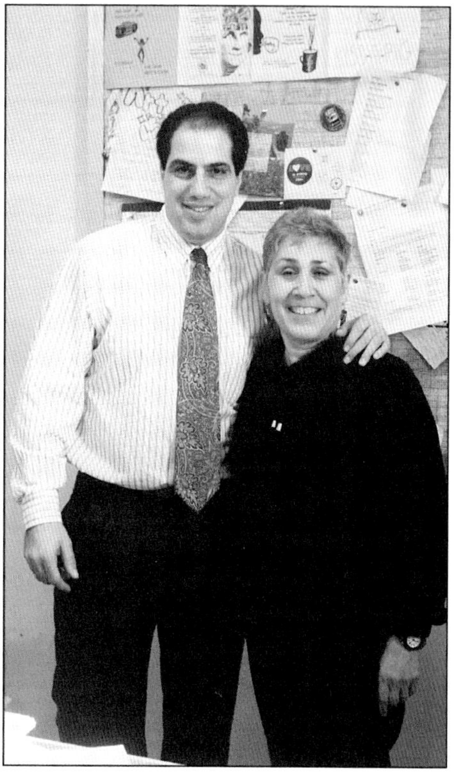

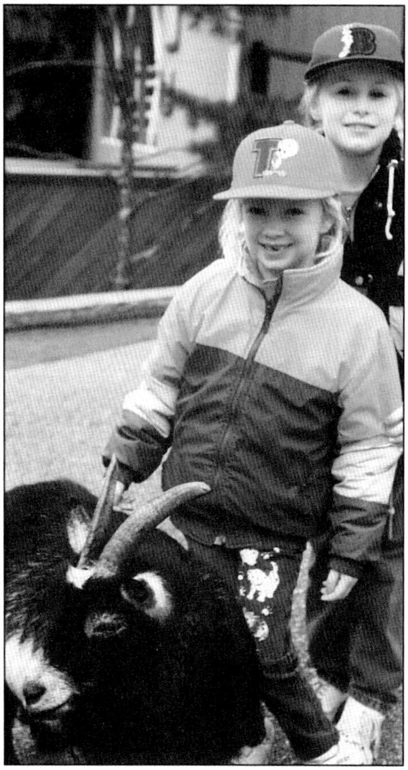

Upper Left: Sports Hall of Fame inductee. In 1995, Bobby Thomson was inducted into the Staten Island Sports Hall of Fame. A dream that was 40 years in the making came to be in December 1995 when the Staten Island Sports Hall of Fame held its first installation ceremony. The Hall of Fame's goal is "to recognize those individuals who have made extraordinary contributions to Staten Island sports history, and by virtue of their accomplishments, service, or force of character, have enriched that history for all time." (Collection of the Baseball Hall of Fame Museum Library.)

Upper Right: George Anthony and Ruth Beyl, teachers at Susan Wagner High School. The school was named for the wife of former New York City Mayor Richard Wagner. Mrs. Beyl, coordinator of student affairs, has been at the school since shortly after it opened. Anthony, a history teacher and coordinator of the Peer Mediation program, was a student of Mrs. Beyl when he attended Wagner High in the 1970s. Such programs are stellar examples of efforts to counteract the increasing violence in our schools and society. (Photograph by Tova Navarra.)

Left: Lauren and Erica Peters make friends with one of the Staten Island Zoo's African pygmy goats. (Photograph by Tova Navarra.)